MAINSTREAMING OF CHILDREN IN SCHOOLS
Research and Programmatic Issues

EDUCATIONAL PSYCHOLOGY

Allen J. Edwards, Series Editor
Department of Psychology
Southwest Missouri State University
Springfield, Missouri

Patricia A. Schmuck and W. W. Charters, Jr. (eds.). Educational Policy and Management: Sex Differentials

Phillip S. Strain and Mary Margaret Kerr. Mainstreaming of Children in Schools: Research and Programmatic Issues

Maureen L-Pope and Terence R. Keen. Personal Construct Psychology and Education

Ronald W. Henderson (ed.). Parent–Child Interaction: Theory, Research, and Prospects

W. Ray Rhine (ed.). Making Schools More Effective: New Directions from Follow Through

Herbert J. Klausmeier and Thomas S. Sipple. Learning and Teaching Concepts: A Strategy for Testing Applications of Theory

James H. McMillan (ed.). The Social Psychology of School Learning

M. C. Wittrock (ed.). The Brain and Psychology

Marvin J. Fine (ed.). Handbook on Parent Education

Dale G. Range, James R. Layton, and Darrell L. Roubinek (eds.). Aspects of Early Childhood Education: Theory to Research to Practice

Jean Stockard, Patricia A. Schmuck, Ken Kempner, Peg Williams, Sakre K. Edson, and Mary Ann Smith. Sex Equity in Education

James R. Layton. The Psychology of Learning to Read

Thomas E. Jordan. Development in the Preschool Years: Birth to Age Five

Gary D. Phye and Daniel J. Reschly (eds.). School Psychology: Perspectives and Issues

Norman Steinaker and M. Robert Bell. The Experiential Taxonomy: A New Approach to Teaching and Learning

J. P. Das, John R. Kirby, and Ronald F. Jarman. Simultaneous and Successive Cognitive Processes

Herbert J. Klausmeier and Patricia S. Allen. Cognitive Development of Children and Youth: A Longitudinal Study

Victor M. Agruso, Jr. Learning in the Later Years: Principles of Educational Gerontology

The list of titles in this series continues on the last page of this volume.

MAINSTREAMING OF CHILDREN IN SCHOOLS
Research and Programmatic Issues

PHILLIP S. STRAIN
Department of Psychiatry
Western Psychiatric Institute and Clinic
University of Pittsburgh
School of Medicine
Pittsburgh, Pennsylvania

MARY MARGARET KERR
Department of Psychiatry
Western Psychiatric Institute and Clinic
University of Pittsburgh
School of Medicine
Pittsburgh, Pennsylvania

With a Contributed Chapter by

ANN P. TURNBULL
School of Education
and Bureau of Child Research
University of Kansas
Lawrence, Kansas

JAN BLACHER-DIXON
Department of Education
University of California, Riverside
Riverside, California

 1981

ACADEMIC PRESS
A Subsidiary of Harcourt Brace Jovanovich, Publishers
New York   London   Toronto   Sydney   San Francisco

ACADEMIC PRESS, INC.
111 Fifth Avenue, New York, New York 10003

United Kingdom Edition published by
ACADEMIC PRESS, INC. (LONDON) LTD.
24/28 Oval Road, London NW1   7DX

Library of Congress Cataloging in Publication Data

Strain, Phillip S.
  Mainstreaming of children in schools.

  (Educational psychology)
  Includes bibliographies and index.
  1. Mainstreaming in education--United States.
2. Mentally handicapped children--Education--United
States. I. Kerr, Mary Margaret. II. Title. III. Series.
LC4631.S77   371.9   80-70666
ISBN 0-12-673460-7   AACR2

81 82 83 84   9 8 7 6 5 4 3 2 1

To Alexa, Eleanor, George, and Guy—
Our first and best teachers

Contents

Preface   *xi*

1   Efficacy of Special Class Placement for Educable Mentally Retarded Children

Introduction   1
Academic Consequences of Educational Placement   1
Major Findings on Educational Effects   8
Social Consequences of Educational Placement   10
Major Findings on Social Effects   22
Methodological Issues in Efficacy Research   25
Conclusions   31
Reference Note   33
References   33

2   Attitudes toward Mentally Retarded Persons and the Concept of Mainstreaming

Introduction   37
Attitudinal Research Paradigms   38
Community Attitudes toward the Mentally Retarded   41
Professionals' Attitudes toward the Mentally Retarded   44

Peers' Attitudes toward Mentally Retarded Children   57
Summary and Conclusions   65
Reference Notes   66
References   67

3   Preschool Mainstreaming: An Empirical and Conceptual Review

Ann P. Turnbull and Jan Blacher-Dixon

Introduction   71
Review of the Literature   73
Program Outcomes   78
Child Outcomes   85
Teacher Variables   89
Effects on Parents and Family   91
Conclusions   93
Reference Notes   95
References   96

4   Peer Social Behavior in Integrated Preschool Settings: Developmental and Instructional Potentials

Introduction   101
Peer Relations and Behavioral Development   102
Behavioral Processes of Peer Influence   104
Summary and Conclusions   121
Reference Notes   123
References   123

5   Management of Problem Behaviors in Regular Classrooms

Introduction   129
Teacher Talk: Approval and Disapproval in the Classroom   129
Standards for Performance: Classroom Rules   131
Good Behavior Game Procedure   134
Peer-Mediated Feedback Strategies   136
Time Out Procedures   137
Self-Management Procedures   140
Contingency Contracting   145
Home-Based Reporting   146

Token Reinforcement Systems 148
Teacher Training: Consultation Programs 152
Concluding Remarks 158
Reference Notes 159
References 159

6   Academic Instruction of Children in Mainstream Classes

Introduction 165
Arithmetic 166
Reading 176
Spelling 186
Handwriting 192
Creative Writing 200
Concluding Remarks 204
Reference Notes 205
References 205

Subject Index   *211*

Preface

In the fall of 1977 we surveyed a group of 20 leading professionals in special education regarding the issues they felt were most critical to mainstreaming exceptional children into regular classroom settings. Several topics were mentioned repeatedly by these educators, including (a) a concern that the special education efficacy literature could not be used with confidence to promote either integrated or segregated educational programming; (b) a concern that the generally negative attitudes and opinions toward exceptional children would be a major roadblock to successful mainstreaming; (c) a concern about how to promote social integration, particularly among preschool-age exceptional and normal children; (d) a basic concern about the available technology for the academic instruction of mainstreamed exceptional children; and (e) a concern that regular class teachers would not be able to manage the disruptive behavior of mainstreamed children.

This volume was designed to provide beginning answers to these specific concerns and to bring an added measure of empirical decision making to an educational process that often elicits more emotion and rhetoric than sound data. As will be noted throughout this volume, the answers to these concerns are tentative at best, and considerable scientific and political debate surrounds these and other issues related to mainstreaming. Within such a context, bias is unquestionably present. In reviewing the literature on the various issues presented in this volume, the following biases were operative. First, we sought to report both the findings of relevant research and the conceptual and methodological adequacy of the data. Second, we attempted to translate, where appropriate, the results of empirical study to the everyday operation of mainstream educational settings. Third, we purposefully omitted from the chapters any evidence that represented pure opinion, speculation, theory building, or position taking. We purposefully included "evidence" that was based on an empirical analysis.

Efficacy of Special Class Placement for Educable Mentally Retarded Children — 1

Introduction

The purpose of this chapter is to provide a critical review of research related to the efficacy of special class placement for educable mentally retarded (EMR) children. One of the many complex and confusing issues in this body of research is the large number of dependent measures used to assess placement effects. These indices range from sociometrics to direct observation procedures, from achievement tests to projective techniques. In sum, the vast majority of these dependent measures may be divided into two broad categories: academic and social. In order to clarify discussion, this review is divided into studies that (a) examined academic consequences of educational placement; and (b) examined social consequences of educational placement. Within each division, studies are reviewed in chronological order. Particular emphasis is given to methodological issues as they impact on the interpretation of results and the general credibility of research findings.

Academic Consequences of Educational Placement

In one of the earliest studies on academic outcomes of placement, Bennett (1932) compared the reading, arithmetic, mechanical, and spelling performance of children attending regular classes and those in special classes. Fifty youngsters in each placement, ranging in age from $12\frac{1}{2}$ to $13\frac{1}{2}$ years were matched for chronological age (CA), mental age (MA), and IQ. The level of handicap ranged from mild to moderate retardation. On measures of reading, arithmetic, and spelling the regular class children were superior. The groups were equal in mechanical ability. At a more fine-grain level of analysis, Bennett noted that no relationship was found between retarded academic performance and length of time in special class.

Various problems in subject selection and matching are evident with this study. More than one-half of the children in special classes had attended regular classes in the same school system prior to their placement in segregated classes. The question remains unanswered as to what uncontrolled characteristics of the special class students led to their differential treatment. One possibility was the disproportionate number of health-related and sensory impairments evidenced by special class children. Of course, these factors alone could operate to depress achievement scores. As is the case with the vast majority of efficacy studies, this investigation does not offer more than a nominal description of the independent variable—special versus regular class placement. Critical issues including teachers' credentials and training, specification of curriculum, and instructional interaction patterns were not addressed.

The next efficacy study related to academic outcomes was conducted by Pertsch (1936). The design closely replicated that employed by Bennett. Educable mentally retarded children in regular and special classes were matched for CA, MA, IQ, sex, and race. The 278 children were tested on educational achievement, mechanical aptitude, and personal adjustment; then, they were retested 6 months later. At both assessment points, children in the regular classes were superior in reading comprehension, arithmetic computation, arithmetic reasoning, and personal adjustment. As Bennett also found, the groups were relatively equal in mechanical aptitude.

Cowen (1938) provided a thorough critique of Pertsch's work along with sample reanalyses of data that favored special class students. As regards subject selection, members of regular classes were superior to their special class peers at the outset of the study. Thus, when Cowen compared gain scores rather than absolute scores for both groups, special class children tended to make greater gains. As was the case in Bennett's study, design and analysis problems severely limit the believability of the results.

Almost 20 years elapsed before the next efficacy study on academic achievement appeared. Elenbogen (1957) administered the Stanford Achievement Test to children who had spent the last 2 academic years in either special or regular classes. The subjects were matched for CA, IQ, sex, and school district. On measures of paragraph meaning, word meaning, arithmetic computation, and arithmetic reasoning, the regular class children performed in a superior fashion. The mean scores for the groups were statistically significant on paragraph meaning, word meaning, and arithmetic computation indices. Elenbogen proposed, in the absence of any empirical evidence, that these results favoring regular class students were the result of academic competition between these subjects and their regular class peers. Although Elenbogen's explanation is certainly a logically sound one, other factors also may have been influential. For example, it is possible that the groups were not equivalent on test-taking experience or ability, that the curriculum in regular classes more closely matched the content of the Stanford Achievement Test, or that examiner effects may have biased the results.

In an attempt to correct some of the subject selection problems in earlier studies, Blatt (1958) compared regular and special class EMR children from separate county school systems. The 75 special education students were chosen on three bases: (*a*) at least 2 years' attendance in special classes; (*b*) CA between 8½ and 16 years; and (*c*) diagnosis of EMR by a certified psychometrician using an individual intelligence test. The 50 regular class subjects were selected on the following bases: (*a*) never having been in a special class; (*b*) living in a community that had no special classes; and (*c*) diagnosis of EMR by a certified psychometrician using an individual intelligence test. The total population of special and regular class children was then matched for CA, MA, IQ, and sex. Achievement data from the California Achievement Test indicated no significant differences between groups on reading, arithmetic, and language scales. There was also a trend for special class children to show more absolute gain in achievement test scores from one year to the next. This later finding was most pronounced in reading achievement.

Blatt's results were the first pieces of evidence disputing the academic superiority of EMR children in regular classes. Unfortunately, any direct comparison of these data with earlier studies can be only speculative in nature. A number of factors limit such a comparison. First, it can be argued that Blatt's population was less handicapped than those employed earlier. For example, both regular and special class children achieved significantly better than would have been expected for their MAs. Second, it seems reasonable to expect that the nature of special class services would have changed over the 25-year period between Bennett's (1932) initial study and Blatt's investigation. Finally, as with all the research reviewed to this point, lack of specificity regarding the independent variable of placement makes scientific replication and valid comparisons impossible.

Cassidy and Stanton (1959) closely followed Blatt's (1958) subject selection procedures in their comparison of 100 special class and 94-regular-class EMR children. All youngsters had Stanford–Binet IQ scores between 50 and 75, and they ranged in age from 12 to 14 years. Members of the special class group had been enrolled at least 2 years in a segregated placement within the same community. Regular class children were selected from school systems that did not offer special classes. Results on academic achievement tests showed the regular class group to be superior. Cassidy and Stanton maintain that the primary difference between placements was the greater emphasis placed upon reading, spelling, and arithmetic in regular classes. Like Elenbogen's (1957) notion of peer competition improving performance in regular classes, this statement of differential emphasis on academic achievement does not have direct empirical support.

Cassidy and Stanton were the first to provide information regarding the possible interaction between degree of handicap and educational placement. Subanalyses were conducted across three IQ levels (50–59, 60–69, 70–79). At all levels, regular class students were superior. However, there were few children in regular classes within the 50–59 IQ range, and the variability in achievement for this group was extreme.

Thurstone (1959) examined the achievement scores of 1273 students in regular and special classes. Stanford–Binet IQ scores ranged from 50–79, and CA ranged from 9 years 4 months to 14 years 11 months. All subjects were tested initially on the Stanford Achievement Test, with the special class children scoring significantly below regular class youngsters. A second test 1 year later showed regular class children's gain scores to be superior in all areas except arithmetic. A third test, given 2 years later, showed no significant differences between gain scores. As in all studies, with the exception of Blatt (1958), both groups achieved below their expected MA level. In this study, subanalyses across IQ levels (50–59 and 60–69) revealed differential results. Low-range children in special classes had superior gain scores in all areas except arithmetic. Since the initial academic profiles of special and regular class students showed equally poor achievement across academic areas, it seems likely that uncontrolled variables related to academic curriculum or teaching methods were responsible for the differential effects across the IQ ranges.

The first attempt to systematically evaluate a range of placement alternatives was undertaken by Ainsworth (1959). The author compared the academic performance of children in regular classes, special classes, and regular classes with periodic instruction by itinerant teachers with special education training. The children ranged in IQ from 50 to 75. All subjects were matched for CA, IQ, sex, and rural–urban dimensions. Unlike previous research, Ainsworth reported that all teachers were fully certified. Children were given a battery of tests, including the California Achievement Test, Gates Primary Reading Tests, and author-constructed tests related to knowledge of numbers and writing proficiency. After a year, all groups had improved significantly; there were marginal differences between the groups. On writing skills, the special and regular class children were significantly better than the itinerant teacher group.

One difficulty in interpreting the results of this study is the uncertain distinction between regular class and regular class plus itinerant teacher placement. It is not clear exactly what role the itinerant teacher played vis-à-vis the ongoing regular class curriculum, how often instruction was provided, or whether the format of this periodic instruction was one-to-one or small group.

In a study quite similar to that conducted by Thurstone (1959), Mullen and Itkin (1961) compared the academic achievement scores of 140 pairs of EMR children in regular and special classes. The subjects were matched for age, IQ, sex, socioeconomic status, reading achievement, and foreign language spoken in the home. At the end of 1 year, the groups were equal in academic achievement with the exception of greater arithmetic gains by regular class children. At the end of 2 years, there were no significant differences between the groups. However, regular class children performed consistently better than special class children in reading. These results are clearly at variance with the dominant trend for regular class EMR children to show superior academic achievement as compared to special class retarded youngsters (e.g., Bennett, 1932; Cassidy & Stanton, 1959; Elenbogen, 1957; Thurstone, 1959). Mullen and Itkin suggest that the high rate of teacher attrition in regular classes may have influenced the results of their study. The authors also indicate that a clear bias was evident in the placement process such that it would be difficult to judge special and regular class EMR children as equivalent.

Studies by Warren (1962) and Bacher (1964) also suggest little if any difference between the academic achievement of special and regular class EMR children. Warren studied 24 children placed in special classes and 24 children who were slated for placement but for various reasons were not transferred. The subjects were matched for IQ, CA, sex, years in school, and socioeconomic status. At the end of 1 year, California Achievement Test scores were equivalent for both groups. Similarly, Bacher measured the achievement scores of children classified as slow learners who were either in slow learner classes or in regular classes. The children ranged in IQ from 75 to 95 and scored at least 1 year below expected CA level in reading. Stanford Achievement Test scores were not significantly different across groups.

In one of the most methodologically sound studies conducted to date, Goldstein, Moss, and Jordan (1965) examined the academic achievement of 130 children over a 4-year period. Goldstein *et al.*'s study was unique for several reasons. First, they were the first not to compare in situ groups of children. Instead, their subjects were tested upon entry into first grade; then, those children scoring below 85 were assigned randomly to either special or regular classes. Not only did this procedure alleviate the active subject selection bias in other investigations, but it also afforded the opportunity to study a younger group of children than had been involved previously in efficacy research. The study was also unique in the specification and attempted control of curriculum and teacher variables. A statewide curriculum guide was employed, and specially trained teachers were provided with continuing supervision over the course of the study.

Achievement results from this study are nondefinitive. At the second year testing, regular class EMR children scored higher in reading; however, this trend was not evident at the end of the study. In agreement with Thurstone's (1959) findings, there was a general pattern of higher achievement by low-IQ children in special as opposed to regular classes. Goldstein *et al.* argued that these equivocal results, obtained under tightly controlled conditions, suggest that special class placement for EMR children has no empirical support.

Although the Goldstein *et al.* study clearly is more sophisticated in design than most efficacy studies, the rather bold conclusions of the authors should be viewed in light of several methodological problems. First, there was considerable subject attrition across the 4 years of the study, with approximately one-fourth of the original population available at the 4-year mark. Second, it is not clear to what extent and with what level of skills teachers employed the same curriculum guide. In the final analysis, one must depend upon direct observation of instructional interaction to make definite statements on the comparability of instruction across classes and across time. Finally, there is no evidence provided to support the appropriateness of the curriculum guide employed by special class teachers.

Evidence of the importance of curriculum in efficacy studies was provided by Jordan (1965). Using a random assignment procedure similar to that employed by Goldstein *et al.* (1965), Jordan analyzed the reading achievement of special and regular class EMR children across the first four grades. The special class children were exposed, almost exclusively, to readiness materials during Year 1. The regular class children were instructed in a standard basal-reading series during this time. In grades 2, 3, and 4 all children used a basal reader. During the first grade, regular class children were superior in reading achievement; however, there were no differences in performance by the end of the fourth grade. Jordan's study is particularly valuable because it highlights the transient nature of achievement differences and suggests that differential content emphasis can account for such differences.

Hoeltke (1966) compared the academic achievement of 122 regular and special class EMR children. All special class students had been enrolled in this placement for at least 3 years. Regular class students had never attended special classes. Wide Range Achievement Test scores revealed that the regular class children were significantly superior in reading, spelling, and arithmetic. Ironically, Hoeltke also reported that teachers viewed special class children as superior in achievement.

Data reported by Smith and Kennedy (1967) also show little support for the formation of special classes. Ninety-six EMR children were assigned randomly to one of three groups: (*a*) 45 min of specialized instruction and attention daily in special education classes; (*b*) 45 min of instruction and attention daily in a small group format; and (*c*) only regular class assignment. California Achievement Test scores revealed that no significant differences were obtained after 2 years. The authors provide little information regarding the content of instruction, the process of instruction, or the rationale for selecting a daily 45-min period for specialized training. In the absence of such data, it is difficult to evaluate the general finding of "no difference."

Carroll (1967) examined one variation on the typical regular versus special class placement design. Here, the academic achievement of special class EMR children was compared to that of youngsters who spent one-half of their school day in a special class and the other half integrated in a regular class. After 1 year, Wide Range Achievement Test scores indicated that the partially integrated group was superior in reading (word recognition on this test). Although change scores were not significant, special class youngsters were ahead slightly in spelling and arithmetic. The inconsistency of these academic data would seem to suggest that differential curriculum and/or instructional approaches and not administrative arrangements were responsible for the achievement scores.

Lewis (1973) has provided further information on the academic achievement of children from a range of integrated services. Educable mentally retarded children were selected from four settings: (a) regular classes; (b) self-contained special classes; (c) special classes with partial integration for academic instruction; and (d) regular classes with daily resource room instruction. All children ranged in age from 6 years to 10 years 9 months. Metropolitan Achievement Test scores revealed no differences among the groups. Separate analyses across sex showed that girls in regular classes, special classes, and special classes with partial integration were superior to boys in reading. There were no differences between the academic performance of males and females in resource placement. These results on sex differences are particularly important because they highlight the necessity of considering learner characteristics when evaluating any administrative arrangement.

Bradfield, Brown, Kaplan, Rickert, and Stannard (1973) tested the academic performance of children in self-contained special classes and those in regular classes where the instructional process had been individualized via learning centers and precision teaching techniques. California Achievement Test scores on third-grade children revealed no significant differences between the groups. Wide Range Achievement Test data on fourth-grade children showed that regular class children were superior in reading and arithmetic. Bradfield *et al.*'s study represents one of the most thorough attempts to regulate the instructional process in special and/or regular classes. However, since the precision teaching format was employed only in the regular classes, the results shed no light on the effects of regular versus special class placement. Also, one would expect that teachers who employed the precision teaching format for academic instruction generally were more skillful in motivating a wide array of other school-appropriate behaviors.

Additional evidence against the educational efficacy of special classes was presented by Walker (1974). Stanford Achievement Test scores were compared after children had been placed for 2 years in either self-contained classes or regular classes with resource room support. Children were matched for CA, IQ, and reading level. There were no significant differences in change scores for arithmetic; however, the children with resource room experience performed significantly better on word reading and vocabulary subtests.

Walker's study is illustrative of the need to control curriculum content and instructional interaction in efficacy research. For example, it is reasonable to conclude that variables such as (a) individualized instruction; (b) increased instructional time; and (c) specialized curriculum content were responsible for the observed differences in achievement. Without a total effort to assess and equate the curriculum and instructional process across settings, the results of comparative efficacy studies are confounded inextricably.

Major Findings on Educational Effects

Some 40 years of efficacy research related to educational outcomes has produced a largely ambiguous, methodologically suspect body of knowledge. Three general trends across studies have emerged. These trends are reviewed briefly below.

First, EMR children in special classes do not appear to demonstrate significantly better educational achievement than EMR children in regular class placement. In fact, the dominant trend in efficacy research has favored regular class children (Bennett, 1932; Cassidy & Stanton, 1959; Elenbogen, 1957; Thurstone, 1959).

There are a wide variety of factors that likely contribute to this trend. First, it has been proposed that the regular class setting creates a social climate that encourages academic competition and that this competition leads to superior performance by regular as opposed to special class children (Elenbogen, 1957). Certainly, no one would argue that EMR children in regular classes are more likely to be exposed to classmates who are achieving at expected or advanced grade levels. Whether the disparity in performance encourages better performance by EMR children remains essentially unknown.

Variation in curriculum content also has been considered an important factor in regular class EMR children's superior academic performance (Cassidy & Stanton, 1959; Lewis, 1973). Cassidy and Stanton state:

> Placement of the mentally retarded child in a regular classroom presumably means that greater emphasis is placed upon the individual's acquiring competency in reading, spelling, and arithmetic. Differences in the two types of educational settings, as indicated by the results obtained from the various psychological instruments and other materials used, picture the special classroom as being the more concerned with the overall personal development and growth of the child but lowest in the academic areas which are commonly developed within an educational framework [p. 42].

From the perspective offered by these authors, there are inherent differences in the curriculum goals of special and regular classes. If this is the case, then efficacy research based upon academic achievement indeed is biased against special class placement.

A final factor considered to be critical in understanding the superior academic performance of regular class EMR children is selective placement. With very few exceptions (e.g., Goldstein *et al.*, 1965), efficacy studies have not demonstrated clearly that groups of children were relatively equivalent on critical indices related to academic achievement. In an early critique, Cowen (1938) wrote:

> the graded group had not been chosen for special class placement because it consisted of pupils whose will-to-do, whose drive-to-accomplish, whose emotional balance, whose personality adjustment, whose school achievement and whose mechanical ability were superior to those for special class placement [p. 27].

Goldstein *et al.* (1965) and Mullen and Itkin (1961) have noted also that the superior academic achievement of EMR children in regular classes results from selective placement. Random assignment is one method of reducing selectivity, but as will be discussed later in this chapter, the procedure is not without shortcomings.

To summarize, there has been little empirical support for the educational efficacy of special class placement. In fact, it can be argued, at least from a resource allocation vviewpoint, that EMR children can be educated as well in regular class placements. It also seems important to realize that investigating the relative merits of administrative arrangements logically should follow positive findings on a number of essential prior questions. Such questions would include:

1. Are there validated curricula available for EMR children?
2. Are there replicable teaching/instructional activities that lead to positive behavior change by EMR children?
3. Are there teacher competencies particular to this population? Do teachers presently engage in these activities at a satisfactory level?

A *second, general trend related to educational outcomes is the evident superiority of children who receive individualized instruction* (e.g., Bruininks, Rynders, & Gross, 1974; Smith & Kennedy, 1967; Walker, 1974). Of course, one of the initial arguments for the creation of special classes was that low pupil–teacher ratios would lead to individualization. At least in the special education settings included in efficacy research, it would appear that little individualization obtained. Effective individualization was demonstrated only in those regular class settings with supplemental, tutorial-like services added.

With the mandate for individualization such a fundamental part of PL 94–142, it may be that other methods of instruction will become historical relics. Whether increased individualization follows an orderly, educationally helpful path will depend in large part on the development of a technology for individualizing beyond one or two children. It should be remembered that the positive effects of individualization in efficacy studies have been accomplished by teachers *not* responsible for an entire classroom of children. Some progress is clearly being made toward the identification and development of those skills necessary for classroom-wide individualization (Kerr & Nelson, in press), but this effort is in its preliminary stage.

A *final, general trend in efficacy research related to educational outcomes is the consistency with which EMR children in any administrative setting achieve below expected grade or MA level.* In only one study conducted to date (Blatt, 1958), has the achievement level of EMR students approached that of non-retarded, equivalent-MA-level children. This finding indicates that no mere manipulation of placement can be viewed as a legitimate, educational intervention. Also, it is apparent from this trend that a number of critical educational issues transcend the simple question of special versus regular class placement. For example, such issues would include (a) the relationship between degree of handicap and placement options; (b) the relationship between the level of academic achievement and children's personality/social development; and (c) the relationship between motivational variables and children's level of achievement.

Social Consequences of Educational Placement

Research that will be considered under the general rubric of social consequences covers three rather independent areas of study: (a) patterns of social interaction between EMR children and their classmates; (b) measures of the social status or acceptance of EMR children as judged by teachers and classmates; and (c) measures of EMR children's personal evaluations of themselves. In many of the studies to be reviewed, investigators have focused on more than one of these areas.

In terms of initial intent, special classes were begun, in part, in order to provide EMR children with a learning environment free of the frustration, shame, and ridicule resulting from competition with intellectually superior peers (Cegelka & Tyler, 1970). As might be expected, the empirical evidence does not reflect so clear a picture.

Bennett (1932) was the first to consider the social status of EMR children. Teachers were asked to rate special and regular class EMR children on a number of personal and school-related attributes. Special class EMR children generally were rated higher in oral discussion skills, in thrift, in care for school property, in adherence to school rules, in clear speech, in personal cleanliness, and in cooperation with teachers. In evaluating these results, it is important to realize that the comparability of children in both groups was never established.

Johnson (1950) has provided a rather thorough examination of the social status of EMR children in regular classes. Children from two communities where no special classes were available served as subjects. Interviews were conducted in a total of 25 classes, with five classes each at grade levels 1–5. Each class had at least one EMR child who scored 69 or below on the Stanford–Binet. Children were asked a series of questions about who their best friends were and who they liked least. Two trends were quite clear. First, EMR children seldom were identified as friends and often identified as least liked. Second, more low-IQ EMR children were rejected than higher-IQ handicapped youngsters. When asked to describe why they disliked their EMR peers, children specified such behaviors as fighting, showing off, cheating, and generally breaking classroom rules.

Although regular class children tended to express quite specific acts that brought disfavor to their EMR classmates, one cannot be certain that the handicapped children in fact engaged in relatively higher rates of the designated noxious behaviors. If their behavior patterns were fundamentally different, then reducing the rate of these behaviors should bring about more active friendships and less rejection between EMR and regular class peers. It is also quite possible that the regular class children's list of deviant behaviors represented a rationalization for overt prejudice toward EMR children. Drabman, Spitalnik, and Spitalnik (1976) have demonstrated that children's sociometric ratings are not related to the actual level of disruptive behavior by peers. Rather, children seem to rate each other on the basis of expected norms that they create for individual class members.

Lapp (1957) employed Johnson's (1950) sociometric device to study the social status of EMR children in special class and those who had been integrated partially into regular classes. Sixteen children from one special class served as subjects. Twelve of the children were integrated daily for physical education, music, art, social studies and/or science activities. The remaining four children were instructed in the special class. The questionnaire was administered to the children in the spring of 2 consecutive years. A somewhat inconsistent pattern of results was found. First, children who were integrated partially were more accepted than totally segregated youngsters. In terms of active rejection, there was no difference between the groups. Second, integrated children were more isolated from regular class peers than they were rejected openly by these children. Lapp proposed that the relative passivity of integrated EMR children likely was responsible for their social isolation.

Lapp's data on relative social status cannot be interpreted to support regular class placement. Since in situ groups were used, it is most probable that there were substantial differences in the academic and social competencies of segregated and partially integrated students. It should be remembered also that the integrated students were not present, as they were in Johnson's (1950) study, for reading, math, or spelling instruction.

In another study of the social status and adjustment of EMR children in special and regular classes, Elenbogen (1957) reported significant differences in favor of special class children. Teachers administered rating scales and a structured interview. Children in special classes tended to express more realistic vocational goals, have more after-school jobs and friends, participate in more school functions, and express more favorable opinions of school. No reliability of ratings was reported by Elenbogen; and thus it is impossible to judge the "truthfulness" or the stability of teachers' perceptions. Generally speaking, however, it has been shown that teachers are quite poor judges of the traits investigated by Elenbogen (see Greenwood, Walker, & Hops, 1977).

Baldwin (1958) examined the social status of 31 EMR children in regular classes. Three separate assessment procedures were used: (*a*) the Ohio Social Acceptance Scale; (*b*) the Ohio Social Recognition Scale; and (*c*) interviews with teachers and regular class pupils. The results were similar, in part, to those obtained by Johnson (1950). EMR children in regular class were accepted significantly less than their classroom peers. Unlike Johnson, however, Baldwin did not find that lower-IQ EMR children were accepted less than higher-IQ EMR youngsters. Interview data revealed that teachers and fellow pupils most often listed the antisocial behaviors of EMR children as most disturbing.

Taken together, the work of Johnson (1950) and Baldwin (1958) clearly would suggest that physical integration does not lead to desirable social integration. In fact, data from these studies reveal that the regular class may be experienced by EMR children as a hostile, rejecting environment. Just to what extent any overt behaviors by EMR children lead to their rejection cannot be fully understood by the interview methodology employed. This general type of social acceptance study, as exemplified by Johnson's and Baldwin's research, needs also to be viewed as representing only one-half of the social interactants of concern. It would be most valuable to know, for example, how EMR children in regular classes accepted each other and nonhandicapped peers, how EMR children evaluated themselves on a comparative basis, and how these youngsters perceived their teachers' behavior with regard to themselves and classmates.

At a much different level of analysis, Porter and Milazzo (1958) examined the adult social adjustment and economic standing of EMR children who had attended either special or regular class. All subjects were at least 18-years-old; and, they were matched for IQ and years in class. The 12 special class subjects had attended a university demonstration school, while the 12 regular class children were drawn from public schools in the same city. An interview format was used to secure the judgments of subjects, their parents, acquaintances, neighbors, and employers.

On measures of social competence the former special class students were more stable, lived in a more desirable physical location, and attended church more often. Additionally, no special class individual had been arrested, while one-third of the regular class subjects had criminal records. In terms of potential for economic self-sufficiency, only one special class member was unemployed, whereas eight former regular class members were unemployed.

Porter and Milazzo's results are most provocative. However, generalizations to other populations are quite limited. First, it is not clear whether or not any differential selection process was operative across the demonstration school and the public schools. Second, it seems reasonable to assume that there would be structural, if not functional differences between the university-based class and public school programs. For example, one would expect lower pupil–teacher ratios in the university program, possibly more individualized instruction in this setting, and more expansive budgets for educational hardware and software in the demonstration setting. Finally, generalization to other sites is limited severely by the lack of information regarding the curriculum employed in both settings. The tendency for special class pupils to be more socially and vocationally competent could well be the result of training aimed specially at these skill areas.

Blatt (1958) examined the social adjustment and social behavior of EMR children from special and regular classes. When the 75 special class childrens' adjustment was compared to that of 50 matched, regular class youngsters, no differences were noted. Using the California Test of Personality, both groups revealed more personal and social problems than norms of higher-IQ children would predict. On the New York City Scales of Social Maturity and Emotional Stability, special class students were found to have more part-time jobs and to be less likely to have been classified as truant.

On the vast majority of indices, there were no differences between the groups. For example, the two groups were essentially equal on indices of (a) delinquency; (b) stealing in school; (c) number of contacts with police; (d) number of suspensions from school; (e) length of time in detention homes; and (f) attendance at church Sunday school.

Those differences and similarities that emerged on the New York scales must be viewed with considerable caution since teachers were the primary source for these data. A considerable body of attitudinal research has shown that teachers with special training and experience hold more favorable opinions of handicapped children than do regular class teachers (Alexander & Strain, 1978; Mandell & Strain, 1978). Thus, the apparent superiority in social adjustment of special class children may have been due to teachers' differential acceptance of EMR youngsters.

Ainsworth (1959) attempted to examine the social consequences for EMR students in regular class, special class, and regular class with itinerant teacher support. On measures of deviant behavior across a 1-year period, regular class youngsters demonstrated a significant decrease. Special and regular class students with itinerant teacher support showed no differences in the frequency of deviant behaviors across this time period. Teachers' ratings of 14 personal characteristics revealed no differences either across time or groups of children.

Ainsworth's study is subject to serious methodological criticisms, including no standardization of assessment procedures, exclusively teacher-administered tests, and subjects' switching classes and teachers during the year. Nonetheless, a number of corollary findings are noteworthy. First, reliability between teachers' ratings were extremely low. Second, there were low correlations between ratings and actual behaviors observed. Viewed together, these findings suggest that sociometric assessments of adjustment often yield data of doubtful reliability and validity.

Sociometric devices were used also by Thurstone (1959) to examine the social acceptance and school adjustment of regular and special class EMR youngsters. Both high- and low-IQ children in regular classes received much more lower favorability scores than did normal classmates. Teachers and peers both judged the EMR children in a similar fashion. Special class children also were found to enjoy school more, have more friends, and engage in more school-related activities than regular class EMR youngsters.

The close agreement in sociometric ratings between teachers and peers is subject to a variety of interpretations. First of all, it is possible that teachers held certain biases toward EMR youngsters, responded differentially toward them, and thus helped to set the occasion for peers to develop similar biases. On the other hand, one might suspect that peers' social rejection of EMR youngsters could have influenced teachers' negative perceptions of retarded youngsters. Likely, both explanations reflect some part of the process by which reciprocal influence is maintained between teachers and students.

Cassidy and Stanton (1959) have provided information that indicates how teachers' perceptions and biases may affect the social adjustment of EMR children. Using the California Test of Personality, special class EMR children were found to be better adjusted than regular class EMR youngsters. When the expectations of regular and special class teachers were examined, it was found that regular class teachers were concerned more with students' academic performance, whereas special class teachers were concerned more with social skills, physical appearance, and habits of conduct. Although regular class teachers were quite concerned with EMR children's academic success, they did not feel that these youngsters would ever be successful in academic settings and that they likely would become delinquent, incorrigible youths. Although Cassidy and Stanton (1959) did not document directly any differential teacher behaviors toward regular or special class children, it seems reasonable to conclude that teachers with such drastically disparate perceptions of EMR youngsters would interact and communicate in fundamentally different ways with these children.

One likely implication of Cassidy and Stanton's (1959) study is that there would be a positive correlation between regular class children's academic performance or IQ and the degree of social acceptance (e.g., Johnson, 1950). Jordan (1960) has provided evidence that such a pattern of acceptance–rejection also operates in special classes. A total of 349 EMR students from 22 classes were asked to rate their classmates according to whom they most and least liked. Lower-IQ children were found to be rejected more and to receive lower overall ratings than higher-IQ classmates.

A clear pattern of social acceptance–rejection is evident across both special and regular class settings. It appears that less-skilled, less-intelligent children are rejected actively by their classmates. Thus, the critical issue related to peer acceptance is not what educational placement leads to social integration, but what intervention tactics can be employed to increase the likelihood of positive interaction between children who exhibit various levels of behavioral development (see Chapter 5).

Mullen and Itkin (1961) compared the personal adjustment of regular and special class EMR children over a 2-year period. At the end of the first year, there were no differences between the groups on personal adjustment. After 2 years, regular class teachers ranked their students higher in classroom adjustment than did special class teachers. On behavior checklist data, special class children showed a significant decrease in hostile–aggressive activity in school after 2 years. Children from high-risk families also were found to make better personal adjustments in special as opposed to regular classes.

Mullen and Itkin's (1961) data are suggestive of a differential teacher expectation pattern similar to that identified by Cassidy and Stanton (1959), namely, that special class teachers are, in general, more accepting and responsive than regular class teachers to the social limitations and needs of EMR children. It is not clear, however, whether EMR children in special class in fact behave in a more adjusted fashion or whether special class teachers simply are more tolerant than regular class teachers of suspected deficiencies and more optimistic about educational outcomes.

Further evidence of the superior social acceptance of EMR children in self-contained classes is provided by Johnson (1961). In what represents one of the better controlled investigations conducted to date, Johnson compared the personal and social adjustment and social acceptance of 16 matched pairs of subjects. Children in self-contained classes came from a school district in which all children classified as EMR were served in special classes only. The regular class students were selected from districts in which no special classes were available. On the Syracuse Scales of Social Relations, EMR children in self-contained classes were significantly higher in social acceptance. No differences were detected, however, on measures of personal and social adjustment.

Kern and Pfaeffle (1963) administered the California Test of Personality to EMR children in three educational placements: (*a*) a segregated school for the mentally retarded; (*b*) special classes; and (*c*) regular classes. The authors maintain that since the regular class children were all on waiting lists to enter segregated classes, these two groups may be equated legitimately. Special school youngsters were found to have the highest overall adjustment scores, followed by special class then regular class children.

Caution should be exercised in viewing these results as predictive of personal or social adjustment beyond the confines of the special school or classroom.

It can be argued, at least from a logical standpoint, that adjustment to and exclusive experience in the relatively controlled and limited special school environment would be counterproductive as EMR children move into larger, more complex, and likely more demanding community settings. Clearly, if the schooling experience is held to be significant for social skills development and social adjustment outside of the 6-hr school day, then evaluative research must include measures of placement effects in a variety of extraschool settings.

Meyerowitz (1962) was one of the first to examine the self-concept scores of EMR children. In fact, this was the first efficacy study to use self-concept scores as a dependent measure. The study is noteworthy also due to the rigorous subject selection procedures. One hundred and twenty EMR children were assigned randomly to special or regular classes at the beginning of the first grade. The control group, composed of 60 children of normal intelligence, was matched on the following dimensions: area of residence, father's occupation, and family income. Meyerowitz administered the Illinois Index of Self-Derogation to all subjects. The testing format includes 30 items composed of two self-descriptive statements. One statement reflects socially desirable or neutral content. The other statement represents clearly undesirable content. Subjects are asked to choose which statement best reflects the way they feel about themselves. Two clear findings emerged. First, EMR children attributed significantly more undesirable descriptions to themselves than did normal youngsters. Second, significantly more derogatory comments were used by special as opposed to regular class EMR children.

In reviewing the results of this study, Meyerowitz suggests that the apparent superiority of regular class EMR children on this self-concept measure may reflect a transient phenomenon. He further states that as EMR children in regular classes are faced with more complex learning tasks than those demanded in first grade, failure experiences may well produce very negative self-perceptions. Of course, to begin to answer fully questions regarding the interaction between length of time in educational setting and personal–social development would require extensive longitudinal study.

A slightly different model of the usual efficacy study was conducted by Bacher (1964). Here, children with IQ scores between 75 and 95 and members of either regular classes or classes for slow learners were studied. Self-concept was assessed on the Columbia Classroom Social Distance Scale and the students' "I Think Score" on the Davidson–Long Checklist of Trait Names. On both these indices, no differences were found between the groups. Moreover, no significant differences were found between these low-IQ subjects and normal subjects in regular classes. Social adjustment was measured also by the Columbia Classroom Social Distance Scale. Children in classes for slow learners were accepted more by their peers than were equivalent-IQ youngsters in regular classes. Additionally, slow learner subjects were more accepting of their peers than were regular class children.

Bacher's (1964) study particularly is important because of the reciprocal acceptance–rejection patterns identified. If both exceptional and normal children reject each other, then efforts to improve the quality of interaction must focus on the attitudes and behaviors of both parties.

Goldstein *et al.* (1965) were the first to consider extraschool outcomes of special versus regular class placement. Mothers of special class EMR children attributed fewer derogatory descriptions to their children. Unfortunately, no measurement of mothers' perceptions were made prior to the school experience. Thus, the exact role of class placement cannot be separated from other variables that may influence mothers' opinions of their children. Somewhat conflicting results were obtained from neighborhood sociometric ratings. Here, regular class children interacted more in a positive fashion than did special class youngsters. Neither group was rejected overtly by neighborhood members. As Bacher's (1964) research points to the necessity to consider and intervene in regard to the attitudes and behaviors of both exceptional and normal youngsters, Goldstein *et al.*'s data suggests that efforts to alter the social interaction patterns of EMR children must target on relevant family and community members as well.

Welch's (1966) study of self-concept development in special class and partially integrated EMR children closely replicated Meyerowitz's (1962) findings. Again, the Illinois Index of Self-Derogation was used to assess self-concept. The test was administered when children first entered the contrasting placements and then 8 months later. No pre–post differences were noted for the segregated group or a group of normal controls. Partially integrated children offered fewer derogatory comments about themselves as they interacted more with normal children. Overall, segregated children tended to describe themselves in more derogatory terms than did integrated or normal youngsters.

The hypothesis offered by Meyerowitz (1962) that the self-concept of EMR children would change over time has been investigated by Mayer (1966). One hundred EMR children in special classes served as subjects. The children were divided into those who were placed in special classes during the first three grades, during the fourth through sixth grades, and during the seventh through ninth grades. Mayer proposed that children placed in the early grades would have better self-concepts than children placed later. Two indices of self-concept were employed: (*a*) The Children's Self Concept Scale; and (*b*) The Way I Feel About Myself. No differences were found in self-concept scores across EMR groups. An important secondary finding was the similarity between the self-concept scores of normal children in the standardization sample and the EMR children. Mayer interpreted these results to indicate that long-term experience in special classes may have a positive effect on self-concept.

In an additional study of self-concept, Hoeltke (1966) tested special class EMR children who had been in segregated settings for at least 3 years and EMR children who had never been in a special class. Teacher ratings were employed with specific attention to attitudes toward the teacher and self-concept as a learner. Special class children were found to be more positive toward themselves as learners than regular class EMR youngsters. There were no differences between the two groups in their attitudes toward their teachers. These results closely parallel earlier findings in which teacher ratings have been employed (e.g., Cassidy & Stanton, 1959; Johnson, 1950).

Measures of self-concept comparing special class and partially integrated EMR children by Carroll (1967) are in close agreement with Meyerowitz's (1962) findings. The Illinois Index of Self-Derogation was administered to subjects at the beginning and end of 1 school year. Across this time period, there was a significant reduction in the number of self-derogatory statements by partially integrated children.

Additional evidence of potential support for regular class placement for EMR children is provided by Fine and Caldwell (1967). Here, 42 EMR children along with their teachers were administered a questionnaire that addressed the students' perceptions of themselves vis-à-vis reading, arithmetic, and general ability. Regular class children tended to rate themselves as equal or superior to their classroom and school peers in all areas. Teachers, on the other hand, typically rated EMR children below class peers in all areas.

Fine and Caldwell (1967) interpret these data to indicate that regular class EMR children maintain a healthy self-concept in this setting. One could argue, however, that no inaccurate self-evaluation can be considered healthy or desirable. Possibly the key ingredient in the EMR child's development of a "healthy" self-concept or accurate self-evaluation lies in encouraging an analysis of past and present skills rather than a comparison with others.

Towne, Joiner, and Schurr (Note l) have reported results that strongly conflict with those data presented by Fine and Caldwell (1967). Sixty-two EMR children were given an eight-item self-concept scale on five separate occasions. On the first testing, all children were in regular classes, awaiting placement in segrated special classes. The remaining four testing times were distributed evenly across the first year of special class placement. All test items were designed to probe students' evaluation of their school performance. The results indicated that when students were placed in special classes they viewed themselves as more competent than when they were in regular classes. This trend diminished toward the end of the first year.

A study by Monroe and Howe (1971) addressed the social acceptance of integrated EMR adolescents. All 70 boys were integrated for varying amounts of time during the school day. Also, the boys varied in the length of time they had been involved in the integrated program from 1 to 3 years. The Ohio Social Acceptance Scale was administered to members of the subjects' physical education classes. Educable mentally retarded children generally received lower scores than nonretarded peers. There were also no significant differences in scores for groups of EMR subjects who had been integrated for 1, 2, or 3 years. Monroe and Howe were interested also in the relationship between socioeconomic status and peer acceptance. The highest acceptance scores were obtained by nonretarded children in the high socioeconomic group and the lowest scores were obtained by EMR children in the low socioeconomic group. Although Monroe and Howe did not specifically study the relationship between socioeconomic status and the EMR label itself, one might suspect that low socioeconomic status is a strong predictor of EMR status (Cohen & DeYoung, 1973; Dunn, 1968).

Lewis (1973) investigated the self-concept and social adjustment of EMR children across four administrative arrangements. In the first setting, children had been screened into special classes but the placement had not been finalized. Another group of students were enrolled in self-contained classes. The third group was composed of students who were enrolled in special classes but who also participated in many school activities with regular class youngsters. The final group was composed of regular class students who attended resource rooms or learning centers for most academic instruction. On the self-concept measure, the Way I Feel About Myself, no significant differences were found between the four groups. Similarly, no differences were found between the groups on self-reports of attitude toward school. The teacher who had the most regular contact with each student provided reports on students' level of social adaptation. Results indicated that children in segregated classes were viewed as less socially competent than children in any of the other three placements. Also, segregated children were seen by teachers as less self-directed than other EMR youngsters.

Bradfield *et al.* (1973) compared the self-concept and behavior rating scores of EMR and educationally handicapped children in segregated classes and those in regular classes. The regular classes were conducted so that individualized instruction was maximized via learning centers and precision teaching techniques. On the semantic differential measure of self-concept there were no differences between the groups in attitudes toward self, family, or authority figures. Teachers' ratings from the Quay–Peterson Behavior Problem Checklist indicated that both EMR and educationally handicapped children in the regular classes showed a more marked improvement than children in special classes after a 7-month period. It should also be pointed out that the regular class children initially were considered by their teachers to exhibit significantly more behavior problems than special class youngsters.

In a most unique study of placement effects, Warner, Thrapp, and Walsh (1973) examined the attitudes of special class EMR children toward their placement. The children were asked five questions:

1. Do you like being in a special class?
2. Would you rather be in some other class in this school?
3. Why do you think you are in a special class?
4. What do you like most about being in a special class?
5. What do you like least about being in a special class?

The majority (61%) of the 369 students interviewed said they liked being in a special class. Only 26% of the respondents indicated that they wanted to be in another class, and several of these children expressed a wish to be in a different special class. A majority (53%) of elementary-age children felt they were in special classes in order "to learn," "to read," "to catch up." However, fewer junior high (34%) and high school (18%) students expressed such an opinion. Less than 10% of all children attributed their placement in special classes to mental retardation. Most of the respondents indicated that academic work was what they liked most about the special class; the disruptive behavior of their classmates was what they most disliked.

Sheare (1974) examined the social acceptance of EMR adolescents in segregated and integrated classes. The subjects were 400 ninth-grade children of normal intelligence. One-half of this group was assigned randomly to classes in which EMR children (not more than three) were present. The other half was assigned to classes in which no EMR students were present. After approximately 4 months, all nonretarded children were administered a 25-item social acceptance scale. Items on the scale included such statements as: "Special-class teenagers should be educated in special schools away from normal teenagers" and "A special-class teenager can be as useful to the school as any other teenager."

Two significant findings emerged from this study. First, subjects who were exposed to EMR students in their classes were more accepting and positive toward these students than were youngsters without direct classroom exposure. Second, females were most positive in their attitudes than were males. The author interprets these findings as support for the notion that lack of interaction with and knowledge of EMR children is responsible for negative, pejorative attitudes.

Gampel, Gottlieb, and Harrison (1974) examined the social behavior of segregated and integrated EMR children who all were formerly segregated. A total of 55 children were included in the study. The first group was composed of 12 EMR children enrolled full-time in a segregated class. The second group was composed of 14 EMR children who were enrolled full-time in regular classes. The third group was composed of 18 low-IQ children who had never been identified for special class placement. The final group was composed of 11 normal-IQ children who attended the same classes with integrated EMR children. A time-sampling technique was employed whereby all subjects were observed in their classroom setting across a 6-week period. The following behaviors were recorded: attention, distraction, out of seat, restlessness, self-stimulation, uncoordinated motor response, aggressive behavior to peer, aggressive behavior from peer, positive verbal response to peer, negative verbal response to peer, positive verbal response from peer, and negative verbal response from peer.

The results indicated that segregated children engaged in more restless behavior and more negative verbal responses to peers and received more negative verbal responses from peers than did integrated EMR youngsters. No other comparison across groups was significant. In general, these data indicate that integrated EMR children engage in more appropriate and positive social interaction than do segregated youngsters.

Walker (1974) employed a variation of the Illinois Index of Self-Derogation to assess the self-concept and social adjustment of EMR children in resource rooms and those in segregated classes. Twenty-nine children assigned to resource rooms and 41 children assigned to segregated classes were matched for chronological age, IQ, and reading level. At the end of a 2-year period, there were no statistically significant differences between the groups on the measure of self-concept.

Bruininks *el al.* (1974) examined the effects of school location (suburban versus inner-city) and sex of normal peer on the social acceptance ratings of EMR children. The handicapped youngsters were enrolled in regular classes with resource learning center assistance. Acceptance scores were derived from a version of the Ohio Social Acceptance Scale. Educable mentally retarded children attending inner-city schools received significantly higher ratings than nonretarded children of the same sex. In contrast, EMR youngsters in suburban schools were given significantly lower ratings than nonretarded children of the same sex. Pooled data across sex revealed no differences in social acceptance between retarded and nonretarded children.

Haring and Krug (1975) examined the social adaptation of 13 regular class EMR children who had received individualized instruction in a special class for 1 year. The initial subject population was composed of 48 elementary-age EMR children who resided in an economically depressed area. The 24 children who were assigned to the experimental classrooms received individualized instruction via precision teaching techniques. All children used the Distar and Sullivan Programmed Reading Series for reading instruction and the Suppes Sets and Numbers for math instruction. Student motivation was maintained by the use of token economy programs with contingencies imposed for accurate academic performance.

After 1 year of this special class intervention, 13 students were placed in regular classes. At the end of 1 year in regular classes, teachers ranked EMR students on social competency in the upper $\frac{2}{3}$ of the class. When asked about the future placement of EMR students, teachers indicated that $\frac{3}{4}$ of the experimental subjects could remain in regular class. No student was seen as needing special class placement. The authors propose that rigorous, individualized instruction in special classes can help prepare EMR children to cope adequately with the academic and social demands of the regular classroom.

Budoff and Gottlieb (1976) conducted a particularly thorough study of the self-concept and social adjustment of segregated and integrated EMR children. Seventeen of the 31 EMR subjects were assigned to a regular class with support from a learning center. The student–teacher ratio in the special class and integrated settings was approximately 7 to 1. An extensive battery of instruments was used to assess the subjects' social functioning. A school morale scale was developed from Wrightsman's School Morale Scale, which previously had been shown to discriminate differences in attitudes between special and regular class children (Gottlieb & Budoff, 1973). From a factor analysis of the Laurelton Self-Concept Scale the authors developed a 28-item academic self-concept instrument. A 60-item self-concept scale also was developed for this study. Forty-eight of the items were designed to measure how children felt about themselves and 12 items were designed to find out how children felt that their peers perceived them. A measure of locus of control also was employed to determine whether children perceived themselves to be the primary controlling agent in the situations described. Two scales related to children's anxiety and their tendency to deny such negative feelings also were administered.

After 1 school year, integrated students felt more positive about their prospects in school, expressed more of a sense of control over their environment, and viewed themselves as more competent learners.

Major Findings on Social Effects

The body of research on social outcomes of educational placement is best characterized by the ambiguity of results. There are, however, at least two trends that seem fairly reliable.

First, there is a clear relationship between the era in which studies on social adjustment and social status were conducted and the direction of results. In only one study (Mullen & Itkin, 1961) from Bennett's (1932) initial investigation to the 1970s did any study report that integrated EMR children received higher ratings from classroom peers or teachers than special class youngsters. Goldstein *et al.* (1965) did find that neighborhood peers gave higher social ratings to integrated EMR children than to special class EMR youngsters. All studies reported from the 1970s found that integrated EMR children were viewed more favorably than their special class counterparts.

A variety of factors may have operated to produce these time-dependent results. First, the structure and function of both regular and special class placement for EMR youngsters underwent profound change across the 40-plus-year period in question. During the first 3 decades, special classes were being developed actively with assistance and political pressure from parent groups, professional organizations, federal and state law, and litigation. In this climate, one must seriously question the comparability of placements, particularly in designs in which one school system offered special classes and the other(s) did not (e.g., Johnson, 1950, 1961; Kern & Pfaeffle, 1963). In such cases, it seems unlikely that EMR children were in regular classes because these settings were judged by school officials to be the most educationally sound alternative. More likely, financial considerations and teacher availability were overriding concerns. Thus, it seems reasonable to assume that school systems offering special class placement for EMR children during the 1930s, 1940s, 1950s, and 1960s were better funded, better equipped, and better staffed to meet the needs of these children than systems not providing such services.

It should be noted also that one of the initial and principal goals of special class placement was to offer EMR children a learning atmosphere free of the suspected frustration, ridicule, and shame associated with academic competition in regular classrooms. Given this charge, one would expect that special class teachers would be concerned particularly with the social–affective dimension of the educational experience. Indeed, Cassidy and Stanton (1959) and Mullen and Itkin (1961) suggest that special class teachers' concern for the social adjustment of EMR children is translated directly into curriculum goals that differ substantially from the academic emphasis of most regular class curricula.

In conclusion then, the superior social acceptance and adjustment of segregated EMR children evident in early efficacy studies likely resulted from the following circumstances: (*a*) the suspected inadequacy of early regular class services for EMR children; and (*b*) a clear difference in the instructional goals for regular and special class EMR youngsters.

In studies conducted during the 1970s (e.g., Bradfield *et al.*, 1973; Budoff & Gottlieb, 1976; Haring & Krug, 1975) EMR children in regular classes were provided with specialized and/or individualized instruction. Moreover, the political climate through the mid-1970s was such that segregated placement was criticized actively and public school resources for the education of EMR children were being shifted to regular class arrangements. Thus, the superior social adjustment of EMR children studied in the 1970s must be examined in light of the same lack of comparability between regular and special class placement that operated during preceding decades.

The second major trend regarding social outcomes concerns the apparent superiority in self-concept of integrated EMR children. Emphasis should be placed on *apparent* as the data are admittedly less than unequivocal. Of the 12 studies conducted on the self-concept of EMR children in various educational settings, 6 studies report results in favor of integrated students, 4 report no differences, and 2 indicate more positive self-concept scores by segregated youngsters. Both studies that reported results favoring special class EMR children, Hoeltke (1966) and Towne *et al.* (1967), employed what may be termed "limited" self-concept indices. Specifically, both studies measured the subjects' self-perception as it related exclusively to learner competence. Although other investigators employed self-concept indices that included evaluations of self regarding academic skills, this certainly was not the primary focus of assessment. Areas in which integrated children rated themselves higher than special class peers included physical attractiveness, physical prowess and skill, social competence and popularity, and ability to influence others (e.g., Budoff & Gottlieb, 1976; Meyerowitz, 1962; Welch, 1965).

As was noted earlier, a higher self-concept rating may not always translate directly into better or more healthy personal and social adjustment. The basic issue here is the degree of match between one's self-perceptions, others' views, and the reality of the situation. Take, for example, the finding of higher scores in self-concept as a learner for special class EMR children. On balance, the efficacy research shows that integrated EMR children tend to achieve better academically than segregated peers. One could argue that self-perception as a learner is dependent upon the immediately present referent group; however, the social context of the special class is a relatively limited and brief environment in the total social ecology of mildly handicapped children, particularly when possibilities for future regular class placement are considered.

Although they may be stated as working hypotheses only, a number of factors appear to be important in understanding the general trend toward high self-concept scores by integrated EMR children. First, it is important to note that segregated and integrated EMR children usually differ in terms of formalized, school system recognition as being of below normal intelligence. Thus, segregated children, without exception, have been labeled as retarded. This is not necessarily the case with regular class children of equal intelligence.

Research on the label *mentally retarded* and its effects on persons' attitudes toward the recipient suggests a general pattern of stereotyped perceptions and negative behavior toward mentally retarded persons (Dokecki, Anderson, & Strain, 1977). As regards EMR children, there is considerable evidence to suggest that labeled children are (*a*) generally viewed as less competent socially and academically than their performance would indicate (Severance & Gastrom, 1977); (*b*) viewed by age-peers as less socially attractive than nonlabeled children of equal intelligence (Johnson, 1950); and (*c*) viewed as less likely to make satisfactory later life adjustment than nonlabeled youngsters (Cassidy & Stanton, 1959). Moreover, research on the relationship between attitudes held and interpersonal behaviors directed toward the referent has shown that individuals (teachers in particular) are less positive and supportive of children for whom they have low expectations for success (Brophy & Good, 1970).

Another factor potentially related to the superior self-concept of regular class EMR children is the dehumanization process associated with placement in settings designed exclusively for the mentally retarded. First, it has been inevitable in the assignment of the label *mentally retarded*, and even to a greater extent in the label *special class EMR* that an illusion of homogeneity follows. In their sociological research on special classes, Edgerton and Edgerton (1973) propose that teachers and administrators tend to conceal the heterogeneity of strengths and weaknesses among labeled children and thus inadvertently prohibit individualized solutions to academic and social deficits.

⬥ Besides losing one's individual identity in the placement process, certain civil liberties have been restricted in special class settings. Indeed, current case law clearly considers placement in special classes as a potential deprivation of basic rights (see Cohen & DeYoung, 1973). Often, special class placement means limited access to such specialized or extracurricular activities as organized sports, art, music, and social clubs. The racial and ethnic representation of many EMR classes also suggests that special classes have promoted de facto racial segregation (*Larry P. v. Riles*, 1971) and used testing procedures that are culturally biased against children who do not use English as a first language (*Arreola v. Board of Education*, 1968). Although many of these discriminatory practices have been curtailed in recent years, they were in full operation when the studies on self-concept were conducted. Although no one can delineate with precise accuracy the mechanisms by which biased and demeaning actions affect children's self-concept, there can be little doubt that the results are often destructive.

Methodological Issues in Efficacy Research

Throughout this review essential methodological problems associated with individual studies have been highlighted. In this section, the following design issues common to most of the literature reviewed will be considered: specification of independent variable, subject selection, and choice of outcome measures.

SPECIFICATION OF INDEPENDENT VARIABLE

Sidman (1960) notes that the heart of scientific verification is the replication of phenomena across time, across experimenters, and across laboratories. The primary prerequisite for replication is a precise description of the independent variable. If the scientist is uncertain as to the exact conditions presented to the subjects, replication, and thus scientific verification, cannot occur. As regards the efficacy literature, it is difficult to conclude that *any* systematic replications have occurred.

One of the major stumbling blocks to replication in this area of research is the use of terms such as *regular class placement* and *special class placement* in a way that assumes homogeneity and singularity of function. For example, generalizations are made from these data (cf. Dunn, 1968; Smith & Arkans,

1974) as if there were some consensual agreement across schools regarding the structure and function of special and regular class services for EMR children. One need only to review the method sections of efficacy studies to see the consistent *lack* of similarity in services that share the titles *regular class* or *special class*. There are few instances in the efficacy literature (e.g., Bradfield *et al.*, 1973; Goldstein *et al.*, 1965; Haring & Krug, 1975) in which placement alternatives are not considered as unitary variables. Yet, it is clear that many separate components of educational service delivery are subsumed under these labels. For example, curricula employed, pupil–teacher ratio, teacher competency, and motivational incentives for students are some of the more salient components of placement alternatives that likely contribute to academic and social outcomes. As early as 1959, Goldstein stated:

> Nowhere in the research does one find any information that sheds any light on the critical characteristics of the programs. Thus it is not only impossible to ascertain just what is being compared, but it is also impossible for another researcher to replicate the study [p. 342].

A number of researchers have attempted to delineate and control the various functional components of placement alternatives. For example, Goldstein *et al.* (1965) had all teachers in their study use the *Illinois Curriculum Guide for Teachers of the Educable Mentally Handicapped*. This procedure allowed for some standardization in curriculum goals related to arithmetic, fine arts, language arts, physical education, practical arts, science, and social relationships. Moreover, these authors took several steps in hope of insuring that teachers actually employed the curriculum guide in an appropriate and similar fashion. First, all special class teachers had state certification in mental retardation. Second, close classroom supervision was maintained. Finally, teachers met at 6-week intervals during the school year and at the end of each year to discuss teaching plans and evaluate child performance and curriculum items. These efforts are certainly commendable. However, in the absence of direct observational data on instructional interaction patterns, possible behavioral differences between teachers cannot be addressed satisfactorily.

Bradfield *et al.* (1973) and Haring and Krug (1975) both handled the curriculum issue by employing behavioral teaching strategies. Parts of the instructional process standardized by such an approach include (*a*) the specification of curriculum goals and assessment procedures in precise behavioral terms; (*b*) the specification of performance criteria for meeting goals; (*c*) regularization of teacher planning by control of antecedent and consequent events; and (*d*) use of motivational incentives to encourage on-task behavior and develop discriminated responding (see Kerr & Strain, 1978, for a thorough discussion of these procedures). No study addressed procedures to control for differences in teacher expectations and assessments of appropriate and inappropriate child behavior. However, the standardization of reliable child performance indices and the focus on teacher-manipulated variables that control child performance may, in practice, reduce the influence of teacher expectation and bias.

Two historical footnotes should also be added to this discussion of independent variable control. First, many of the efficacy studies reported were conducted during a time when few teachers of exceptional children were certified. Indeed, there were relatively few training opportunities for special educators. Second, active research on instructional materials and procedures in special education postdated many efficacy studies. Thus, the technology of sound, empirically supported instruction for EMR children was not available until the 1960s. Moreover, this technology is still undergoing rapid change and refinement today (Stowitschek, 1978).

As is most always the case, criticism of methodology is a far simpler task than offering sound alternatives. The difficulty is not so much due to design complexities as it is the result of necessary methodological compromise when one asks questions outside the confines of a laboratory. Probably nowhere is this dilemma more clear than in efforts to specify independent variables. For example, the laboratory scientist interested in the effects of food deprivation on the activity level of a particular species has a number of reliable, calibrated indices by which to describe the independent variable (food deprivation). First, the scientist might measure precise amounts of nutritive substances and administer these directly to the animals. Second, the scientist can further describe the independent variable by body weight measures of each animal. In so doing, other experimenters can readily understand and produce the same manipulations. The applied scientist interested in the educational and social outcomes of educational placement must be far more elaborate and speculative in describing the independent variable. It does not follow, however, that the applied researcher is less of a scientist. If anything, the applied scientist must be *more* vigilant, rigorous, and cautious in collecting and interpreting data.

With the goal of replication in mind, the following suggestions for better specifying the independent variable in efficacy research are offered. First, it would be most advantageous to control teacher variance by observing teachers who have either graduated from the same program or, better yet, met similar instructional competencies. It also seems most important to sample the direct instructional behaviors of teachers in both regular and special class settings.

Efforts to equate or at least better describe instructional objectives across administrative arrangements are clearly needed. A number of distinct items are relevant here. First, it is necessary to specify the content and rate of presentation of instructional material. Also, ideally there should be common, reliable performance criteria by which students are evaluated and by which they progress through a series of instructional steps. A number of teacher-tested curriculum development and evaluation models are available that meet the standards given above (see Kerr & Strain, 1978).

SUBJECT SELECTION

The vast majority of efficacy studies have employed subject selection procedures that bring the validity of results into question. There have been three primary approaches to subject selection employed. The first approach has been to compare segregated EMR children from school systems not offering integrated placement with EMR children from school systems only serving such youngsters in regular classrooms. The second approach has been to compare segregated and integrated EMR children from the same school system. The final and least used approach has been to screen initially and then randomly assign children to newly created integrated and segregated placements.

In the first approach one must accept the dubious proposition that school systems that provide special services are fundamentally equivalent to those that do not. Earlier it was noted that school systems formerly not offering special class placement tend to be smaller, poorer, and generally more limited in the range of services provided to any subpopulation of children. Moreover, one must also assume that children from the systems utilizing special classes had an equal likelihood of placement, given IQ scores within a designated range. There is, however, general professional consensus and a large volume of demographic data that points to special class placement decisions being made on the basis of problem behaviors, accompanying physical handicaps, and social class status (Blatt, 1958; Mercer, 1973; Quay, 1963).

Similar methodological issues exist when comparing the performance of segregated and integrated EMR children from the same school system. In order to control for nonrandom placement effects, investigators have sought to match children for CA, MA, and IQ, for example. Yet, matching would seem to represent an endless task when one considers the variety of economic, personality, and motivational factors that impinge on academic success and social adjustment. One must also consider that the progressive addition of variables along which subjects are matched likely represents a parallel reduction in the validity of generalizations to the total population of unmatched, segregated and integrated youngsters.

Goldstein *et al.* (1965) conducted one of the few studies in which children were assigned randomly to previously unavailable segregated and integrated programs. Not only did this procedure control for differential placement effects, but by employing first graders it was possible to eliminate the confounding effects of educational history. This subject selection procedure certainly offers the most methodologically sound approach to efficacy research. However, such an approach is limited in its feasibility and today there may be legal restrictions against random assignment of public school students.

DEPENDENT MEASURES

Regardless of the elegance of experimental design, the utility of any data rests with the appropriateness of the dependent measures. A number of factors are problematic with dependent measures used in efficacy research. First, there is reasonable doubt that standard tests of achievement reflect the content of curricula across special and regular class placements. Clearly, standardized achievement scores bear little relationship to prevocational, vocational, or self-care goals that are prevalent in many special classes for EMR children. Even if both regular and special classes had similar, academic curriculum goals, there is still some doubt as to whether the standardized achievement tests constitute a representative sampling of learned material. To make such a judgment it would be necessary to correlate precise instructional objectives with items on the test. In the case of standardized achievement tests, this is yet to be accomplished.

In addition to the lack of congruence between what is taught and what is tested, problems may also arise from the differential experience of regular and special class children with achievement testing per se. In special classrooms, for example, yearly and, in some cases, twice yearly achievement testing might well be replaced with a more informal and more continuous system of performance feedback. Thus, one could argue that regular class EMR children are more "test-wise" than their special class counterparts or that they are more likely to have developed a negative set toward achievement testing. With either arrangement the basic issue remains the same, namely, that differential experience with achievement testing confounds any differences observed between regular and special class EMR children.

A final issue related to achievement measures concerns the possible bias against the disproportionate number of segregated EMR children who come from low-income, cultural minority families. The normative research on the major achievement tests (e.g., Stanford Achievement Test, California Achievement Test, Wide Range Achievement Test, and Metropolitan Achievement Test) has essentially ignored social class differences and in so doing has created instruments of doubtful validity for most special class EMR children.

When one considers the lack of match between special class curricula and achievement test content, the possible novelty of achievement testing for special class children, and the lack of achievement test norms for other than white, middle-class youth, it seems possible that the achievement levels of segregated EMR children are underestimated in the efficacy literature.

There have been three basic kinds of social adjustment indices employed in efficacy studies: self-ratings, ratings by others, and direct observations of child behavior. In the area of self-ratings, many interpretation problems exist. For example, there is little, if any, data to substantiate the relative stability of self-ratings over time. On a closely related point, it is not clear whether such ratings are sensitive to change in self-perception. Also, where data are available, there appears to be a very weak relationship between self-ratings and the behavioral manifestation of these judgments (Greenwood et al., 1977). Finally, recall that self-ratings are based on a negative–positive metric rather than an accurate–inaccurate one. Therefore, children may claim many friendships, state that they are competent learners, and see themselves as having control over their environment, none of which may represent the current reality. Indeed, it seems dangerous to boast that any educational arrangement leads to improved self-ratings without having a direct and independent measure of the social processes the child personally has assessed.

Sociometric ratings of EMR children by peers and adults have been a widely used measurement technique. An enormous volume of research outside of the efficacy literature has employed sociometrics as well. Typical retest reliability coefficients have ranged between .30 and .70. Although these coefficients may be satisfactory to establish general population descriptors, they are wholly inadequate for prediction of individual child social status and adjustment across time. In addition to their overall lack of stability, sociometric ratings of popularity are poorly correlated with behavioral measures of interaction (Greenwood et al., 1977). This finding is in agreement with the reported incongruence between children's general verbal reports and their actual behavior. Finally, Quay (1963) has described two weaknesses of sociometrics as applied to efficacy research. First, peer preference scores derived from special and regular class children are based on quite different reference groups. Specifically, it seems likely that segregated children will limit their preference choices to their EMR peers in the special class. Integrated EMR children's scores, however, will likely reflect choices among normal as well as EMR youngsters. Second, Quay proposed that differences in teacher ratings across settings may reflect lower norms for acceptable social behavior by special class teachers.

Direct observations of EMR children's social behaviors have been rare, yet the results of such research have been remarkably consistent. Specifically, there is little evidence to suggest any behavioral differences between integrated and segregated EMR children (Corman & Gottlieb, 1978). The direct observational research has been characterized by the use of several positive and negative behavior categories time-sampled across a number of sessions. Although these procedures are certainly to be recommended over sociometric devices, two procedural problems are common across observational studies. First, the use of time-sampling procedures obviates the measurement of behavior sequences and thus it is not possible to determine the effects of EMR children's behavior on peers and vice versa. Second, behavior categories have been selected on an a priori rather than an empirical basis. In this regard, an analysis of several important information sources seems to be a logical prerequisite to the development of social behavior categories. At one level of analysis, behavior categories may be developed through systematic interviews with children regarding the behaviors of peers that they most and least like. At a more fine-grain level of analysis, continuous recording of the identified behaviors could be made to verify those child behaviors that set the occasion for positive peer responding and those child behaviors that are ignored or lead to negative interaction. The utility of this approach for behavior category identification has been documented previously by Gable, Hendrickson, and Strain (1978) and Strain, Shores, and Kerr (1976). With such precise behavioral data at hand, it then would be possible to train children to engage in positive approach behaviors and, in turn, be responsive to positive overtures from peers.

Conclusions

Through almost a half century of research on special versus regular class placement for EMR children the "unknowns" far outweigh the "knowns." There seem to be at least three reasons for the lack of a reliable data base for making placement decisions regarding EMR youngsters. The first reason is a reflection of a long-standing, conceptual incongruity between educational practice and education research. In educational practice, particularly that espoused by special educators, the proper unit of measurement and concern is the individual child. We test individuals, write Individualized Educational Plans (IEPs), implement one-to-one instruction where possible, and compare a child's progress to his or her prior level or rate of attainment. Yet, when it is time to evaluate an educational procedure or administrative arrangement, the lure of large group designs is great. It is no longer the case that alternatives are lacking, but these intensive, single-subject designs are considered by some to be less than true experimental procedures. If we closely examine the methodological shortfalls of the efficacy literature, however, it becomes evident that one problem is a lack of fit between the question under study and the selection of group design procedures. For example, the statistical necessity for homogeneous groups, random assignment of subjects, and normally distributed scores sharply conflicts with the educational reality of heterogeneous groups of children, anything but random assignment of students, and the absence of testing norms for many EMR pupils. To meet the group design requirements, the investigator must create a hybrid class structure whose generalization to the real world is highly suspect. Further, the placement decision of everyday concern to the on-line educator is not what category of exceptional child will be served in this or that setting but what setting is most suitable for Ted, Marcy, Bill, and Karen. To best answer that question we need to utilize experimental designs that highlight, not obscure, the variability of individual child behavior.

In addition to experimental design problems, the paucity of usable data from the efficacy literature reflects a limited view of the antecedents and outcomes of educational placement. Until recent court actions (see Cohen & DeYoung, 1973), the composition of many segregated EMR classes suggested that racial, family income, and social class characteristics were as much responsible for special class placement as was low IQ. Clearly, it is important to consider the question of special or regular class placement as demanding more than achievement and IQ data. Placement is as much a sociological, ecological, and legal issue as it is an educational one. In order to fully understand placement outcomes (regardless of setting) and thus make more rational and humane decisions it is important to know the following: How might important others (friends, family, human service delivery professionals) in the child's environment respond to a particular placement decision? What social sanctions or values in the child's culture impinge on placement decisions? How do the curriculum goals of various placements correspond to the values held by the child, his or her family, and their community? If a placement decision demands a physical relocation, how might this affect the child's family? Are there alternatives available that *functionally*, not just structurally, meet the criteria implied by the doctrine of "least restrictive setting?"

Finally, it seems clear that the efficacy literature has suffered from a "simple solution to a complex problem syndrome" that has been perpetuated by educational decision makers. Several researchers have broken out of the standard mold of comparing regular versus special class placement, and thus we are acquiring a valuable (albeit meager at this point) literature on the effects of partial integration during the school day (Carroll, 1967), resource room support (Kern & Pfaeffle, 1963), and special tutorial services (Ainsworth, 1959). Of course, the range of placement alternatives studied reflects the notions of researchers as well as educational decision makers regarding the types of services that are potentially suitable for EMR children. If one accepts the notion that 40 years of efficacy research is yet to demonstrate satisfactory child outcomes associated with either special or regular class placement, then it is most difficult to understand how the present trend toward placement in a regular class can be taken as prima facie evidence of movement from a more to a less restrictive educational environment. Special educators of today would do well to reexamine the efficacy literature and also attend to the fact that the least restrictive alternative has yet to be equated with the best alternative.

Reference Note

1. Towne, R. C., Joiner, J. M., & Schurr, T. *The effects of special classes on the self-concepts of academic ability of the educable mentally retarded.* Paper presented at the forty-fifth annual convention of the Council for Exceptional Children, St. Louis, April 1967.

References

Ainsworth, S. H. *An exploratory study of educational, social, and emotional factors in the education of mentally retarded children in Georgia public schools.* Athens: The University of Georgia, 1959.

Alexander, C., & Strain, P. S. A review of educators' attitudes toward handicapped children and the concept of mainstreaming. *Psychology in the Schools,* 1978, *15,* 390–396.

Arreola v. Board of Education Case No. 160–577, Superior Ct., Orange City, Calif., 1968.

Bacher, J. *The effect of special class placement on the self-concept, social adjustment, and reading growth of slow learners.* Unpublished doctoral dissertation, New York University, 1964.

Baldwin, W. K. The educable mentally retarded child in the regular grades. *Exceptional Children,* 1958, *25,* 106–108.

Bennett, A. A comparative study of subnormal children in the elementary grades. New York: Teachers College, Columbia University, 1932.

Blatt, B. The physical, personality, and academic status of children who are mentally retarded attending special classes as compared with children who are mentally retarded attending regular classes. *American Journal of Mental Deficiency,* 1958, *62,* 810–818.

Bradfield, R. H., Brown, J., Kaplan, P., Rickert, E., & Stannard, R. The special child in the regular classroom. *Exceptional Children,* 1973, *39,* 384–390.

Brophy, J. E., & Good, J. L. Teachers' communication of differential expectations for children's classroom performance. *Journal of Educational Psychology,* 1970, *61,* 365–374.

Bruininks, R. H., Rynders, J. E., & Gross, J. C. Social acceptance of mildly retarded pupils in resource rooms and regular classes. *American Journal of Mental Deficiency,* 1974, *78,* 377–383.

Budoff, M., & Gottlieb, J. Special-class EMR children mainstreamed: A study of an aptitude (learning potential) × treatment interaction. *American Journal of Mental Deficiency,* 1976, *81,* 1–11.

Carroll, A. W. The effects of segregated and partially integrated school programs on self-concept and academic achievement of educable mentally retardates. *Exceptional Children,* 1967, *34,* 93–99.

Cassidy, V. M., & Stanton, J. E. *An investigation of factors involved in the educational placement of mentally retarded children.* Columbus, Ohio: Ohio State University Press, 1959.

Cegelka, W. J., & Tyler, J. L. The efficacy of special class placement for the mentally retarded in proper perspective. *Training School Bulletin,* 1970, *67,* 33–68.

Cohen, J. S., & DeYoung, H. The role of litigation in the improvement of programming for the handicapped. In L. Mann & D. A. Sabatino (Eds.), *The first review of special education* (Vol. 2). Philadelphia: Buttonwood Farms, 1973.

Corman, L., & Gottlieb, J. Mainstreaming mentally retarded children: A review of research. In N. Ellis (Ed.), *International review of research in mental retardation.* New York: Academic Press, 1978.

Cowen, P. A. Special class vs. grade groups for subnormal pupils. *School and Society,* 1938, *48,* 27–28.

Dokecki, P. R., Anderson, B. J., & Strain, P. S. Stigmatization and labeling. In J. L. Paul, D.

J. Stedman, & G. R. Neufeld (Eds.), Deinstitutionalization: Program and policy development. Syracuse: Syracuse University Press, 1977.

Drabman, R. S., Spitalnik, R., & Spitalnik, K. Sociometric and disruptive behavior as a function of four types of token reinforcement programs. Journal of Applied Behavior Analysis, 1976, 9, 31–40.

Dunn, L. M. Special education for the mildly retarded: Is much of it justifiable? Exceptional Children, 1968, 35, 5–22.

Edgerton, R. B., & Edgerton, C. R. Becoming retarded in a Hawaiian School. In D. E. Meyers (Ed.), Sociobehavioral studies in mental retardation. Los Angeles: American Association on Mental Deficiency, 1973.

Elenbogen, M. L. A comparative study of some aspects of academic and social adjustment of two groups of mentally retarded children in special classes and in regular grades. Dissertation Abstracts, 1957, 17, 2496.

Fine, M. J., & Caldwell, T. E. Self evaluation of school related behavior of educable mentally retarded children: A preliminary report. Exceptional Children, 1967, 33, 324.

Gable, R. A., Hendrickson, J. M., & Strain, P. S. Assessment, modification, and generalization of social interaction among multihandicapped children. Education and Training of the Mentally Retarded, 1978, 13, 279–286.

Gampel, D. H., Gottlieb, J., & Harrison, R. H. A comparison of the classroom behaviors of special class EMR, integrated EMR, low IQ, and nonretarded children. American Journal of Mental Deficiency, 1974, 79, 16–21.

Goldstein, H. Methodological problems in research in the educational programs for the treatment and habilitation of the mentally retarded. American Journal of Mental Deficiency, 1959, 64, 341–345.

Goldstein, H., Moss, J. W., & Jordan, L. The efficacy of special class training of the development of mentally retarded children. U. S. Office of Education, Cooperative Research Project Report No. 619. Urbana: University of Illinois, 1965.

Gottlieb, J., & Budoff, M. Social acceptability of retarded children in nongraded schools differing in architecture. American Journal of Mental Deficiency, 1973, 78, 15–19.

Johnson, G. O. A study of the social position of mentally handicapped children in the regular grades. American Journal of Mental Deficiency, 1950, 55, 60–89.

Johnson, G. O. A comparative study of the personal and social adjustment of mentally handicapped children placed in special classes with mentally handicapped children who remain in regular classes. Syracuse, N.Y.: Syracuse University, 1961.

Jordan, J. B. Intelligence as a factor in social position: A sociometric study in special classes for the mentally handicapped. Dissertation Abstracts, 1960, 21, 2987–2988.

Jordan, L. J. Verbal readiness training for slow-learning children. Mental Retardation, 1965, 3, 19–22.

Kern, W. H., & Pfaeffle, H. A. A comparison of social adjustment of mentally retarded children in various educational settings. American Journal of Mental Deficiency, 1963, 67, 407–413.

Kerr, M. M., & Nelson, C. M. Behavior problems of children and youth: Classroom strategies. Columbus, Ohio: Charles E. Merrill, in press.

Kerr, M. M., & Strain, P. S. Use of precision planning techniques by teacher trainees with behaviorally disordered pupils. Behavioral Disorders, 1978, 1, 93–106.

Lapp, E. R. A study of the social adjustment of slow-learning children who were assigned part-time to regular classes. American Journal of Mental Deficiency, 1957, 62, 254–262.

Larry P. v. Riles. Civil Action No. 71–2270, N.D., Calif., 1971.

Lewis, M. A comparison of self-concept, academic achievement, attitude toward school and adaptive behavior of elementary school children identified as educable mentally retarded in four different school environments. Unpublished doctoral dissertation, University of Michigan, 1973.

Mandell, C. J., & Strain, P. S. An analysis of factors related to the attitudes of regular classroom teachers toward mainstreaming mildly handicapped children. *Contemporary Education Psychology*, 1978, 3, 154–162.

Mayer, C. L. The relationship of early special class placement and self-concepts of mentally handicapped children. *Exceptional Children*, 1966, 33, 77–81.

Mercer, J. R. *Labeling the mentally retarded*. Berkeley: University of California Press, 1973.

Meyerowitz, J. H. Self-derogations in young retardates and special class placement. *Child Development*, 1962, 33, 443–451.

Monroe, J. D., & Howe, C. E. The effects of integration and social class on the acceptance of retarded adolescents. *Education and Training of the Mentally Retarded*, 1971, 6, 20–23.

Mullen, F. A., & Itkin, W. *Achievement and adjustment of educable mentally handicapped children in special classes and in regular classes*. Chicago: Chicago Board of Education, 1961.

Pertsch, C. F. *A comparative study of the progress of subnormal pupils in the grades and in special classes*. New York: Teachers College, Columbia University, 1936.

Porter, R. B., & Milazzo, T. C. A comparison of mentally retarded adults who attended a special class with those who attended regular school classes. *Exceptional Children*, 1958, 24, 410–412.

Quay, L. C. Academic skills. In N. R. Ellis (Ed.), *Handbook of mental deficiency*. New York: McGraw-Hill, 1963.

Severance, L., & Gastrom, L. Effects of the label "mentally retarded" on causal explanations for success and failure outcomes. *American Journal of Mental Deficiency*, 1977, 81, 547–555.

Sheare, J. B. Social acceptance of EMR adolescents in integrated programs. *American Journal of Mental Deficiency*, 1974, 78, 678–682.

Sidman, M. *Tactics of scientific research*. New York: Ronald Press, 1960.

Smith, J. O., & Arkans, J. Now more than ever: A case for the special class. *Exceptional Children*, 1974, 41, 497–502.

Smith, H. W., & Kennedy, W. A. Effects of three educational programs on mentally retarded children. *Perceptual and Motor skills*, 1967, 24, 174.

Stowitschek, J. Applying programming principles to remedial handwriting practice. *Journal of Special Education Technology*, 1978, 1, 21–26.

Strain, P. S., Shores, R. E., & Kerr, M. M. An experimental analysis of "spillover" effects on social interaction among behaviorally handicapped preschool children. *Journal of Applied Behavior Analysis*, 1976, 9, 31–40.

Thurstone, T. G. *An evaluation of educating mentally handicapped children in special classes and in regular grades*. Chapel Hill: University of North Carolina, 1959.

Walker, V. S. The efficacy of the resource room for educating retarded children. *Exceptional Children*, 1974, 40, 288–289.

Warner, F., Thrapp, R., & Walsh, S. Attitudes of children toward their special class placement. *Exceptional Children*, 1973, 40, 37–38.

Warren, K. An investigation of the effectiveness of educational placement of mentally retarded children in a special class. *Dissertation Abstracts*, 1962, 23, 2211.

Welch, E. A. The effects of segregated and partially integrated school programs on self-concept and academic achievement of educable mental retardates. *Dissertation Abstracts*, 1965, 26, 5533–5534.

Attitudes toward Mentally Retarded Persons and the Concept of Mainstreaming

2

Introduction

The history of care and treatment afforded to handicapped individuals has been controlled largely by the prevailing attitudes of society toward its atypical or deviant members. Although recent legislative and court action may reflect a movement in the direction of more favorable and factual opinions toward handicapped citizens, a social history highlighted by the eugenics movement, custodial care, and segregated class placement will not be easily or quickly changed.

Today, handicapped individuals, with varying levels of competence, are afforded opportunities to interact with normal and less-handicapped peers. For example, group home and halfway house placements are expanding for previously institutionalized persons. Likewise, public schools have greatly intensified their efforts to mainstream handicapped children into regular classes. For these service delivery innovations to succeed, it seems necessary that the general public, teaching professionals, and classroom peers hold favorable attitudes toward these integrated programs and the individuals they serve.

The purpose of this chapter is to review attitudinal studies toward handicapped individuals. By and large, this literature is dominated by studies concerned with attitudes toward mentally retarded persons. Therefore, attitudinal research on other handicapping conditions is not considered in this review.

Attitudinal Research Paradigms

At least six research strategies can be identified in the attitudinal literature. They include (*a*) public opinion survey; (*b*) investigations of stereotypes; (*c*) attitude scaling; (*d*) attitude modification; (*e*) sociometric rating; and (*f*) expectancy paradigm. Although these research tactics share many methodological points, they are considered separately to clarify discussion.

Public opinion surveys generally monitor the factual bases of persons' knowledge about handicapping conditions in general. The most popular research tactic has been to construct a series of statements regarding causative and treatment issues related to a handicapping condition. Respondents then mark those statements they feel to be factual and/or reflective of their beliefs. In a representative study, Connaughton (1974) surveyed physicians' beliefs about the etiology and treatment of mental retardation. Physicians were found to be quite competent in their understanding of genetic and biochemical insults to normal development; however, they demonstrated limited knowledge of educational and psychological issues related to retardation.

Data derived from opinion surveys present a number of interpretation problems. First, surveys do not typically define or behaviorally describe the handicapping condition under study. It is very likely that respondents react to global labels such as *mentally retarded, emotionally disturbed,* and *learning disabled* in many different ways, and that they may in fact totally misinterpret the nature of the handicapping condition (Gottlieb, 1975). Survey tactics also limit the range of beliefs and information that can be abstracted. It is possible, for example, for a respondent to agree with many items on a survey, although the survey does not at all represent the beliefs and opinions most firmly held by that individual. Finally, by using a global, nonpersonal referent (e.g., *the mentally retarded*), attitude surveys are unable to discriminate between opinions that are held for a general handicapped population and for a specific handicapped individual.

Investigations of stereotypes differ primarily from survey research in that they are not concerned with the proportion of people who believe this or that, but with beliefs held about different groups. Whereas surveys determine on an a priori basis the range of beliefs or opinions studied, stereotype investigations provide open-ended stimulus items. Gottwald (1970), for example, asked respondents to describe what the phrase *mentally retarded* meant to them and Willey and McCandless (1973) used a similar tactic to study traits most frequently assigned to special class educable mentally retarded (EMR) children and nonhandicapped children in regular classes. This open-ended perspective on attitude study, as compared with typical survey paradigms, potentially offers a more personal and accurate estimate of respondents' actual beliefs. However, data summarization and reduction problems severely limit the clarity of results.

Any number of respondents may hold the same opinion or belief, yet subtle, semantic differences in their responses may be subject to varied interpretation. Similarly, respondents may actually hold quite different beliefs, but express them in linguistic forms that are indistinguishable.

In contrast to survey and stereotype paradigms, which highlight the content of beliefs, attitude-scaling research has focused on an analysis of differences between respondents based upon an overall favorability score. Individual scores are obtained by statistical scaling procedures such as those of Guttman, Likert, or Thurstone. This quantification of attitude allows one to compare the mean scores of groups of respondents such as regular and special class teachers, or examine variables that correlate with certain attitude scores. In a study employing a variety of scaling tactics, Mandell and Strain (1978) examined the effects of principals' attitude, special class teachers' attitude, educational background, and classroom environment on regular class teachers' attitude toward mainstreaming mildly handicapped children. A 5-point Likert scale was employed to assess the attitudes of each group of educators. The favorability score for regular teachers was then employed as a criterion variable in a multiple linear regression procedure to determine if principals' attitude, special class teachers' attitude, educational background, and classroom environment were predictive of a positive attitude toward mainstreaming. In this study, as in most scaling research, summarized favorability scores were derived from subjects' responses to opinionnaire items with which they either agreed or disagreed.

Scaling studies, like public opinion surveys, employ similar attitude sampling tactics, and both methods are limited by the use of global attitude referents and the imposed limitation on the range of opinions monitored. Additionally, scaling studies also mask considerable inter- and intrarespondent variability in opinions. Two or more respondents may thus receive equal favorability scores, yet disagree on most or all items on the sampling instrument. Knowing the precise nature of respondents' beliefs is, of course, particularly vital in efforts to improve opinions toward handicapped individuals.

Studies of attitude modification have been designed primarily to evaluate the effects of exposure to handicapped individuals or information about handicapped individuals on subjects' responses to opinionnaire items. Pretest–posttest designs with appropriate control or comparisons groups are most common. For example, Cleland and Cochran (1961) used an institutional tour (Group 1) and written information about the institution (Group 2) in an attempt to modify the attitudes of high school students toward the mentally retarded.

Attitudinal change studies have produced conflicting results, and a number of methodological problems are likely responsible. First, it is difficult to replicate the procedures employed in individual studies. For example, subjects are seldom described in sufficient detail to permit replication. The actual interventions employed are similarly unclear. Stating only that subjects were exposed to a tour or didactic information guarantees considerable variance in the content of tours and didactic training across studies. Another methodological limitation concerns pre- and posttest comparisons based upon group or pooled data. Here, dramatic change by a few subjects in a group may produce statistically significant change for the entire group. It is also quite possible that individuals with positive pretest attitudes and those with negative pretest attitudes will be affected differentially by the various treatments. Specifically, Gottlieb (1975) has stated that subjects whose initial attitudes are negative may use an institutional tour experience to confirm, rather than change, their attitudes. Finally, by using "closed" attitude sampling indices, it is possible that interventions may affect significantly attitudes that are not measured directly.

Whereas previously discussed research paradigms have measured attitudes with reference to categories of handicapping conditions, the sociometric rating strategy uses handicapped individuals known to the respondents as the attitudinal referent. In the typical study, each subject in a group is asked to rank in order those peers with whom she or he would most like to interact. Instead of a respondent obtaining a score, the referent's favorability as a social partner is evaluated (e.g., Gottlieb & Davis, 1973; Meyerowitz, 1967). The sociometric rating paradigm has been particularly popular in evaluating the social status of handicapped individuals in various educational settings (e.g., segregated class, regular class, resource room). Generally, results indicate that handicapped children receive lower sociometric rankings than their nonhandicapped or less handicapped peers (Baldwin, 1958; Heber, 1956; Johnson, 1950).

Sociometric ratings do leave a number of critical issues related to social choice and social status unanswered. The most often voiced criticism of sociometric tactics is the unclear relationship between ratings and actual patterns of interaction (Strain & Carr, 1975). In one of the most exhaustive reviews of attitudinal research conducted to date, Gottlieb (1975) concludes that research is insufficient to substantiate a positive correlation between respondents' ratings of peers and their social behavior directed toward these same youngsters. Another major criticism of sociometric ratings is poor test–retest reliability (Greenwood, Walker, & Hops, 1977). Finally, the typical rating tactic that offers respondents the simultaneous choice of all peers with whom to interact is a circumstance that is rarely available in the natural environment. More often, the choice of social partners is limited, moment to moment, by physical space, other ongoing interactions, and subjects' past history of reinforcement associated with interactions (Lott & Lott, 1974).

One of the more active and controversial areas of attitudinal research has involved the expectancy paradigm. In this procedure, the experimenter attempts to control the attitude or expectancy of subjects (usually teachers) by labeling various children and then examines the effects of the label on teacher and child behavior. Since Rosenthal and Jacobson's (1968) landmark study of teacher

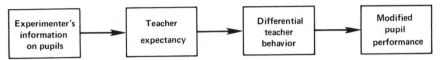

Figure 2.1 Schematic representation of teacher expectancy effects.

expectations, few studies have replicated their dramatic results, and many criticisms have been leveled at this paradigm.

Expectancy research has in large part been predicated on an ubiquitous, cause–effect conceptualization of the self-fulfilling prophecy. Herein lies the major limitation of this research paradigm. The typical model of teacher expectancy effects is depicted in Figure 2.1. In this model, individual variability in pupils' perception of teacher cues and teachers' individual variability in behavior as a function of the type of information provided are not considered. Moreover, the majority of studies have employed contrived as opposed to naturalistic information sources to produce differential perceptions. It seems likely that teachers develop or alter perceptions of students based upon a variety of information sources, including (*a*) parent conferences; (*b*) cumulative records; (*c*) behavioral records; (*d*) standardized test information; and (*e*) those physical–personal characteristics of sex, attractiveness, motivation, economic status, and race. Regrettably, these naturally occurring data sources have been rarely considered.

Although heated conceptual and methodological arguments have characterized much of the teacher expectancy research, it is important to note that even the staunchest critics of this research tactic (e.g., Snow, 1969) do not deny the reality of expectancy effects.

In summary, this brief review of popular research paradigms in the study of attitudes toward the handicapped should not be viewed as a complete methodological treatise. Rather, the intent has been to provide the reader of the following attitudinal research with the analytic perspective necessary to unravel an often confusing and conflicting body of knowledge.

Community Attitudes toward the Mentally Retarded

Generally speaking, the attitudes of the American public toward the mentally retarded are characterized by lack of factual information, confusion with other handicapping conditions, and pejorative stereotypes.

In one of the most extensive studies of community attitudes, Gottwald (1970) asked 1515 respondents to describe what the phrase *mentally retarded* meant to them. Of particular interest are those responses related to etiology and level of retardation. The majority of subjects who offered a causative response indicated that mental retardation could be attributed primarily to various physical trauma including birth injury, defects, or brain damage. In a related area, approximately 1% of the respondents produced answers that discriminated between levels of severity in mental retardation. Taken together, these results suggest that the common conception of mental retardation is limited to that statistical minority of all cases of mental retardation characterized by moderate to severe deficits.

Further evidence of the general public's limited view of mental retardation was provided by Begab (1970). In an attempt to improve the attitudes of social work students toward mental retardation, Begab found that the majority of his subjects viewed the mentally retarded as physically sick and damaged. Here again, there was no indication that respondents differentiated between levels of retardation or that they were even aware of mild mental retardation and its prevalence.

This general view of the mentally retarded as physically damaged, sick individuals most certainly contributes to the negative stereotypes associated with mental retardation. For example, Winthrop and Taylor (1957) asked 133 subjects to agree or disagree with nine stereotypic misconceptions regarding "feeblemindedness." Among the beliefs supported by these subjects were the views that feeblemindedness results from mental disease and that sterilization is the best treatment approach.

Similar community attitudes were reported by Greenbaum and Wang (1965). These investigators obtained attitudinal responses from 330 subjects regarding the following categories: mentally retarded, moron, imbecile, and idiot. In general, attitudes toward these categories were more negative than those held toward mental illness. These data also support Gottwald's (1970) and Begab's (1970) findings that few individuals differentiate between levels of retardation. Thus, it appears that referents such as feebleminded, mentally retarded, moron, imbecile, and idiot elicit similar public reaction, and that this reaction is limited to attitudes and beliefs directed specifically toward more severe levels of behavioral handicap.

Other labels also have been employed that resulted in stereotypic responses. Hollinger and Jones (1970) administered two social distance scales to their subjects ($N = 114$), one referring to mentally retarded people, the other to "slow learners." On all but one comparison, slow learners were judged more favorably. In explaining the difference between slow learners and mentally retarded, the respondents equated mental retardation with physical disability and mental illness. Slow learners, on the other hand, were characterized by general "slowness" that was not associated with physical defect or limited intellectual ability. The more favorable status of slow learners in this study may have been due to the existence in the target community of special classes for slow learners. In other settings, children enrolled in such classes would likely be labeled EMR.

The possibility of label × community subgroups interaction related to attitudes was highlighted by Meyers, Sitkei, and Watts (1966). Attitudes toward mildly and severely retarded children were sampled from a random group of adults ($N = 188$) and a specially selected group ($N = 24$) of adults who had children enrolled in classes for the mentally retarded. Unlike previously described research, these authors provided respondents with brief, behavioral descriptions of mildly and severely retarded individuals. Mildly retarded people were described as slow learners who as adults will function in a manner academically and socially similar to a normal 9-year-old. Severely retarded people were described as never being able to dress or feed themselves and always needing custodial-like care. Both groups of respondents agreed that the public schools should provide educational services for mildly handicapped children. The groups differed, however, in their reaction to severely retarded individuals. The majority of the random sample did not feel that the public school should provide educational programs, whereas the parents of retarded children were equally divided on the issue of public school classes for the severely retarded. At least for this investigation, it appears that when the general public is provided with behavioral descriptors rather than labels of retardation, they display attitudes that discriminate across levels of competency.

In further work on the relationship between attitude referents and expressed feelings, Gottlieb and Siperstein (1976) administered four instruments to female undergraduate education majors. Subjects were assigned to one of five conditions (descriptors of attitude referent). The conditions were (a) "mentally retarded persons"; (b) a severely retarded child between the ages of 9 and 12 residing in an institution; (c) a mildly retarded child between the ages of 9 and 12 attending a special class; (d) a severely retarded young adult who was just released from an institution; and (e) a mildly retarded young adult who just completed a vocational education program. Results indicate that the subjects were most favorable toward mildly retarded individuals, regardless of age, and least favorable toward severely retarded referents, regardless of age. Attitudes toward the "mentally retarded person" were intermediate between the mildly and severely retarded referents.

Research is available also that indicates how an individual's attitude or perceptions of a person's performance is altered by specific referents. Severance and Gastrom (1977) conducted a study based on attribution theory regarding the effects of the label *mentally retarded* on the perceptions of observers. When attribution theory is applied to studying the effects of a label it focuses on the explanations made by others to account for behavior outcomes by persons with or without the label. If a "mentally retarded" person succeeds at a task one would predict that the label will restrict the likelihood of a person's success being credited to ability but enhance the likelihood of its being credited to factors of effort or luck. In comparison, a person not so labeled who succeeds at the same task would be more likely to elicit causal explanations that involve the ability factor. Conversely, if a "mentally retarded" fails, this outcome would be attributed to the stable factor of ability. However, if a nonretarded person fails at the same task, observer explanations would include factors such as bad luck, high task difficulty, and lack of effort. The subjects, 96 female undergraduate students, were presented with descriptions of a target person with varying characteristics. The label was varied (*mentally retarded* versus no label), as was the task outcome (success versus failure), and sex. The subjects were given a paragraph describing the target person, task, and outcome; then they were asked to give a reason for the outcome. Each of the predicted (and stereotyped) causal explanations were offered readily by subjects for success and failure outcomes.

Although the content of community members' attitudes toward mentally retarded individuals have been studied extensively for over 20 years, it is extremely difficult to draw any firm conclusions from this line of research. The absence of descriptive information to accompany specific attitude referents has been particularly problematic. Also, since researchers have employed divergent methods of eliciting attitudes, it is next to impossible to compare and contrast findings across studies. Indeed, Gottlieb and Siperstein (1976) have reported data suggesting that an individual's apparent attitude toward a specific referent varies significantly across assessment instruments. It would appear, however, that the general public tends to interpret labels such as *mentally retarded* as reflecting severe and profound deficits. Clearly, additional research is required wherein community attitudes are studied with reference to well-specified levels of retardation or other handicapping conditions (e.g., Gottlieb & Siperstein, 1976). Information derived from such work would be of great value in the planning and implementation of integrated services for handicapped individuals. Before one can hope to improve community attitudes, a thorough description of current beliefs and the specific referents to which they apply is required.

Professionals' Attitudes toward the Mentally Retarded

As discussed previously, community members often respond to mentally retarded children on the basis of preconceived notions rather than factual information. The resulting interaction based upon these largely negative and pejorative attitudes often serves to exacerbate a person's handicap. Likely, a very similar process characterizes many of the instructional and social interactions between professionals and mentally retarded children.

There seems to be little doubt that the attitudes of teachers toward exceptional pupils are influential in determining the overall academic and social adjustment of these youngsters. The exact processes by which attitudes may mediate teacher behaviors and thus differentially affect child performance are not clear. However, this fact should not diminish efforts to promote the most favorable and realistic attitudes toward exceptional children and their education in mainstream settings (Corman & Gottlieb, 1978).

Haring (1957) was one of the first to identify the importance of special education teachers' attitudes on subsequent child adjustment. He further proposed that regular class teachers be provided with intensive educational input designed around factual information regarding the characteristics and learning capabilities of exceptional children (Haring, Stern, & Cruickshank, 1958).

Major (1961) observed that teaching experience with exceptional children actually may result in the intensification of negative attitudes. She argues that regular class teachers are seldom provided specific teaching techniques for educating problem children and that these youngsters are perceived as disruptive of the normal classroom structure. One also might speculate that exceptional children may well become a source of professional and personal embarrassment because of poor academic and social performance. Major also warns that the attitudes of regular class teachers will likely not be changed by administrative or legislative fiat or by parental pressures.

Proctor's (1967) study of the attitudes of special class teachers, regular class teachers, and college professors toward integrating exceptional children in the regular grades confirms Major's notions about the attitudes of regular class personnel. Here, special class teachers displayed significantly more factual information regarding exceptional children and more realistic attitudes toward the prospects for and potential outcomes of integration than did regular class teachers. The special class teachers also expressed opinions that closely matched those of college professors. Proctor interprets these findings to suggest that a teacher's type of experience (special versus regular class training) is more relevant to attitudes held than is the quantity of experience.

With regard to the influence of experience on attitudes held, Combs and Harper (1967) have presented data at variance with Major's ideas. The inexperienced subjects in this study were 80 undergraduate education majors, and the 80 experienced subjects were drawn from graduate courses at the same university. Each of the experienced teachers had completed at least 3 years of direct classroom teaching. Subjects were asked to read four actual case histories of children diagnosed as either psychopathic, schizophrenic, mentally deficient, or cerebral palsied. The subjects were then to decide which of 25 adjectives (20 negative, 5 positive) were more or less descriptive of the children. One-half of the experienced and one-half of the inexperienced group were given descriptions that were accompanied by the clinical labels; the other subjects were only given case descriptions to review. The effects of labels were inconsistent across conditions. For the mentally deficient, more negative adjectives were applied when the label was not present. The opposite was true for the other categories. Significantly, there were no differential effects across experienced and inexperienced subjects. Generally, both groups held equally unfavorable attitudes toward all categories of exceptionality. It should be pointed out that the subject selection procedures used by Combs and Harper result in a unique definition of experienced versus inexperienced educators. Specifically, it seems likely that the experienced teachers' attendance in graduate courses would indicate that the groups were different on significant variables other than years in the classroom. Such variables might include, for example, amount and type of university course work, scholarly ability, and commitment to the profession.

Fine (1967) reports that regular and special educators have quite different instructional goals for their class members and different ideas about motivating lower-ability students. The subjects were 13 teachers of elementary-age EMR children and 21 teachers from regular elementary grades in the same school system. Although no specific data are provided, Fine proposes that these teachers were typical of their larger constituent groups. The teachers were asked two specific questions. In the first, they were asked to rank from 1 to 5 in order of importance to them the following classroom goals for students: good citizenship, social adjustment, reading achievement, personal adjustment, and academic performance. The second question asked the teachers to rank on a 5-point scale, from strongly agree to strongly disagree, their judgment of the following statement: "Most children of lower ability would do better if made to try harder." Regular class teachers were found to place more emphasis on academic performance as opposed to social or personal adjustment. Also, the regular class teachers tended to favor "pushing" lower-ability students, while special class teachers tended to reject this notion.

Efron and Efron (1967) have provided a particularly detailed account of the attitudinal differences between persons trained in mental retardation and those not so educated. A 70-item questionnaire (Likert format) was administered to 235 subjects representing the following groups: educators specializing in mental retardation, educators in other fields of special education, educators in other than special education, students in mental retardation, students in other fields of special education, other students in education, students in other than education, and individuals from other occupations. Using a factor analytic technique the authors identified six dimensions of attitudes toward mentally retarded persons. Factor One, Segregation via Institutionalization, indicates that the retarded individuals should be removed from society because they represent a threat to its members. Factor Two, Cultural Deprivation, indicates that cultural or environmental factors play a significant role in retarded development. Factor Three, Noncondemnatory Etiology, reflects a general view of retardation as being no different from any physical handicap. Retardation is not viewed as evidence of God's wrath or parental sinning. Factor Four, Personal Exclusion, is a bipolar factor that is characterized at the negative end of the continuum by an intense desire to avoid intimate contact with retardation and retarded persons. Factor Five, Authoritarianism, represents a view that there would be less retardation if people would obey God. Also, the most important contribution that schooling can make is to be kind to and protect retarded persons. Factor Six, Hopelessness, is another bipolar factor with a negative side that sees retarded persons as incapable of leading successful, happy lives. The various subject groups differed significantly on all factors except Noncondemnatory Etiology. Teachers of the retarded, as compared with general education teachers and individuals from other occupations, were less authoritarian, less prone to promote institutionalization, more accepting of having a retarded person in the family, more likely to ascribe retardation to cultural factors and in more command of factual information about retardation. Students in the field of retardation did not differ on any factor from teachers of the retarded. When compared to teachers and students in general education, students in retardation were less authoritarian, less supportive of institutionalization, more hopeful about the later life adjustment of the retarded, more inclined to support a cultural basis to retardation, and more knowledgeable in general about retardation. These data clearly support the notion that the quality and content of instruction and experience are more powerful determinants of attitudes than are quantitative measures of experience.

Shotel, Iano, and McGettigan (1972) examined the attitudinal differences between teachers in schools with a self-contained special class and a group of teachers participating in an integrative program using resource rooms. The three schools involved in the integrative program were in the first year of this innovation. EMR, emotionally disturbed, and other school peers were assigned for varying lengths of time to the resource rooms. The three schools housing segregated classes were matched with the experimental schools on variables of size and proximity of student population. A yes–no questionnaire was administered that addressed the following attitudes: placement of exceptional children in regular classes with resource room support, exceptional children's potential for age-level achievement, exceptional children's potential for normal social adjustment, the teachers' estimated skills to teach exceptional children, and the need for specialized methods and materials for exceptional children. The questionnaire was administered at the beginning and end of one school year. A number of findings are relevant to the present discussion. First, teachers from resource program schools were initially more favorable toward integration and more optimistic about academic and social adjustment of EMR children than they were at the year's end. Throughout the school year these teachers reported that the EMR students in their regular classes were the lowest in achievement and general class participation. Also, teachers reported that these youngsters were teased often by classmates. There was little disagreement that special methods and materials were required to teach exceptional learners. The authors note that since regular teachers are convinced of the importance of specialized education, it is unlikely that they will readily and confidently accept the responsibility of teaching these children.

In a unique study of attitudinal differences, Alper and Retish (1972) examined the effects of student teaching on students in special education, elementary education, and secondary education. Ten college seniors from each major were administered the Minnesota Teacher Attitude Inventory (MTAI) before and after student teaching. In addition, an 11-item questionnaire designed to measure students' evaluation of the teaching experience was administered after the field experience. Individuals who rank high on the MTAI generally maintain good interpersonal relations with students, enjoy teaching, and emphasize cooperation between themselves and students. On the other hand, teachers who score low generally are a dominant force in the classroom, with such domination based upon a basic fear and distrust of students. With combined scores for all majors, there was a significant decline in MTAI scores after student teaching. Analyses across subgroups indicated that special education majors' scores actually increased slightly, while secondary and elementary education majors' scores decreased. There was a moderately high correlation between MTAI scores and student teachers' evaluations of their field experience. These results indicate that with certain of these student teachers, an experience designed in part to promote positive attitudes toward children was counterproductive. One possible explanation for these results is that prior to student teaching some pre-service teachers may not hold accurate perceptions of the day-to-day experience of classroom instruction. It is also possible that the differential results reflect variations in the curriculum content of teacher preparation programs or differences in personality variables between individuals who select various programs of study.

In further work on attitudinal differences of pre-service teachers, Greene and Retish (1973) administered the MTAI to 29 special education majors and 46 elementary education majors. None of the subjects had participated in student teaching. No significant differences in MTAI scores were found. Considered together, the results of these two studies by Retish and his colleagues would seem to indicate, at least at one particular university, that the student teaching experience may have a significant impact on the formation of teachers' attitudes.

Brooks and Bransford (1971) conducted an initial effort to systematically alter the attitudes of regular classroom teachers toward exceptional children. Thirty professionals took part in a summer workshop that offered practicum placement 5 hr per week plus 9 hr of didactic instruction. Also, the subjects participated in weekly sensitivity training sessions. Pre- and postworkshop responses were collected on a semantic differential instrument designed to measure attitudes toward special education, exceptional children, preventive measures, rehabilitation, level of intelligence, integration into regular classes, and teaching as a profession. Following the workshop, significantly more positive responses were found for concepts of special education, prevention of handicapping conditions, and integration. Attitudes toward the other concepts were quite positive prior to the workshop.

Another formalized effort to alter teacher attitudes was conducted by Glass and Meckler (1972). Eighteen elementary school teachers were enrolled in an 8-week summer workshop in which 38 children with learning and behavior problems also were enrolled. The workshop format provided the participants with (*a*) daily instructional interaction with children; (*b*) problem solving sessions designed to review the workshop format; (*c*) formal instruction sessions related to academic remediation; (*d*) feedback and planning sessions in which instructional interactions with students were reviewed; and (*e*) parent meetings. The MTAI was administered on a pre–post basis along with a self-report inventory. This inventory required the participants to judge their competency on each workshop objective. The results indicated that the particpants saw themselves as more competent to teach handicapped learners and more receptive to the idea of mainstreaming than they did prior to the workshop. The teachers also evaluated themselves at the end of the workshop as better able to assess pupil performance and needs, develop remedial programs, implement behavior management programs, and listen to children. Although a number of serious methodological problems exist in this study—problems such as no control group and nonrandom subject selection—it would appear that practicum-based intervention aimed specifically at improving the skill level of teachers may result in positive, collateral attitude change toward exceptional children.

Yates (1973) also has reported data that confirms the efficacy of hands-on teacher training procedures. In this study, 30 teachers from kindergarten through fifth grade were enrolled in a 100-hr program designed to provide special education skills to regular classroom teachers. Ten teachers served as experimental controls. The intervention was composed primarily of field-based instruction with carefully controlled feedback. Pretest–posttest comparisons indicated that the experimental group was superior in their level of special education information and also felt that intellectually limited children could be successfully educated in regular classes.

In a more recent study, Harasymiw and Horne (1976) examined the effects of teacher retraining workshops, practica, and seminars on attitudes toward exceptional learners and regular classroom integration. One hundred and ninety-one experimental subjects were selected from five schools where mildly handicapped children were enrolled in regular classes. One hundred and sixty-one control teachers were selected from six schools with segregated programs only. The schools served children of similar socioeconomic status. Also, the two groups of teachers did not differ significantly along variables of age, formal educational training in special education, and sex. A 52-item Likert type scale was used to assess attitudes after 1 year of exposure to integrated programming

and accompanying teacher retraining. Experimental teachers expressed significantly more positive attitudes than control teachers on five of eight scales.
Specifically, the former were more positive regarding regular class placement,
felt instruction could be more readily modified to meet educational needs, did
not see integration as in any way harmful to normal children, felt they now
were trained adequately to instruct exceptional learners, and did not view major
changes in the regular classroom routine as following automatically from integration. On other assessment devices several interesting findings emerged.
When asked to judge how positive various groups of professionals felt about
mainstreaming, experimental subjects generally gave more positive assessments
than did control subjects. Significantly, both groups of educators felt that regular
class teachers were the least favorable and most removed from any decision
making regarding integration.

Gickling and Theobald (1975) conducted a large-scale survey of professionals'
attitudes that sheds some light on the alienation that regular class teachers
experience in the mainstreaming process. The survey consisted of 326 respondents representing the following groups: regular classroom teachers, special
education teachers, and regular and special education supervisors–administrators.
Each subject answered a yes–no questionnaire that addressed attitudes toward
(a) how the philosophy of equal educational opportunity is applicable to exceptional children; and (b) their willingness to educate exceptional children in
regular classes with technical support. The questionnaire also investigated how
teachers were informed about exceptional children and involved with related
educational decisions in their school systems. Although most respondents felt
that segregated classes discriminated against exceptional children and did not
affect satisfactory academic progress, they were not prepared to do away with
these self-contained classes. When the data on communication systems were
analyzed, a bleak picture emerged. Two-thirds of the regular education respondents reported that they were not aware of special children in their systems
or what programs were provided now or would be in the future. At least in
these school systems it appears that the special education professionals were
removed from the educational mainstream and that the resulting lack of communication left many regular educators with quite negative and uncertain
feelings regarding exceptional children and mainstreaming.

A few studies have been conducted to date in which the attitudes of teachers
were assessed as a function of various degrees of mainstreaming. Guerin and
Szatlocky (1974), for example, studied professional attitudes in eight school
districts that together used four different models for integrating EMR students.
In the first model all EMR students were enrolled in a special class and then
placed in regular classes for varying time blocks each day. Model 2 found all
EMR children enrolled and attending regular classes throughout the day. Special education funds had been diverted to reduce class size and purchase special

materials. From three to six EMR children were included in the regular classes. In the third model, EMR children were enrolled in regular classes. However, the students were provided with specialized instruction in academic areas by learning center personnel. In the final model, EMR children were enrolled in regular classes and provided with specialized academic instruction by an itinerant teacher. Across all models, administrators were quite positive about the mainstreaming programs. Teachers' attitudes were less consistent. Sixty-two percent expressed positive attitudes while the remaining 38% were evenly split between neutral and negative opinions. Only with the first model, continued special class enrollment, were the attitudes of regular and special class teachers predominantly negative. The authors also note that the attitudes of teachers were remarkably consistent within specific schools.

Meyers, MacMillan, and Yoshida (Note 1) examined the effects of court-ordered decertification of EMR children on the attitudes of regular and special educators from 12 California school systems. The decertification program resulted in approximately one-half of the students in self-contained classes for EMR children being moved to regular classes. Sixty percent of the 200 special educators from self-contained classes reported that the average learning level of their pupils was reduced as a result of the program. Some 25% indicated that the incidence of behavior problems had decreased. Of the 252 regular class teachers in the study, 59% reported that the presence of former EMR pupils had not altered their instruction of other class members.

If there is one consistent pattern to attitudinal studies of exceptional children and mainstreaming, it is the *lack* of consistent and predictable responses to questionnaires by special and regular educators. Clearly, categories of professional personnel do not represent unitary variables about which generalizations can be made. Thus, there is a pressing need to specify the conditions under which educators tend to express various attitudes. Mandell and Strain (1978) have provided an initial step in this process. Specifically, the study addressed the relationship between the predictor variables of (*a*) principals' attitude; (*b*) special educators' attitude; (*c*) educational background; and (*d*) classroom environment and regular educators' attitudes toward mainstreaming mildly handicapped children. Two randomly selected regular classroom teachers were chosen from 54 elementary schools that had at least one self-contained special class. Also, the school principal and one randomly selected special education teacher in the school were asked to participate. All subjects responded to a 20-item Likert scale that assessed their opinions about mainstreaming. Multiple linear regression procedures were used to detect which variables were significant predictors of a positive attitude toward mainstreaming. Neither the principals' or special education teachers' attitudes toward mainstreaming were related to regular class teachers' attitudes. Five educational background factors were related: years of teaching experience (negative correlation), course on diagnosing learning and behavior problems, previous special education teaching experience, number of university courses on exceptional children, and participation in in-service programs focused on exceptional children. Three components of the classroom environment variables were also significant predictors of a positive attitude. These were team teaching, availability of resource teachers, and less than 27 students enrolled. Although replications across other school systems are clearly needed, the present results may be used to begin selecting teachers for mainstreaming programs and arranging classroom environments to maximize the potential for successful integration.

The research reviewed to this point would indicate that regular class teachers may be less than accepting of exceptional children introduced into their class-room. Moreover, this lack of acceptance is often accompanied by a general absence of information regarding the needs and characteristics of exceptional children. One fear that has been voiced (Alexander & Strain, 1978) is that the attitudes held by regular class teachers will adversely affect pupil performance in the regular class. Such a possibility was first presented by Rosenthal and Jacobson (1968). These authors randomly selected approximately 20% of the children in grades 1 through 6 to be identified as youngsters with potential to be "intellectual bloomers." These children and their counterparts had been tested previously with a performance-based intelligence test. The IQ test sub-sequently was administered one semester and 1 and 2 years after the teachers were informed of the predicted intellectual growth. Approximately 50% of the labeled children showed IQ gains of 20 or more points. This study has been at the center of heated scientific and polemical debate for over a decade.

The major methodological shortcomings of the Rosenthal and Jacobson study include the questionable use of statistical procedures, the potentially confound-ing use of teachers as test administrators, the high attrition rate, regression effects for subjects with extreme prelabeling scores, and questionable sampling procedures. In spite of these problems, the "Rosenthal effect" is widely accepted and a considerable body of research supports the basic tenants of this pioneering study.

Even prior to the Rosenthal and Jacobson study, Herriot and St. John (1966) conducted a national survey in which it was observed that teachers working in lower-SES schools were less likely to hold favorable opinions about the motivation and behavior of their pupils than teachers from higher-SES schools. Additionally, the lower-SES-school teachers were more likely to be dissatisfied with their work and anxious to leave their present school. It is significant to note that Jones (Note 2) has reported a strong positive correlation between teachers' satisfaction and students' morale. Of course, these data do not reveal the precise direction or mechanisms of influence between teachers and students.

A number of studies have examined the process by which teacher judgments and evaluations of children may be altered by specific labels assigned to children.

Salvia, Clark, and Ysseldyke (1973) found that teachers continued to hold stereotyped attitudes in the face of conflicting evidence. Teachers were exposed to a normal child who had been labeled improperly as either mentally retarded or gifted. Although the child's behavior did not confirm either label, teachers continued to interpret his behavior as evidence of being either mentally retarded or gifted, depending upon which label was presented.

In further work on this topic, Foster, Ysseldyke, and Reese (1975) randomly assigned 38 college students to one of two treatment conditions, normal expectancy and low expectancy. Both groups initially were asked to complete a pseudo-referral-form. The normal-expectancy group was told to complete the form as they imagine it would appear for a normal fourth grade boy. The low-expectancy group was told to complete the referral for evaluation form as it might appear for an emotionally disturbed fourth grade boy. Next, both groups separately were shown a videotape of a normal fourth grade boy engaged in the following tasks: taking the reading recognition subtest of the Wide Range Achievement Test, taking the Peabody Individual Achievement Test general information subtest, performing various perceptual-motor tasks, and participating in a brief free play period. The normal-expectancy group was told prior to viewing the tape that the child had been evaluated by a clinical team and judged to be normal. The low-expectancy group was told that the child had been evaluated as being emotionally disturbed. After viewing the tape all subjects were asked to complete the referral for evaluation form based upon what they had just observed. On the initial referral form subjects rated a hypothetical disturbed child more negatively than a hypothetical normal child. After viewing the tape, subjects rated the normal-labeled child more positively than when he was labeled emotionally disturbed. Also, the low-expectancy group tended to give more positive ratings to the labeled child after viewing the tape. These data indicate that teacher trainees hold very strong stereotypes about the behavior of emotionally disturbed children, and that those expectations are upheld in the presence of conflicting behavioral evidence.

In a closely related analogue study, Gillung and Rucker (1977) had 176 regular classroom and 82 special class teachers complete the Rucker–Gable Educational Programming Scale to measure the effects of labeled and non-labeled behavioral descriptions on expectations. The scale is composed of a series of brief descriptions of children who actually were referred for special services. The descriptions contain a false name, age or grade, and data related to academic achievement and problem behaviors. The descriptions, in fact, were taken from cases in which the youngsters were identified as either mentally retarded, emotionally disturbed, or learning disabled. After reading the descriptions the respondents were to recommend the most appropriate educational placement, with choices ranging from regular class placement to placement in other than public education facilities. In order to test for labeling effects, appropriate labels were added to the behavioral descriptions. The results indicated that regular class teachers tended to recommend more restrictive educational placements for labeled children than for those with identified behaviors but no labels. This same finding occurred for special education teachers as well. Similar to findings reported by Mandell and Strain (1978) for regular class teachers, there was a negative correlation between years of special education teaching experience and assignment of children to less restrictive placement alternatives.

It has been suggested that subjects in experimental research often behave in the manner that they interpret to be consistent with the hypothesis of the study. If this is indeed the case in attitudinal research, then it is necessary to control for teachers' expectations for appropriate experimental subject behavior. In an attempt to examine the influence of experimental demands on attitudes, Foster and Salvia (1977) exposed 88 randomly selected elementary teachers to one of four experimental conditions: normal label and demand to be objective, normal label and no such demand, learning disabled label and demand to be objective, and learning disabled label with no such demand. The groups then separately viewed a videotape of a fourth-grade boy engaged in academic, motor, and social activities. The subjects were asked to rate the child's grade level on eight academic skills and to estimate the frequency with which he engaged in 24 undesirable behaviors. The boy's academic behavior was, in fact, age- and grade-appropriate. The data indicated that both labels and demands to be objective affected teachers' perceptions. There was a trend for teachers to overestimate problem behaviors when the child was labeled learning disabled and when there was no specific instruction to be objective. When viewing academic behaviors, the normal label combined with the objectivity demand produced conservative grade-level judgments. When teachers were exposed to the learning disabled label plus the objectivity demand, there was a tendency to give liberal grade level judgments. In this study, the demand for objectivity generally resulted in labeled behavior being viewed more accurately, yet still quite negative when compared to nonlabeled behavior.

While the majority of attitudinal studies related to labeling effects have centered on issues of labeled versus nonlabeled children, Algozzine, Mercer, and Countermine (1977) have offered an interesting account of the interplay between different labels of exceptionality. In this study, 128 teachers were asked to rate the relative disturbingness and acceptability of the behavior described in one of four randomly assigned case studies. The case studies depicted the following conditions: learning disabled label with characteristic learning disabled behavior, learning disabled label with characteristic emotionally disturbed behavior, emotionally disturbed label with characteristic emotionally disturbed behavior, and emotionally disturbed label with characteristic learning disabled behavior. Behaviors characteristic of emotional disturbance were rated as more disturbing and less acceptable when exhibited by a child labeled as learning disabled. The study suggests that labels may generate different levels of tolerance for the same behavior. Thus, this finding is in close agreement with other studies (e.g., Foster *et al.*, 1975; Gillung & Rucker, 1977) that found labels to be as or more critical to teacher judgments than actual behavior.

In addition to the analogue research showing differential teacher judgments of children as a function of diagnostic labels, there is a large body of research that substantiates changes in teachers' instructional behaviors following exposure to various labels or evaluations. In an early study in this area, Beez (1968) tested the effects of teacher expectations on students' achievement at an identification task. Sixty Head Start teachers and 60 students participated. The teachers were asked to instruct the children to correctly label a symbol. Thirty teachers were told that the child they were to instruct was quite intelligent and could be expected to do well at the task. The remaining teachers were told that they could expect poor performance from their tutee. The results indicated that 77% of the children who were prejudged to be competent learners acquired five or more symbol meanings, whereas only 13% of those children described as poor learners reached this level of performance. Also, teachers of favorably labeled children actually attempted to teach more symbol meanings than did teachers of negatively labeled children.

Brophy and Good (1970) proposed that the self-fulfilling prophesy begins when teachers form differential expectations for individual students. Because of these expectations, they treat children differently. Children in turn tend to respond in line with their differential treatment, and thus the original expectations are confirmed. To test this notion, Brophy and Good observed the instructional interaction between teachers and children they judged to be high and low in academic achievement. Teachers gave more opportunities to respond correctly to highly judged children. They did this by continuing to prompt these youngsters when correct answers were not immediately forthcoming. In contrast, these same teachers tended to criticize low achievers when they made incorrect responses.

A more fine-grain observational procedure was used by Khleif (1976) to examine the instructional behaviors of 10 teachers as they interacted with normal and slow-learning children. When the teachers were with slow learners they showed a lack of instructional clarity, were inconsistent in their judgments of permitted classroom behavior, and engaged in an increased level of sarcasm and threats.

A study by Farina, Thaw, Felner, and Hust (1976) indicated that retarded individuals may be perceived as less likely than persons labeled mentally ill or normal to succeed at simple learning tasks. Here, college students were told that they were to participate in a study at a state training school designed to determine what kind of students could work best with what kind of person.

The students were told that they would be helping either a mentally retarded, mentally ill, or normal individual to master two learning tasks. Actually, the learners were confederates who did not display behaviors indicative of retardation or mental illness. On one task the students were to administer contingent shock when errors were made. The students could adjust both the magnitude and the duration of the shock. However, no shock was actually delivered to the learners. The confederates identified as mentally retarded generally received less intense shock of shorter duration than either normal or mentally ill confederates. The authors interpret these results to indicate that the college students expected less of the mentally retarded confederates and were thus reluctant to punish their incorrect responses.

Several teacher bias studies have been conducted also with retarded children as subjects. The results of these studies are quite ambiguous. In an initial effort, Haskett (1968) examined 32 special class teachers and their 264 EMR pupils. All subjects were tested initially on the Metropolitan Achievement Tests (MAT) and the Syracuse Scales of Social Relations (SSSR). The investigator reported factual MAT scores to the teachers but falsified SSSR scores such that one-half of the children were given higher scores and the other half were given lower scores than they actually achieved. Five months later, both tests were administered again. No relationship was noted between MAT scores and teacher expectancy. However, there was a significant correlation between SSSR posttest scores and experimenter-induced bias.

Gozali and Meyen (1970) attempted to replicate the basic design of the Rosenthal and Jacobson (1968) study with EMR pupils. Sixteen teachers and 162 subjects participated. All children were administered the Stanford Achievement Test at the beginning and end of one academic year. After the pretest 20% of the subjects were assigned randomly to the experimental group. Teachers were informed that these youngsters had been identified by achievement testing as having "hidden potential" relative to academic performance. No performance differences were detected between experimental and control subjects.

Similar results were obtained by Soule (1972), who attempted to modify the performance of severely retarded children by influencing cottage parents' judgments of learning potential. Twenty-four of the more highly functioning children in a residential facility participated. All children were pretested using the Peabody Picture Vocabulary Test, Slosson Intelligence Test, and a locally developed behavior checklist. Cottage parents responsible for the 12 experimental subjects were told that the psychology department had determined that these children had the potential to perform at a much higher level than they currently exhibited. In a posttesting 6 months later, the Peabody, Slosson, and checklist were given again, plus the Stanford–Binet and Cattell Intelligence Test if a basal age could not be determined on the Binet. In addition to these measures, the Meacham Verbal Language Development Scale was administered and counts were made of the transfers to a higher functioning school program, referrals to a higher functioning living unit, and number of cottage-parent–child interactions during 20-min observation sessions across 5 days. Analysis of covariance revealed no significant differences between experimental and control subjects.

Peers' Attitudes toward Mentally Retarded Children

The body of research on peer attitudes has followed three basic paths: (*a*) description of attitudes toward EMR children; (*b*) assessment of social standing; and (*c*) remediation of negative attitudes.

DESCRIPTION OF PEERS' ATTITUDES

Clark (1964) was the first to examine the attitudes of normal children toward EMR peers. Specifically, 214 children in fourth and fifth grade classes were shown photographs of 10 male and 3 female special class pupils from the same school building. The special class children were identified only as "children in the school." The subjects were asked to select which child they knew best and to describe him or her. Generally, the descriptions of EMR children seldom were associated with their special class placement; rather they were described as former classmates, fellow schoolmates, or acquaintances in the community. Few descriptions included judgments of academic or intellectual ability. Rather, physical appearance and athletic ability were the most often mentioned attributes. Consistent with research on normal populations, few cross-sex choices were made. Although few negative attributes and no evidence of social rejection emerged from this study, it is important to remember that no comparison was provided between attitudes toward the special class children and normal peers. Also, it is possible that when asked to select the child they knew best, the normal peers picked the child they liked best.

Renz and Simensen (1969) added a normal comparison group to the design and methods employed by Clark (1964). A random sample of 100 seventh grade students was selected. In order to participate in the study these children had to be able to recognize 1 of 14 photographs of EMR peers. Fifty-seven children met this criterion. These children were asked to select one child from each group that they knew best and to describe the selected peers as thoroughly as possible. No evaluation differences emerged between normal and EMR reference groups.

Gottlieb (1974) conducted a pair of experiments to examine the effects of labeling and academic performance on normal children's judgments of retarded youngsters. In the first study, 48 fourth grade pupils from affluent homes were shown one of two videotapes. In the first tape, one-half of the subjects saw a confederate peer perform as an incompetent speller. The other subjects saw the confederate peer portray a competent speller. The labeling effect was determined by telling one-half of the subjects that the boy on the videotape was mentally retarded and a member of a special class. The other one-half was told that the boy was a fifth grade pupil. Immediately after viewing the tape the subjects filled out a modified social distance scale and an attitudinal questionnaire. Only the competence–incompetence dimension was associated with significant changes in expressed attitudes. Specifically, more positive attributes were associated with the confederate peer when he performed in a competent fashion. Labeling the child as mentally retarded did not affect the subjects' judgments.

In the second study, the procedures were replicated with 40 fourth grade pupils from low income families. This time no significant effects for competence or label dimensions were observed. The results indicate that for fourth grade children the label *mentally retarded* does not act as a stimulus for negative judgments and attitudes.

Several studies have examined the influence of various rater characteristics on attitudes toward EMR peers. For example, Jaffe (1966) measured the attitudes of 240 high school seniors toward behavioral descriptions that either did or did not contain information about the person being mentally retarded. The findings indicate that the labeling condition did not affect the subjects' level of negative statements, level of favorable traits, and social distance directed toward the described person. Subjects did view the retarded person as weaker, smaller, more passive, and more suggestible than the nonretarded person. There was a trend for subjects with greater contact with retarded individuals to attribute more favorable traits to the retarded stimulus person.

A similar study was conducted by Strauch (1970), who selected junior high subjects from two types of schools. In the first type, EMR students took part in industrial arts, homemaking, art, music, and physical education classes with normal peers. In the other schools, EMR children were enrolled in essentially self-contained programs. The subjects were administered a semantic differential instrument composed of 20 adjective pairs. The data did not yield significant differences related to attitudes toward the concepts *mentally retarded* and *special class pupil*. There was, however, a trend for contact subjects to offer more favorable attitudes than noncontact subjects regarding these concepts.

Peterson (1974) studied the relationship between contact with EMR peers, IQ, CA, and educational level of parents on respondents' expressed attitudes. A total of 420 nonretarded children attending the fifth through eighth grades participated. Subjects were asked whether they agreed or disagreed with 16 statements regarding children in special class. Items included such statements as, "Nobody cares about them in school" and "They often fight with other children." The subjects also completed an adjective pair scale in which they rated special class children along dimensions of happy–sad, smart–dumb, and kind–cruel. The notion that contact with an EMR child would positively affect attitudes was supported by the agree–disagree scale but not the adjective pair index. Also, there was a tendency for older children to express more favorable opinions of EMR youngsters. Finally, there was a significant negative correlation between parental educational level and the expression of positive attitudes.

An additional study of the relationship between contact and attitudes held was conducted by Cook and Wollersheim (1976). Subjects were drawn from three schools that differed in services to mentally retarded youngsters. One school offered EMR classes, another had services for Trainable Mentally Retarded (TMR) youngsters, and the third school had no such services. Subjects from these settings were exposed to either of two experimental conditions. In the first, the control condition, subjects responded to a description of a 12-year-old boy. In the labeling condition, subjects were told that the boy attended a special class for the mentally retarded. Four dependent measures were used to assess attitudes. The first two involved semantic differential measures taken from Jaffe (1966). On the evaluation measure, subjects responded to 11 pairs of adjectives including valuable–worthless, clean–dirty, tasteful–distasteful, warm–cold, deep–shallow, easy to get along with–hard to get along with, self-reliant–dependent, neat–sloppy, not dangerous–dangerous, and employable–unemployable. On the strength activity measure, four adjective pairs were used: active–passive, large–small, strong–weak, and independent–suggestible. The third dependent measure was composed of 20 behaviors taken from an adaptive behavior scale. On a 6-point scale, the subjects indicated how sure they were that the described person displayed these behaviors. The final measure was used to assess how willing the subjects were to volunteer to work with mentally retarded children from special classes. On balance, the labeling of the behavioral description produced more negative responses on the dependent measures. For the nonlabeling groups, contact did not significantly affect attitudinal scores. There was a trend, however, for students with EMR contact *not* to discriminate between labeled and nonlabeled descriptions.

Gottlieb, Cohen, and Goldstein (1974) have shown that no contact with EMR pupils may be associated with more positive attitudes than daily contact at school. The study involved two separate experiments with the intent of replication across socioeconomic levels. In the initial assessment, 284 lower-middle-class children from three elementary schools were administered an adjective rating scale. Contact with EMR children differed across the schools. In one setting, subjects attended a no-interior-wall school where the behavior of 19 EMR children could be observed readily. Another setting had integrated 7 EMR children in regular classes and 12 others in a segregated placement. The final school setting contained no EMR pupils. The most favorable attitudes were expressed by students from the no-contact school. There were no differences in attitudes across the two settings containing EMR students. Almost identical results were obtained in a replication with upper-middle-income students.

Siperstein and Gottlieb (1977) found that rater characteristics of sex and popularity affected children's expressed attitudes toward retarded youngsters. Thirty-four male and 38 female elementary-age children from an upper-middle-class school participated. The subjects were assigned randomly to one of four treatment conditions that were mediated by audiotape. The tapes portrayed (a) a competent speller of normal physical appearance; (b) a competent speller with Down's syndrome; (c) an incompetent speller with normal appearance; and (d) an incompetent speller with Down's syndrome. Several interesting findings related to rater characteristics emerged. First, regardless of sex, the child on the audiotape was viewed to be in a higher grade when he performed competently. On an adjective checklist, females were significantly more positive than males in the competent condition, while their responses were quite similar in the incompetent condition. On a social distance scale composed of items involving a desire to interact with the audiotaped child, females were less accepting than males. Two significant findings emerged related to social status. Initially, high-status children were less accepting than low-status children of a normal looking competent speller. Also, high-status children were more accepting of an incompetent speller who looked normal than were low-status youngsters.

SOCIAL STANDING OF EMR CHILDREN

Gottlieb and his colleagues have conducted an extensive and methodologically sound group of studies in which segregated and integrated EMR children have been rated by children of comparable ability.

In an initial study, Goodman, Gottlieb, and Harrison (1972) sampled the opinions of 20 male and 20 female children from primary and intermediate units of a suburban elementary school. The reference groups were (a) non-EMR children; (b) EMR children who were integrated into the academic routine of the school; and (c) EMR children who were in a self-contained class in the school. Each subject completed a sociometric device composed of 35 stimulus sets. Each set was composed of three stick figures: (a) two children playing ball together (labeled "friend"); (b) two children at a blackboard (labeled "alright"); and (c) two children with their backs toward each other (labeled "wouldn't like"). The children were read a list of 35 names and asked if they knew each child mentioned. The list was then read a second time omitting the children who were not known to the subjects. Each subject was asked to state how he or she felt about the named children by circling the appropriate stick figure. The results indicated that EMR children were chosen less often as friends and rejected more often than non-EMR youngsters. Also, integrated EMR children were rejected more often than segregated youngsters by males but not by females. This finding followed a general trend for females to be less harsh in their judgments of EMR children than males. The authors proposed that the increased rejection of integrated EMR children was a result of their being perceived as nonretarded and expecting them to conform to the behavioral standards of normal children.

In a systematic replication effort, Gottlieb and Budoff (1973) compared the social standing of EMR children in a traditional school building with those in a no-interior-wall school. Forty males and 40 females were selected randomly from the open-environment school and 28 boys and 28 girls were selected from the traditional school. Each subject rated the social position of partially integrated and segregated children in their respective schools. The sociometric instrument used by Goodman *et al.* (1972) was employed. Findings related to school differences indicated that EMR children in the traditional school were more often unknown than were their peers in the open school. Also, EMR children from the open school were rejected more often than EMR youngsters in the traditional school. In support of Goodman's findings, integrated EMR children in both settings held a lower social position than their segregated peers.

In order to determine whether the sociometric rejection of EMR children corresponds with overt, behavioral rejection, Gottlieb and Davis (1973) designed a forced-choice situation in which a non-EMR child was asked to select a playmate. Twenty-six boys and 16 girls from one elementary school served as subjects. These subjects were assigned randomly to one of three treatment conditions: (*a*) selecting a playmate between an average-IQ child and a segregated EMR child; (*b*) selecting between an average-IQ child and an integrated EMR child; or (*c*) selecting between a segregated and integrated EMR child. The results indicated that non-EMR children were selected significantly more often than segregated and integrated EMR children. Viewed together, this series of studies by Gottlieb and his colleagues clearly shows that increased contact between EMR and normal children does not lead to social acceptance of retarded youngsters. This is not to say, however, that contact could not be programmed in such a way as to facilitate the social relationship between EMR and normal peers.

Iano, Ayers, Heller, McGettigan, and Walker (1974) examined the social status of former special class EMR students who now were in regular classes with resource room support. Also studied was the social status of pupils referred for resource room services who had not been identified previously as exceptional.

In order to determine sociometric status, 40 former EMR children, 606 regular class pupils, and 80 regular class children receiving resource support were presented with six questions and asked to name classmates for each question. The questions were:

1. Who are the children in your class that you like the best?
2. If you were to have your seats changed, who would you like to have sit in the next seat?
3. Who are the children in your class that you like to play with the best?
4. If you were to have your seats changed, who wouldn't you like to have sit next to you?
5. Who are the children in your class that you do not like to play with?
6. Who are the children in your class that you do not like?

Former special class pupils received the most unfavorable ratings, while normal children in regular classes received the most positive ratings. There was no difference in the social standing of children diagnosed as EMR and those not so diagnosed but receiving resource room support. These data indicate that variables other than the label *EMR* are responsible for the social rejection of exceptional children.

Further work on the social standing of EMR children receiving resource room support was provided by Bruininks, Rynders, and Gross (1974). Specifically, the authors assessed the social standing of EMR children enrolled in regular classes with resource center support. The schools were located in either inner-city or suburban districts. Since other evidence (Mercer, Note 3) was available to indicate substantial demographic differences between mildly handicapped children living in urban and suburban settings, it was predicted that the similarities between inner-city EMR children and their normal peers would result in a more favorable social standing for these retarded youngsters. Sixty-five EMR children and 1234 nonretarded pupils from one inner-city and one suburban school district participated. The subjects completed a sociometric questionnaire on each child in their class. The instrument was identical to that used by Gottlieb and his colleagues, in which a child was labeled either as "friend," "alright," or "wouldn't like." In contrast to other research findings, inner-city EMR children received more favorable ratings than their nonretarded peers when judged by same-sex children. However, suburban EMR children were rated significantly lower than normal peers.

The vast majority of the sociometric research on EMR children indicates that individuals who are more visible to nonretarded peers are more often rejected than isolated retarded youngsters. These data suggest that as the amount of time spent in integrated settings increases, the retarded child's social standing will diminish accordingly. Gottlieb and Baker (Note 4) investigated this relationship by assessing the social standing of 300 EMR children who were scheduled for different amounts of time in regular class. However, no significant relationship was noted between time in regular class and social standing. This result was replicated by Gottlieb (Note 5), who also found that perceived behavior, not time spent in regular class, was a major predictor of social standing. Teachers' and peers' perceptions of academic competence did not relate to rejection, but did predict the degree of social acceptance.

An interesting variation on the issue of EMR children's social status was provided by Strichart and Gottlieb (1975), who assessed the extent to which nonretarded children would imitate the behavior of EMR age-peers. Previous research on imitation clearly indicates that among normal children there is a linear relationship between the social standing of a "model" child and the extent to which peers will imitate his or her behavior. Sixty normal children and 20 EMR youngsters participated. All subjects attended the same school and the EMR children attended segregated classes. Three treatment conditions were established in which a non-EMR child had the opportunity to model the behavior of a same-sex and same-age EMR peer. The treatment conditions represented experimenter-manipulated variations in the competence of EMR children as they performed a motor coordination task. Later, the non-EMR children were asked to select a playmate for a future task that was similar to the one completed earlier. The EMR children were found to be imitated most often when they performed in a competent fashion and least often when they did not perform in a competent manner. These data suggest that providing EMR children with adaptive skills may result in improved social standing.

REMEDIATION OF NEGATIVE ATTITUDES

The first reported attempt to improve the social standing of EMR pupils was conducted by Chennault (1967). Two hundred and eighty-two children in eight intermediate and eight junior high school classes for EMR youngsters participated. One-half of the intermediate and one-half of the junior high classes were provided with the experimental treatment. From each experimental class, four children with the lowest sociometric rating participated along with two pupils with high ratings. The treatment was composed of a group activity involving a dramatic skit. For 5 weeks, 15 min twice weekly, the students were taken from their class to plan and rehearse the skit, which eventually was presented to the entire class. Results indicated that experimental subjects' social standing improved significantly as did their judgment of their social position. These changes were significantly greater than those evidenced by control children.

A systematic replication of Chennault's work was conducted by Rucker and Vincenzo (1970). The primary issue of concern was whether or not the sociometric changes produced by mutual activities would maintain in the absence of intervention. A subject selection procedure similar to that employed by Chennault was used. In this case, the experimental subjects met for 45 min twice a week for 2 weeks to plan a carnival for their class. The first session focused on planning the activities of the carnival. During the second and third sessions the students made necessary items and planned the management of the carnival. The carnival was given on the fourth session. Immediately following the group experience, the experimental subjects' social standing had improved significantly over the pretest. When the sociometric device was given 1 month later, however, there were no differences in the social standing of experimental and control subjects.

In further work on the relationship between improved social standing and participation in planned activities, McDaniel (1970) provided basketball and square-dancing activities for 16 EMR children, while 16 other youngsters served as untreated controls. The basketball and square-dancing activities lasted for 30 min each day for 6 weeks. Four major findings emerged:

1. The initial social rejection of the experimental subjects as seating companions was quite high at first, but it decreased and stabilized across the 6-week period.
2. The social rejection of the experimental subjects as playing companions was also high at first but decreased and leveled off across the treatment period.
3. The initial social rejection of the control subjects as seating companions was somewhat below the experimental subjects at first but increased over the course of the study.
4. The initial social rejection of the control subjects as playmates was low, but it generally increased over the 6-week period.

Those studies of social standing change reviewed thus far applied intervention strategies so broad that it is impossible to delineate the variable(s) responsible for sociometric change. In order to isolate potentially functional components of the activity interventions, Lilly (1971) assigned eight low-achieving students to one of six treatment conditions. The first condition, labeled Full Impact Treatment, saw two low-status students removed from each of four classes twice weekly for 15-min periods to work with the experimenter and two popular classmates on a 5-week movie project. In the second condition, Experimenter Impact Treatment, the experimenter attempted to play a minimal role in the project, with the direction assigned to one of the popular peers. In the Peer Impact Treatment, no popular peers were included in the groups; instead, four low-status peers worked together with the experimenter on the project. In the Minimal Impact Treatment, the low-status children participated with unknown, high-status children at a location away from their school. In the Within Classroom Treatment, two low-status children were seated within their regular class next to high-status children. In addition, these youngsters participated together in a group project selected by the teacher. In the final condition, Full Control, low-status children were identified but did not receive any special treatment. Sociometric ratings were conducted 5 to 7 days following the treatment conditions and again 6 to 7 weeks following this assignment. The results indicated that low-status subjects assigned to the treatment groups had significantly greater posttreatment sociometric gains when compared to control subjects. These gains did not persist across the 6- to 7-week follow-up period. There were no differences in the sociometric status of children in the various treatment groups.

Summary and Conclusions

In reviewing the data on community members' attitudes toward mentally retarded persons, four trends are evident. First, it is generally felt that mental retardation is a unitary condition of primarily biological etiology. This perspective is certainly not surprising when one considers the second major trend, namely, that the condition of mental retardation is equated with severe and profound disability. The third general trend reflects a clear bias against spending public education dollars for severely retarded children. Even when parents of retarded children are questioned, a considerable percentage do not view public education as appropriate for these youngsters (Meyers *et al.*, 1966). Finally, when retarded persons engage in competent behavior, it is not taken as evidence of general ability. Rather, variables of luck and extreme effort are invoked to explain inconsistencies between actual behaviors and stereotypes.

Taken together, the attitudes held by the general public toward the mentally retarded can be viewed only as contributors to the limited adaptive behavior of labeled individuals. Indeed, if handicapped children and adults are to be afforded least restrictive living opportunities beyond the school environment, then an intensive effort must be undertaken to reeducate community members.

An examination of the attitudes of professionals toward mentally retarded students reveals four significant trends. First, regular class teachers are generally less favorable than special educators in their opinions of mentally retarded students and the concept of mainstreaming. Second, both positive and negative attitudes appear to be dependent upon the quality or type of educational and teaching experience rather than the quantity of such experience. Third, those successful attempts to improve the attitudes of regular class teachers have emphasized hands-on teaching experiences with exceptional learners. Finally, there is overwhelming evidence from both analogue and direct instructional situations that diagnostic labels have a negative effect on the perceptions and behaviors of teachers.

Looking toward the development of integrated services for exceptional children, the foregoing trends suggest that regular class teachers who are scheduled to receive former special class students will likely need considerable instructional assistance. Currently available data indicate that specific instructional procedures related to the following areas would be most useful: (*a*) targeting behaviors; (*b*) task analysis; (*c*) assessment of performance; and (*d*) programming antecedent and consequent events (Kerr, Shores, & Stowitschek, 1978).

The attitudes of peers toward their mentally retarded age-mates may be summarized as follows. First, there does not appear to be the clear bias toward labeled individuals that exists among community members and professionals. Although there is some evidence to document certain negative stereotypes held by peers, observed behavior seems to affect their judgments more than labels. Second, when the social standing of EMR and non-EMR children has been compared, EMR youngsters invariably have held lower social positions. This trend apparently is exacerbated when the behavior of EMR children is readily observable. Finally, positive albeit temporary attitude change has been reported when EMR and non-EMR children have been afforded an opportunity to interact around structured group projects and activities.

In summary, this review of community, professional, and peer attitudes toward mentally retarded persons clearly indicates that systematic efforts to improve attitudes must be an integral part of any successful mainstreaming program.

Reference Notes

1. Meyers, C. E., MacMillan, D. L., & Yoshida, R. K. Correlates of success in transition of MR to regular class. (Final Report, Grant No. OEG-0-73-5263). Pomona, Calif., U.S. Department of Health, Education, and Welfare, 1975.
2. Jones, R. L. Student attitudes and motivation. In Ohio State University Advisory Commission on Problems Facing the Columbus Schools (Ed.), *A report to the Columbus Board of Education.* Columbus: The Ohio State University, 1968.
3. Mercer, J. R. *The labeling process.* Paper presented at the Joseph P. Kennedy, Jr. Foundation International Symposium on Human Rights, Retardation, and Research, Washington, D.C., October 1971.
4. Gottlieb, J., & Baker, J. L. *The relationship between amount of integration and the sociometric status of retarded children.* Paper presented at the meeting of the American Educational Research Association, Washington, D.C., March 1975.
5. Gottlieb, J. *Predictors of social status among mainstreamed mentally retarded pupils.* Paper presented at the meeting of the American Association on Mental Deficiency, Portland, Oreg., June 1975.

References

Alexander, C., & Strain, P. S. A review of educators' attitudes toward handicapped children and the concept of mainstreaming. *Psychology in the Schools*, 1978, *15*, 390–396.

Algozzine, B., Mercer, C. D., & Countermine, T. The effects of labels and behavior on teacher expectations. *Exceptional Children*, 1977, *44*, 131–132.

Alper, S., Retish, P. M. A comparative study of the effects of student teaching on the attitudes of students in special education, elementary education, and secondary education. *Training School Bulletin*, 1972, *69*, 70–77.

Baldwin, W. D. The social position of the educable mentally retarded in the regular grades in the public schools. *Exceptional Children*, 1958, *25*, 106–108.

Beez, W. V. Influence of biased psychological reports on teacher behavior and pupil performance. *Proceedings of the 76th Annual Convention of the American Psychological Association*, 1968, *76*, 605–606.

Begab, M. J. Impact of education on social work students' knowledge and attitudes about mental retardation. *American Journal of Mental Deficiency*, 1970, *74*, 801–808.

Brooks, B. L., & Bransford, L. A. Modification of teachers' attitudes toward exceptional children. *Exceptional Children*, 1971, *38*, 259–260.

Brophy, J. E., & Good, T. L. Teachers' communication of differential expectation for children's classroom performance: Some behavioral data. *Journal of Educational Psychology*, 1970, *61*, 365–374.

Bruininks, R. H., Rynders, J. E., & Gross, J. C. Social acceptance of mildly retarded pupils in resource rooms and regular classes. *American Journal of Mental Deficiency*, 1974,*78*, 377–383.

Chennault, M. Improving the social acceptance of unpopular educable mentally retarded pupils in special classes. *American Journal of Mental Deficiency*, 1967, *72*, 455–458.

Clark, E. T. Children's perceptions of educable mentally retarded children. *American Journal of Mental Deficiency*, 1964, *68*, 602–611.

Cleland, C., & Cochran, I. The effects of institutional tours on attitudes of high school seniors. *American Journal of Mental Deficiency*, 1961, *65*, 473–481.

Combs, R. H., & Harper, J. L. Effects of labels on attitudes of educators toward handicapped children. *Exceptional Children*, 1967, *33*, 399–403.

Connaughton, M. C. *Physician's understanding of MR and their advice to parents of MR children.* Unpublished doctoral dissertation, Indiana University, 1974.

Cook, J. W., & Wollersheim, J. P. The effect of labeling of special education students on the perceptions of contact versus non-contact normal peers. *Journal of Special Education*, 1976, *10*, 187–198.

Corman, L., & Gottlieb, J. Mainstreaming mentally retarded children: A review of research. In N. Ellis (Ed.), *International review of research in mental retardation*. New York: Academic Press, 1978.

Efron, R. E., & Efron, H. Y. Measurement of attitudes toward the retarded and an application with educators. *American Journal of Mental Deficiency*, 1967, *72*, 100–107.

Farina, A., Thaw, J., Felner, R. D., & Hust, B. E. Some interpersonal consequences of being mentally ill or mentally retarded. *American Journal of Mental Deficiency*, 1976, *80*, 414–422.

Fine, M. J. Attitudes of regular and special class teachers toward the educable mentally retarded child. *Exceptional Children*, 1967, *33*, 429–430.

Foster, G. G., & Salvia, J. Teacher response to label of learning disabled as a function of demand characteristics. *Exceptional Children*, 1977, *43*, 533–534.

Foster, G. G., Ysseldyke, J. E., & Reese, J. H. I wouldn't have seen it if I hadn't believed it. *Exceptional Children*, 1975, *41*, 469–473.

Gickling, E. E., & Theobald, J. T. Mainstreaming: Affect or effect. *Journal of Special Education,* 1975, *9,* 317–328.

Gillung, T. B., & Rucker, C. N. Labels and teacher expectations. *Exceptional Children,* 1977, *43,* 464–465.

Glass, R. M., & Meckler, R. S. Preparing elementary teachers to instruct mildly handicapped children in regular classrooms: A summer workshop. *Exceptional Children,* 1972, *39,* 152–156.

Goodman, H., Gottlieb, J., & Harrison, R. H. Social acceptance of EMRs integrated into a nongraded elementary school. *American Journal of Mental Deficiency,* 1972, *76,* 412–417.

Gottlieb, J. Attitudes toward retarded children: Effects of labeling and academic performance. *American Journal of Mental Deficiency,* 1974, *79,* 268–273.

Gottlieb, J. Public, peer, and professional attitudes toward mentally retarded persons. In M. J. Begab & S. A. Richardson (Eds.), *The mentally retarded and society.* Baltimore: University Park Press, 1975.

Gottlieb, J., & Budoff, M. Social acceptability of retarded children in nongraded schools differing in architecture. *American Journal of Mental Deficiency,* 1973, *78,* 15–19.

Gottlieb, J., Cohen, L., & Goldstein, L. Social contact and personal adjustment as variables relating to attitudes toward EMR children. *Training School Bulletin,* 1974, *71,* 9–16.

Gottlieb, J., & Davis, J. E. Social acceptance of EMRs during overt behavioral interaction. *American Journal of Mental Deficiency,* 1973, *78,* 141–143.

Gottlieb, J., & Siperstein, G. N. Attitudes toward mentally retarded persons: Effects of attitude referent specificity. *American Journal of Mental Deficiency,* 1976, *80,* 376–381.

Gottwald, H. Public awareness about mental retardation. *Research Monograph of the Council for Exceptional Children,* 1970.

Greenbaum, J. J., & Wang, D. D. A semantic-differential study of the concepts of mental retardation. *Journal of Genetic Psychology,* 1965, *73,* 257–272.

Gozali, J., & Meyen, E. L. The influence of the teacher expectancy phenomenon on the academic performances of educable mentally retarded pupils in special classes. *Journal of Special Education,* 1970, *4,* 417–424.

Greene, M. A., & Retish, P. M. A comparative study of attitudes among students in special education and regular education. *Training School Bulletin,* 1973, *70,* 10–14.

Greenwood, C. R., Walker, H. M. & Hops, H. Issues in social interaction/withdrawal assessment. *Exceptional Children,* 1977, *43,* 490–499.

Guerin, G. R., & Szatlocky, K. Integration programs for the mentally retarded. *Exceptional Children,* 1974, *41,* 173–177.

Harasymiw, S., & Horne, M. Teacher attitudes toward handicapped children and regular class integration. *Journal of Special Education,* 1976, *10,* 393–400.

Haring, N. G. A study of classroom teachers' attitudes toward exceptional children. *Dissertation Abstracts,* 1957, *17,* 103–104.

Haring, N. G., Stern, G. G., & Cruickshank, W. M. *Attitudes of educators toward exceptional children.* Syracuse, N.Y.: Syracuse University Press, 1958.

Haskett, M. S. *An investigation of the relationship between teacher expectancy and pupil achievement in the special education class.* Unpublished doctoral dissertation, University of Wisconsin, Madison, 1968.

Heber, R. F. The relation of intelligence and physical maturity to social status of children. *Journal of Educational Psychology,* 1956, *47,* 158–162.

Herriot, R. & St. John, N. H. *Social class and the urban school.* New York: Wiley, 1966.

Hollinger, C. S., & Jones, R. L. Community attitudes toward slow learners and mental retardates: What's in a name? *Mental Retardation,* 1970, *8,* 19–23.

Iano, R. P., Ayers, D., Heller, H. B., McGettigan, J. F., & Walker, V. S. Sociometric status of retarded children in an integrative program. *Exceptional Children,* 1974, *40,* 267–271.

Jaffe, J. Attitudes of adolescents toward the mentally retarded. *American Journal of Mental Deficiency*, 1966, 70, 907–912.

Johnson, G. O. Social position of mentally handicapped children in regular grades. *American Journal of Mental Deficiency*, 1950, 55, 60–89.

Kerr, M. M., Shores, R. E., & Stowitschek, J. J. Peabody's field-based special teacher education program: A model for evaluating competency-based training. In C. M. Nelson (Ed.), *Field-based teacher training: Applications in special education*. Minneapolis: Advanced Training Institute, 1978.

Khleif, B. B. Role distance of classroom teachers of slow learners. *Journal of Research and Development in Education*, 1976, 9, 69–73.

Lilly, M. S. Improving social acceptance of low sociometric status, low achieving students. *Exceptional Children*, 1971, 37, 341–348.

Lott, A. J., & Lott, B. F. The role of reward in the formation of positive interpersonal attitudes. In T. L. Huston (Ed.), *Foundations of interpersonal attraction*. New York: Academic Press, 1974.

Major, I. How do we accept the handicapped? *Elementary School Journal*, 1961, 61, 328–330.

Mandell, C., & Strain, P. S. An analysis of factors related to the attitudes of regular classroom teachers toward mainstreaming. *Contemporary Educational Psychology*, 1978, 3, 154–162.

McDaniel, C. O. Participation in extracurricular activities, social acceptance, and social rejection among educable mentally retarded students. *Education and Training of the Mentally Retarded*, 1970, 5, 4–14.

Meyerowitz, J. H. Self-derogations in young retardates and special class placement. *Mental Retardation*, 1967, 5, 23–26.

Meyers, C. E., Sitkei, E. G., & Watts, C. H. Attitudes toward special education and the handicapped in two community groups. *American Journal of Mental Deficiency*, 1966, 71, 78–84.

Peterson, G. F. Factors related to the attitudes of nonretarded children toward their EMR peers. *American Journal of Mental Deficiency*, 1974, 79, 412–416.

Proctor, D. I. An investigation of the relationships between knowledge of exceptional children, kind and amount of experience, and attitudes toward their classroom integration. *Dissertation Abstracts*, 1967, 28, 1721–A.

Renz, P., & Simensen, R. J. The social perception of normals toward their EMR grade-mates. *American Journal of Mental Deficiency*, 1969, 74, 405–408.

Rosenthal, R., & Jacobson, L. *Pygmalion in the classroom: Teacher expectation and pupils' intellectual development*. New York: Holt, 1968.

Rucker, C. N., & Vincenzo, F. M. Maintaining social acceptance gains made by mentally retarded children. *Exceptional Children*, 1970, 36, 679–680.

Salvia, J., Clark, G., & Ysseldyke, J. Teacher retention of stereotypes of exceptionality. *Exceptional Children*, 1973, 40, 651–652.

Severance, L. J., & Gastrom, L. L. Effects of the label "mentally retarded" on causal explanations for success and failure outcomes. *American Journal of Mental Deficiency*, 1977, 81, 547–555.

Shotel, J. R., Iano, R. P., & McGettigan, J. F. Teacher attitudes associated with the integration of handicapped children. *Exceptional Children*, 1972, 38, 677–683.

Siperstein, G. N., & Gottlieb, J. Physical stigma and academic performance as factors affecting children's first impressions of handicapped peers. *American Journal of Mental Deficiency*, 1977, 81, 455–462.

Snow, R. E. Unfinished pygmalion. *Contemporary Psychology*, 1969, 14, 197–199.

Soule, D. Teacher bias effects with severely retarded children. *American Journal of Mental Deficiency*, 1972, 77, 208–211.

Strain, P. S., & Carr, T. H. The observational study of social reciprocity: Implications for the mentally retarded. *Mental Retardation*, 1975, *13*, 18–19.

Strauch, J. D. Social contact as a variable in the exposed attitudes of normal adolescents toward EMR pupils. *Exceptional Children*, 1970, *36*, 485–494.

Strichart, S. S., & Gottlieb, J. Imitation of retarded children by their non-retarded peers. *American Journal of Mental Deficiency*, 1975, *79*, 506–513.

Willey, N. R., & McCandless, B. R. Social streotypes for normal, educable mentally retarded, and orthopedically handicapped children. *Journal of Special Education*, 1973, *7*, 283–288.

Winthrop, H., & Taylor, H. An inquiry concerning the prevalence of popular misconceptions relating to mental deficiency. *American Journal of Mental Deficiency*, 1957, *62*, 344–348.

Yates, J. R. Model for preparing regular teachers for mainstreaming. *Exceptional Children*, 1973, *39*, 471–472.

Preschool Mainstreaming: An Empirical and Conceptual Review[1]　3

Ann P. Turnbull and Jan Blacher-Dixon

Introduction

Although ideas about mainstreaming have been flooding the literature related to special education during the past 10 years, discussions of issues embedded in mainstreaming practices are still timely. Recent applications of the theory, concept, and practice of mainstreaming to early childhood education have highlighted the educational significance of mainstreaming in general and of preschool (age 3–5) mainstreaming in particular. One of the most compelling forces in the history of mainstreaming is the passage of Public Law 94–142, The Education for All Handicapped Children Act. Two of the major principles of this legislation regarding the education of handicapped children are zero reject and least restrictive environment placements. P.L. 94–142 provides a legal mandate to provide *all* handicapped children with a free, appropriate education suited to their individual needs. States that provide preschool pro- gramming to nonhandicapped children are required to serve also handicapped children of the same age ranges in public school programs. In regard to the principle of least restrictive environment, handicapped children are required to be educated in settings with nonhandicapped children to the maximum extent appropriate in light of the individual needs of the handicapped child. Thus, mainstreaming (i.e., the integration of handicapped and nonhandicapped

[1]This research was supported by the Carolina Institute for Research on Early Education for the Handicapped.

children in educational programs and settings) is having significant impact on the early education of both handicapped and nonhandicapped children. As such, preschool mainstreaming has been considered a type of intervention strategy (Guralnick, 1978a) and, like other types of early intervention (Bronfenbrenner, 1975; Karnes & Teska, 1975), is worthy of thorough consideration. The purpose of this review is to evaluate critically both the empirical and conceptual literature on preschool mainstreaming in order to identify and evaluate significant program, child, and family variables that operate in this type of early intervention for handicapped children.

Relative to the amount of literature available on mainstreaming at the elementary level, there is a severe lack of literature dealing with preschool mainstreaming. The literature that does exist may seem particularly sparse because of a lack of common conceptual ground, acceptable methodology, or valued outcome. This state of affairs may be due, in part, to the fairly recent legislative mandate to integrate handicapped and nonhandicapped children when appropriate. The limited literature may also be due to the fact that there are comparatively fewer preschools than elementary schools and consequently fewer preschoolers available for study. Many states do not have laws requiring free public education for handicapped or nonhandicapped children between the ages of 3 and 5. Finally, the paucity of literature in this domain may be due to a failure to identify systematically relevant issues related to preschool mainstreaming.

Some generalizations about the state of the literature on preschool mainstreaming will be set forth here but elaborated upon in later sections of this review. The bulk of this literature is descriptive rather than empirical in nature and is often a published product of individual mainstreaming projects. Thus, it becomes difficult to draw general conclusions and implications from such material. The experimental studies now available in growing numbers need to be tied conceptually to their descriptive counterparts. The differences between the nature and implementation of mainstreaming at the preschool and elementary levels need to be clarified. For example, the goals and curricular organization of preschool education are typically different from those of elementary education. The "subject" population in preschool mainstreaming programs is also clearly different—physically (in terms of growth, stature, locomotion), intellectually (in terms of cognitive development and capacity for academic learning), and socially (in terms of interactions with peers, both handicapped and nonhandicapped). The relationship of parents to preschool programs is often characterized by more direct involvement than parents typically have in elementary schools. Similarly, the relationship of the child to parents and home may be different, that is, one might weight the role of parents and family more heavily in the life of the preschooler than in that of the school-aged child. Consideration of just these few general issues highlights the fact that preschool mainstreaming may be anomalous enough to be considered independently.

This section of the review has been organized into six areas based on the content or topic of the literature. These sections form a kind of naturally occurring taxonomy. The first section presents a detailed *rationale* for preschool mainstreaming and adds a historical, philosophical perspective to this area. The next section contains what may be loosely called the efficacy literature pertaining to mainstreaming on the preschool level, and includes primarily descriptions or project reports of *program success*. The third section focuses on child outcomes or evidence of *child success* as a result of preschool mainstreaming. The fourth section covers literature dealing with *teacher variables* important in preschool mainstreaming. Some hypothesized *effects on parents and family* are outlined in the fifth section, with particular emphasis on possible parental dilemmas that may be caused by mainstreaming preschool children. The final sections contain a summary and some *conclusions* to be drawn from this literature and the implications for theory, for practitioners, and for researchers.

Review of the Literature

RATIONALE

There are two major questions that must be answered in order to provide a rationale for implementing mainstreaming at the preschool level. These are: *What* is mainstreaming? and *Why* do it at the preschool level? A review of current interpretations and definitions of mainstreaming will help to answer the first question. Answers to the latter question will be derived from discussions of the legal, educational, and social aspects of preschool mainstreaming (Bricker, 1978; Meisels, 1977).

Definition

What is mainstreaming? There are numerous definitions of mainstreaming in the literature, most of which pertain to the elementary or secondary level. These definitions vary in the degree of specificity and in the degree of involvement of professionals and services implied. For example, one generally accepted definition of mainstreaming is as follows:

> Mainstreaming means enrolling and teaching exceptional children in regular classes for the majority of the school day under the charge of the regular class teacher, and assuring that the exceptional child receives special education of high quality to the extent it is needed during that time and at any other time it is needed [Birch, Note 1, p. 1].

The critical elements in this definition include the requirements of (*a*) regular class placement; (*b*) for over 50% of the school day; and (*c*) with appropriate special education services available. This is one of the few definitions of mainstreaming that specifies that placement in the regular class must occur for the majority of the school day to qualify as mainstreaming.

In an attempt to add clarity and operational guidelines, Kaufman, Gottlieb, Agard, and Kukic (1975) developed the following more comprehensive definition:

> Mainstreaming refers to the temporal, instructional, and social integration of eligible exceptional children with normal peers based on ongoing, individually determined, educational planning and program process and required clarification of responsibility among regular and special education administrative, instructional, and supportive personnel [pp. 40–41].

The components of this definition include where the child is placed (with normal peers) and for how long (i.e., temporal integration); what the child, and perhaps by implication the teacher, is doing (i.e., instructional integration); and with whom the child is interacting during the school day (i.e., social integration). The operational definition of these components is left undefined. In addition, the definition requires that specific roles and responsibilities of teachers, administrators, and support personnel (e.g., counselors and therapists) be specified to insure that programs are systematically coordinated for each handicapped child individually. However, according to MacMillan and Semmel (1977), if all of these elements must be present, "then no program to date constitutes mainstreaming [p. 3]."

Clearly, issues and definitions related to school-age mainstreaming abound, but it is not the purpose of this review to extricate them. Rather, this chapter is concerned with the extension of such ideas about mainstreaming to the realm of preschool or early education. A survey of the literature specifically on preschool mainstreaming revealed several descriptions of mainstreaming implementation rather than operational definitions of the concept. For example, some preschools may practice *traditional mainstreaming,* in which handicapped children are integrated into preschool classrooms originally designed for nonhandicapped children. Other preschools may adopt a policy of *reverse mainstreaming,* in which nonhandicapped children are integrated into preschool classrooms designated for handicapped children (Wynne, Brown, Dakof, & Ulfelder, 1975).

Why mainstream at the preschool level? As a first step in formulating the answer to this question, consider the following statement by Hobbs (1975):

> The best bet for reducing the rejection and alienation that compound the burden of the handicapped person is to recognize that all children are different, that each child is unique, and to bring together in natural settings (day-care centers, schools, playground) *from the earliest years onward* children called exceptional and children called normal to learn from each other and to nurture respect for each other [p. 15; author's italics].

Children are now, indeed, being mainstreamed from the earliest years (i.e., preschool). The rationale for this decision is fairly complex and involves the consideration of legal, educational, and social factors.

Legal Factors

Among the most compelling forces in support of preschool mainstreaming is the recently passed P.L. 94–142. As previously mentioned, states that offer preschool programming to nonhandicapped children must now offer similar services to handicapped children as young as 3 years of age. Specifically, the law refers to mainstreaming as education in the "least restrictive environment." The explanation of least restrictive contained in the *Federal Register* is as follows:

> 1. That to the maximum extent appropriate, handicapped children, including children in public or private institutions or other care facilities, are educated with children who are not handicapped, and
>
> 2. That special classes, separate schooling or other removal of handicapped children from the regular educational environment occurs only when the nature or severity of the handicap is such that education in regular classes with the use of supplementary aids and services cannot be achieved satisfactorily [August 23, 1977, p. 42497].

The notion of legislating the integration of handicapped and nonhandicapped preschools is not new. A 1972 congressional mandate ordered the Head Start preschool network, which had been serving primarily nonhandicapped children from low-income families, to include handicapped children as well. The population of each Head Start center is required to include 10% handicapped children. The categories of children to be considered in this 10% include auditorially handicapped, chronically ill, emotionally disturbed, mentally retarded, orthopedically handicapped, speech impaired, visually handicapped, and multihandicapped children (Lapides, 1973). According to DeWeerd (1977), mainstreaming represents recognition of the handicapped child's "right to be visible [p. 6]." This recognition was also reflected in legislation requiring the Handicapped Children's Early Education Projects (HCEEP) to "acquaint the community" with their work (DeWeerd, 1977, p. 6), thereby indirectly integrating handicapped preschoolers into a community of nonhandicapped persons. Preschool mainstreaming is still the exception rather than the rule in preschool programming for the handicapped. However, since mainstreaming is a strong legislative preference, it is not viewed as a passing educational fad (Meisels, 1977; Turnbull, 1977).

Educational Factors

There appears to be strong support for preschool mainstreaming from an educational perspective as well. Indeed, one of the original reports on the effectiveness of early intervention programs cautioned that insufficient attention is being paid to the effects of mixing handicapped and nonhandicapped children in the same classroom in order to improve the learning environment in which the intervention program is taking place (Stedman, Anastasiow, Dokecki, Gordon, & Parker, Note 2). To date, there are enough positive effects from regular intervention programs (Bronfenbrenner, 1975; Haskins, Finkelstein, & Stedman, 1977; Karnes & Teska, 1975) to warrant a similar developmental approach to planning, program design, and evaluation for use with handicapped children (Guralnick, 1978b). In a recent book describing a number of types of integrated preschools (Guralnick, 1978a), mainstreaming is presented as a viable educational alternative (Bricker, 1978) and a feasible administrative endeavor (Galloway & Chandler, 1978).

It is important to keep in mind certain educational tenets when considering mainstreaming at the preschool level. For example, in some preschool programs early childhood educational objectives are viewed as the same for nonretarded and retarded children, with variations only in the degree of achievement (Blacher-Dixon & Turnbull, Note 3; Winkelstein, Shapiro, Tucker, & Shapiro, 1974). However, it has been pointed out that a preschool program originally for nonhandicapped children may not meet the needs of a severely delayed child who has deficiencies in two or more critical areas of development (Lillie, 1975).

There is some evidence of academic progress in integrated preschool settings. For example, Rister (1975) reports the results of a longitudinal follow-up study of the achievement and school status of 88 deaf children who had attended integrated preschools. The study revealed that 62% of the original 88 children attended regular classes in elementary schools and only 30% attended special education classes. These findings should be accepted with caution, of course, because the two groups of children may not have had initial equivalency of age, ability levels, etc. The primary support for preschool mainstreaming in the literature to date does not come from documentation of educational gains or school success; rather, it comes from evidence of social and emotional gains, as discussed in the next section.

Social Factors

The rationale for preschool mainstreaming from a social perspective stems from the apparent positive social effects on both handicapped and nonhandicapped children, teachers, and parents. In one integrated summer preschool that included gifted children, "normal" youngsters, and retarded children with various degrees of mobility, the nonhandicapped children were reported to show less selfishness and greater awareness of others (Justice, 1974). Some of the outcomes of mainstreaming are presumed to increase understanding of individual differences by nonhandicapped children, teachers, and parents (Guralnick, 1976; Hennon, 1977; Hobbs, 1975; Justice, 1974; Karnes & Zehrbach, 1977; Snyder, Apolloni, & Cooke, 1977). Placement in a mainstreamed setting is also believed to be important in fostering a positive self-concept for the handicapped child (Kennedy, Northcott, McCauley, & Williams, 1976; Wynne *et al.*, 1975).

No less important than the psychological reasons for mainstreaming preschoolers is the preparation for later life adjustment. The integrated preschool setting offers an opportunity for handicapped children to learn to cope with normal society by preparing them for later participation in regular education and in society in general (Hennon, 1977; Karnes & Zehrbach, 1977; Wynne *et al.*, 1975). The preschool offers handicapped children normal play and learning experiences, as well as opportunities to learn socially appropriate behaviors through imitation or modeling (Cohen, 1975; Cooke, Apolloni, & Cooke, 1977; Devoney, Guralnick, & Rabin, 1974; Guralnick, 1976; Hennon, 1977; Karnes & Zehrbach, 1977; Neisworth & Madle, 1975; Peterson & Haralick, 1977; Peterson, Peterson, & Scriven, 1977; Snyder *et al.*, 1977). When such child interactions are positive, they may help avoid labeling and stigmatizing of handicapped children (Hennon, 1977).

Parents have expressed their support for mainstreaming at the preschool level in recognition of the positive social benefits for themselves and their children (D'Audney, 1976; Dunst, 1976; Garrett & Stovall, 1972; Morton & Hull, 1976; Cansler, Note 4; Grossi, Pinkstaff, Henley, & Sanford, Note 5). Parental participation in the integrated preschool enhances the benefits of the preschool experience for the children by promoting better working relationships between the parents and the preschool staff.

CONCLUSIONS

Although the term mainstreaming is used frequently to describe educational programs, a survey of definitions in the literature reveals that no operational definition exists. What types of educational practices actually qualify as mainstreaming? Further investigation is needed on the precise nature of temporal, instructional, and social integration in order to determine the practices that actually constitute the implementation of this concept.

Rationales for mainstreaming on the preschool level range in type from the pragmatic (compliance with a legal mandate) to the philosophical (perceived benefits) to the empirical (based on research results). Although the literature abounds with philosophical and social support of preschool mainstreaming, further empirical support is clearly needed.

Program Outcomes

The information on the success of preschool mainstreaming programs comes mainly from individual project descriptions and monographs. There are programs that serve children with primarily one type of disorder (e.g., mental retardation and hearing impairment), and programs that serve children who have one or more of any handicapping condition. The most comprehensive body of literature on integrated preschools is composed of reports of Head Start centers and articles on mainstreaming the hearing-impaired preschooler. Thus, literature pertaining to these two areas will be covered in subsequent, separate sections. However, the types of existing programs and variables related to successful preschool mainstreaming will be discussed first.

Unfortunately, the general research on programs for handicapped preschoolers may still be what Ackerman and Moore (1976) characterized as "spotty" and "uncoordinated." A characteristic of preschool programs that has contributed to research complications is the lack of clearly defined service delivery models. Ackerman and Moore (1976) pointed out that in the past specific models have been defined by variables such as the nature of the child's handicapping condition (categorical) and the age of the child. The categorical classification of programs is becoming less prevalent. Major current determinants of program models, as indicated, are age and population distribution. Home interventions, as opposed to center-based programs, are more likely to occur in rural areas and with younger children. Karnes and Zehrbach (1977) presented a detailed outline of critical dimensions of preschool program development (e.g., population served, geographical location), as well as descriptions of service delivery types (e.g., home-based, home followed by center, home- and center-based, center-based, technical assistance and consultative services model, prenatal model, and the intervention into higher level systems model). In their review of preschool programs within the First Chance Network (HCEEP), Karnes and Zehrbach identify three of the types of delivery systems that can incorporate mainstreaming. These include (a) home-based programs; (b) combination center and home approach; and (c) center-based programs. An example of a home-based system that mainstreams would be one in which instruction is delivered to both a handicapped and a nonhandicapped child in the home of the handicapped child. Mainstreaming in the home-followed-by-center model (or combined center and home model) involves serving the handicapped child first in the home and then enrolling the child in some integrated center. The center-based preschool model, which primarily serves children in a classroom-type setting, has the highest potential for mainstreaming; indeed, most of the programs included in this review are center-based.

In addition to being categorized by service delivery type, preschool programs for the handicapped may be distinguished by their philosophical and/or curricular orientation. For example, preschoolers may be integrated in an open education model (Meisels, 1977), a cognitively oriented program (Ipsa & Matz, 1978; Weikart, 1974), a cognitive learning model, cognitive developmental model, behavioral model, or normal developmental model (Anastasiow, 1978). Any of these curricular models may be used in mainstreamed preschools, or in preschools that have the goal of mainstreaming (e.g., some programs that serve only handicapped children have the goal of preparing youngsters with the necessary skills to enter a mainstreamed setting in elementary school). In addition, all of these models differ as to the type of materials, equipment, and facilities needed; the degree of structure imposed; the use of community or outside resources; evaluation procedures used; and the social or linguistic environment of the classroom. There are building and design variables that are also important for an integrated preschool program and that vary from program to program such as thermal, lighting, space, acoustical, and aesthetic characteristics of the classroom environment (Aniello, 1974).

In addition to the constellation of program variables just outlined, there are a number of child, teacher, and parent variables related to successful preschool mainstreaming that will be discussed later in this chapter review. Figure 3.1 summarizes relevant variables that impact on the success of mainstream programs. It should be noted that the literature does not support one "ideal" mode of integration, service delivery, curriculum methods, or techniques (Wynne *et al.*, 1975). Unless indicated otherwise, the information subsequently reported here came from descriptions of the individual projects, many of which used their own evaluation procedures.

Preschoolers with a variety of characteristics and handicapping conditions can be served in preschool mainstreamed programs. For example, there are bilingual preschool programs that serve handicapped and nonhandicapped Mexican–American children (Evans, 1976), programs to serve autistic children in a regular classroom (Painter, 1974), and programs for preschool visually handicapped children (Hull & McCarthy 1973; Tait, 1974).

Relative to the number of nonintegrated preschools, however, mainstreamed ones are rather sparse. Most programs that do include handicapped children integrate these with a variety of mental and/or physically handicapping conditions, unless specified otherwise. For example, Bricker and Bricker (1975) established a form of noncategorical education for the preschool child. They included an equal number of delayed and nondelayed children in the same environmental setting. Among other things, this project was distinguished by its undemanding structure with developmental programming and by its strong parent involvement component.[2] There were problems with this integration

---

[2]Parent involvement has since become a required component of all programs in the Handicapped Children's Early Education Projects network and in the Head Start Network. Additionally, P.L. 94–142 strongly encourages parent involvement in the education of their handicapped children.

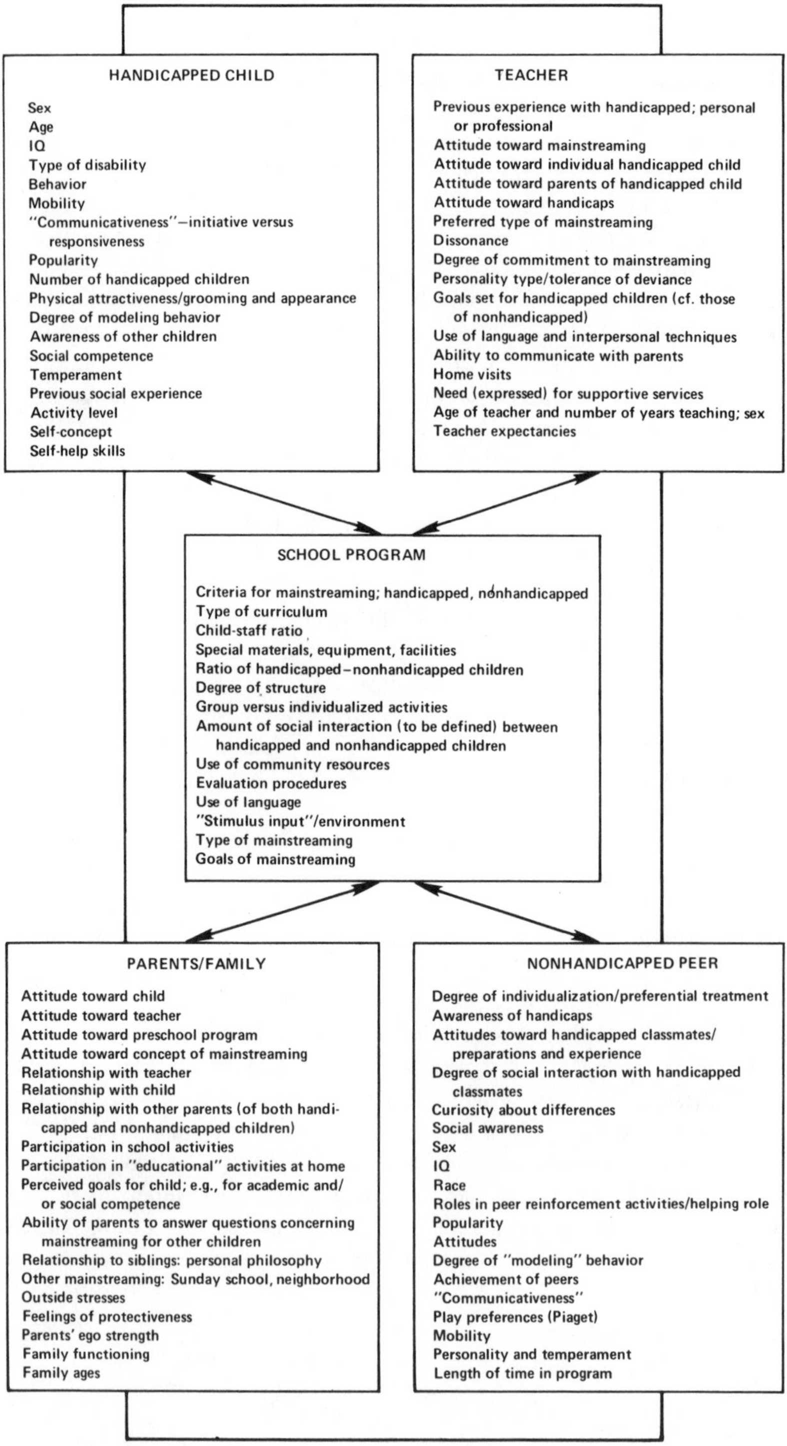

HANDICAPPED CHILD

Sex
Age
IQ
Type of disability
Behavior
Mobility
"Communicativeness"—initiative versus
    responsiveness
Popularity
Number of handicapped children
Physical attractiveness/grooming and appearance
Degree of modeling behavior
Awareness of other children
Social competence
Temperament
Previous social experience
Activity level
Self-concept
Self-help skills

TEACHER

Previous experience with handicapped; personal
    or professional
Attitude toward mainstreaming
Attitude toward individual handicapped child
Attitude toward parents of handicapped child
Attitude toward handicaps
Preferred type of mainstreaming
Dissonance
Degree of commitment to mainstreaming
Personality type/tolerance of deviance
Goals set for handicapped children (cf. those
    of nonhandicapped)
Use of language and interpersonal techniques
Ability to communicate with parents
Home visits
Need (expressed) for supportive services
Age of teacher and number of years teaching; sex
Teacher expectancies

SCHOOL PROGRAM

Criteria for mainstreaming; handicapped, nonhandicapped
Type of curriculum
Child-staff ratio
Special materials, equipment, facilities
Ratio of handicapped–nonhandicapped children
Degree of structure
Group versus individualized activities
Amount of social interaction (to be defined) between
    handicapped and nonhandicapped children
Use of community resources
Evaluation procedures
Use of language
"Stimulus input"/environment
Type of mainstreaming
Goals of mainstreaming

PARENTS/FAMILY

Attitude toward child
Attitude toward teacher
Attitude toward preschool program
Attitude toward concept of mainstreaming
Relationship with teacher
Relationship with child
Relationship with other parents (of both handi-
    capped and nonhandicapped children)
Participation in school activities
Participation in "educational" activities at home
Perceived goals for child; e.g., for academic and/
    or social competence
Ability of parents to answer questions concerning
    mainstreaming for other children
Relationship to siblings: personal philosophy
Other mainstreaming: Sunday school, neighborhood
Outside stresses
Feelings of protectiveness
Parents' ego strength
Family functioning
Family ages

NONHANDICAPPED PEER

Degree of individualization/preferential treatment
Awareness of handicaps
Attitudes toward handicapped classmates/
    preparations and experience
Degree of social interaction with handicapped
    classmates
Curiosity about differences
Social awareness
Sex
IQ
Race
Roles in peer reinforcement activities/helping role
Popularity
Attitudes
Degree of "modeling" behavior
Achievement of peers
"Communicativeness"
Play preferences (Piaget)
Mobility
Personality and temperament
Length of time in program

Figure 3.1. A proposed constellation of variables related to the success of preschool mainstreaming.

model, namely, some initial trouble recruiting nondelayed children because of parental skepticism, and later parent reports that nondelayed children acquired undesirable responses from the delayed children. Nevertheless, all parents sent their children back to this program the following year. Information gathered by the project from a questionnaire indicated that parents of the nondelayed found this preschool to be an "enlightening" experience for themselves and their children; parents of the delayed children chose the integrated program over a segregated one. Clearly, strong parental support contributed to these positive program outcomes.

Similar results were reported from a project integrating emotionally, physically, and mentally handicapped children into regular nursery and kindergarten programs (Buchanan & Mullins, 1968; Lewis, 1973). In this case, nonhandicapped children were strongly encouraged to accept the handicapped children. As a result it was reported that no nonhandicapped children were withdrawn by their parents because of the integrated program. It appears that the success of integrated programs is due, in part, to the opportunity nonhandicapped children have to become acquainted with individual limitations and disabilities.

Some projects that integrate handicapped and nonhandicapped preschool children attribute program success to factors other than parent involvement and child attitudes. These factors include teacher training in the needs and potentials of handicapped children (Korn, 1974; Providing for the Preschool Child, 1975), dissemination of information to parents (Sauer, 1975), and elements of the curriculum such as careful attention to language development prescriptions (Ipsa & Matz, 1978; Special Education Early Childhood Project, 1971).

HEAD START PROGRAMS

The 1972 Congressional mandate requiring Head Start preschool centers to mainstream handicapped children represents the largest-scale preschool mainstreaming effort to date. For the purposes of meeting this mandate, the handicapped preschool child was defined as anyone under age 6 who has a generally recognized and persistent physical or mental defect that prevents him or her from taking part freely in the activities that are so important to all children (Lapides, 1973). Handicapping categories included hearing or visual impairment, crippling deformity, central nervous system or heart damage, and mental retardation or emotional disturbance, as well as less noticeable handicaps that also interfere with success in daily living. Even the most severely impaired children were expected to benefit from integrated preschool programs (Klein, 1975). The following factors have been suggested as critical to successful integration within Head Start: recognizing the feelings of students, parents, and staff about handicapping conditions; maximizing positive interactions between children; maintaining positive student–teacher relationships; appropriately adapting the school environment; and individualizing the regular preschool program to meet the needs of the handicapped children (Cohen, 1975). In order to aid in the implementation of the congressional mandate to integrate handicapped children into Head Start programs, national staff training workshops were held and information on handicapped and nonhandicapped children was provided to Head Start staff, parents, and others (Responding to Individual Needs, Note 6).

The literature on Head Start mainstreaming program success consists of comprehensive national reports, regional reports, and individual project reports. The United States Department of Health, Education, and Welfare has produced yearly annual reports on the services provided to handicapped children through Head Start. Consistently cited as one of the most important services Head Start programs have offered handicapped children is the chance for handicapped and nonhandicapped children to share a developmental environment based on the premise that children are more alike than they are different. The government reports cited individualized educational programming; the provision of special education and health services; help from outside agencies; and parent training, counseling, and support as factors contributing to the success of mainstreaming with Head Start.

A series of reports on the Head Start effort to integrate handicapped and nonhandicapped children by Syracuse University revealed some additional information on mainstreaming success (Final Report on Assessment, 1974a, 1974b). This information was obtained from 52 regular Head Start programs, 14 experimental programs, and 10 selected non-Head-Start preschool enrichment programs. Sources of information included interviews with Head Start directors, classroom observations, and case studies of individual handicapped children. General findings indicated that:

1. Primarily mildly handicapped children, and few severely impaired children, were being served.
2. Few modifications in physical facilities were made for the handicapped children.
3. There appeared to be positive effects for increasing coordinated involvement and effort with families and other community agencies.
4. Teacher attitude is of critical importance.
5. The cost of serving the severely handicapped child exceeded that of serving the typical child.

(Final Report on Assessment, 1974a; 1974b; Final Report on Costs, 1974; The Status of Handicapped Children, Note 7). There are few such cost–benefit analyses of Head Start, and those that exist still favor the inclusion of handicapped children (Feldman, 1974; Final Report on Costs, 1974).

Reports from the Region IV Head Start Network (Grossi *et al.*, Note 5; Head Start is for the Handicapped, Note 8; Sanford, Henley, Fabrizio, & Watkins, Note 9), which includes Alabama, Florida, Georgia, Kentucky, Mississippi, North Carolina, South Carolina, and Tennessee, also provide information on the impact of mainstreaming. A survey, designed to identify the attitudes of Head Start personnel toward mainstreaming handicapped children used a stratified random sample of 1800 respondents. The responses of personnel suggested that mainstreaming (*a*) had a positive effect on the services provided to nonhandicapped children as well; (*b*) enhanced the overall parent program; and (*c*) was perceived by Head Start personnel as a positive influence on the total Head Start program. Furthermore, 60% of Region IV personnel indicated a belief that serving the handicapped increased collaboration with other agencies.

What conclusions can be drawn about mainstreaming within Head Start? It appears to be accepted by project personnel and parents, both handicapped and nonhandicapped children are reported to benefit from it, there is coordinated instructional programming for the handicapped available, and it has been both implemented and evaluated on a large-scale basis. With the passage of P.L. 94–142, Head Start projects may also need to develop procedures for nondiscriminatory testing, re-focus parent involvement activities, place children in the "least restrictive environment," assure the provision of related support services, develop due process procedures, and assure the development of individualized education programs (Sanford *et al.*, Note 9). To date, however, the actual degree to which handicapped children are truly integrated (temporally, socially, and instructionally) within Head Start centers is known only generally. Furthermore, although parent and family cooperation and involvement with Head Start are documented, the effects of mainstreaming on the parents and family are not. Data tends to be embedded in large-scale survey-type evaluations of the programmatic aspects of Head Start.

PROGRAMS FOR THE HEARING-IMPAIRED PRESCHOOLER

The literature on preschool mainstreaming programs for hearing-impaired children is qualitatively different from the other literature reviewed thus far. First of all, there is more of it (Northcott, 1973); secondly, it indicates tremendous support for mainstreaming; thirdly, almost every program bases its success on strong parent involvement as opposed to teacher training, curriculum adaptation, or other factors. Also, most articles define the subject population in terms of the degree of hearing or speech impairment and not in terms of any mental handicap. Thus, one must assume that the subjects involved are otherwise "normal." This situation is in contrast to the noncategorical preschool mainstreaming programs, like Head Start and others, which serve a variety of children with one or more handicaps. Although most of the literature cites examples of traditional mainstreaming, in which handicapped children are integrated into a classroom for nonhandicapped children, there are reports of reverse mainstreaming, in which hearing children participate in preschool classrooms serving the hearing-impaired (Kennedy, 1975; Layman, 1974; Luterman, 1967).

The tremendous communication handicap of prelingually deaf children, the relatively low incidence of deafness, and the need for teachers of the deaf to have special competencies have all been offered as reasons why the special needs of the typical deaf child cannot be met adequately in the regular classroom (Brill, 1975). Despite these negative factors, there are a number of very positive factors in support of mainstreaming. For example, hearing-impaired children in integrated preschool classrooms have a chance to learn to cope with others and to pattern their behavior after the norm (Northcott, 1970; Pollack & Ernst, 1973). The opportunity to interact with nonhandicapped, hearing children may provide the motivation for hearing-impaired children to listen and talk (Northcott, 1978; Pollack & Ernst, 1973; Stern, 1969). Nonhandicapped children may also gain understanding of how children with hearing loss function in social and/or academic activities (How to Integrate Hearing-Impaired Children, 1976).

In addition to presenting a fairly straightforward rationale for mainstreaming hearing-impaired preschoolers, the literature contains some indication of the optimal conditions for such mainstreaming. In general, it is recommended that only one hearing-impaired child be mainstreamed into the preschool classroom (Northcott, 1970), mainly because hearing-impaired children grouped together may reinforce each others silences (Northcott, 1970, 1971). Even some public school administrators recommend mainstreaming the hearing-impaired child as early as possible (Fallis, 1975), although according to Northcott (1978) placement eligibility for such youngsters should depend on a number of other factors as well. For example, the child should be a full-time hearing-aid user, be advanced in the use of audition in language acquisition, and have speech and language skills adequate to promote peer interactions. Some criteria for determining the appropriateness of the integrated preschool setting for hearing-impaired children are as follows: (*a*) opportunity for social interaction with normal peers; (*b*) exposure to peer group models; (*c*) exposure to language models; (*d*) preparation for later integration into the neighborhood, kindergarten or school; and (*e*) adequate teacher preparation and training. The integrated preschool setting, even one that meets all of the optimal conditions, cannot substitute for specific language training, which most hearing-impaired children need to pursue (Estes, 1974; Stern, 1969).

Finally, much of the literature on mainstreaming the hearing-impaired stresses the need for parent participation and support (Fallis, 1975; Luterman, 1967; McCay, 1975; Northcott, 1970, 1971, 1973; Pollack & Ernst, 1973; Rister, 1975; Stack, 1973; Strattner, 1974). By participating in the classroom, parents may see their child in school and assess his or her assets as well as limitations. The degree of parent and special education involvement, rather than the severity of hearing loss, has been said to be the primary determinant of successful integrated nursery school (or preschool) placement (Northcott, 1971). On the other hand, positive parental reactions and attitudes toward preschool mainstreaming have also contributed to successful mainstreaming. Published parental observations of their children (Northcott, 1973), position papers written by parents that "tell it like it is" (Stern, 1969), and involvement of both parents (Luterman, 1967; Strattner, 1974), as well as the entire family (Stack, 1973), in the mainstreaming process are factors that both contribute to and result from program success.

The future of preschool mainstreaming for children with hearing impairments is a positive one, at least according to the articles contained in the professional literature. However, like most of the literature on preschool mainstreaming, this area is embedded in a morass of philosophical position papers and reports of program success lacking in data (e.g., "The program generated a good deal of enthusiasm" [Layman, 1974]). There are two longitudinal studies of deaf children that have implications for preschool mainstreaming (Kennedy, Northcott, McCauley, & Williams, 1976; Rister, 1975). These will be reviewed in detail in the next section, since they are more specific measures of child success.

Child Outcomes

Another mechanism for determining the effectiveness or success of preschool mainstreaming programs is to examine proposed or observed positive child outcomes. Three sources of such data are reviewed here: (*a*) case studies; (*b*) postprogram evaluations or longitudinal studies; and (*c*) analyses of ongoing social interractions.

CASE STUDIES

Historically, the case study approach to evaluating child outcome has been a frequently used measure. Although many project reports contain records of case studies, fewer and fewer are appearing in published articles. Volume II of the *Final Report on Assessment of the Handicapped Effort in Experimental Regular Head Start and Selected Other Exemplary Pre-school Programs Serving the Handicapped* published by Syracuse University (1974) summarizes the case studies of 20 handicapped children participating in Head Start. Such descriptive, anecdotal accounts of success in mainstreaming children have a strong bearing on subsequent funding and policy decisions concerning Head Start. On the other hand, some case study reports have less far-reaching implications. For example, Schramm (1974) reports case histories of two Down's syndrome girls attending a regular Montessori classroom. Although the successful functioning of these two girls in the Montessori environment suggests the feasibility of this educational approach with retarded children, the data are certainly not robust.

Although the case study report method is a valid approach for examining child success in mainstreamed settings, it should probably be used in conjunction with one or more other types of data. The case study approach is subject to criticism due to its lack of generalizability, its basis in anecdote as opposed to data gathered experimentally and its lack of relationship to an established theoretical framework.

POSTPROGRAM EVALUATIONS (LONGITUDINAL STUDIES)

Although the longitudinal research approach is clearly preferable, it is used infrequently for a number of reasons, such as lack of financial or institutional support and lack of appropriate measurement instruments (Gallagher, Ramey, Haskins, & Finkelstein, 1976). Thus, only a few such studies have been reported here. Most postprogram evaluations use future class placement of the handicapped preschooler as a measure of child outcome (Fine, 1974; Howard, 1974; Podell, 1976).

Rister (1975) reports the results of a longitudinal follow-up study of the achievement and school status of 88 deaf children who had attended integrated preschools. The study revealed that 62% of the 88 subjects attended regular education classes and only 30% were in special education classes. Longitudinal sociometric data on 11 severely to profoundly deaf pupils are reported by Kennedy et al. (1976). All subjects had attended a preschool with normal, hearing children. Three years later the peer acceptance and self-perceived status of the mainstreamed deaf children was examined. It was found that the hearing-impaired children were as socially accepted as their classmates and were perceptive of their own status. The authors suggest that the preschool experience was related to this later success in public school elementary classrooms.

Reports on children with handicaps other than hearing impairments also indicate positive child outcomes. For example, the majority of handicapped children who have graduated from First Chance Projects entered regular academic programs as opposed to special class placements (DeWeerd, 1977). The First Chance Projects contain children with a variety of handicapping conditions, and some projects are mainstreamed, containing both handicapped and nonhandicapped children. It is unclear, however, if the mainstreaming aspect of the First Chance programs positively influenced the later regular class placements or not. Thus far, information obtained from the longitudinal approach to studying preschool mainstreaming success is limited.

ANALYSES OF SOCIAL INTERACTIONS

In contrast to both of the above approaches, the analysis of social interactions of children in integrated preschool settings is growing increasingly popular. The need for gathering data on the effects of mainstreaming on actual child behavior has clearly been recognized (Guralnick, 1978a, b). Along with this need has come the development of experimental techniques for collecting and analyzing interactional data. It has been suggested that integrated preschool settings may enhance positive social interactions between handicapped and nonhandicapped children through such mechanisms as peer modeling, reinforcing agents, and generalized imitations (Snyder, *et al.*, 1977). According to Guralnick (1978a, b), there are two ways to maximize such interactions between preschoolers at varying developmental levels. One is to reinforce selective social play activities and the other is to build up the social behavior repertoires of the less socially advanced children. Nonhandicapped peers thus may be used to encourage appropriate social play among their handicapped classmates, to serve as therapeutic agents, and to encourage the spontaneous use of appropriate language and adaptive communication.

A critical point to keep in mind when evaluating the effect of preschool mainstreaming on child behavior is that simply placing handicapped and nonhandicapped children in the same room does not guarantee that any interactions between them will occur. Ray (1974), in fact, compared the free play behavior of developmentally delayed and nondelayed toddlers using ethological methods for collecting naturalistic observations. In general, he found that nondelayed toddlers interacted more with nondelayed peers than with delayed toddlers, who exhibited less object-related play and nonverbal signals and less laughing and talking. Delayed children were more likely to be found in "separate" as opposed to "peer-related" contexts.

Specific intervention by the teacher may be required to facilitate peer imitation and social interaction (Cooke *et al.*, 1977; Devoney *et al.*, 1974). For example, several studies have examined aspects of play behavior of handicapped and nonhandicapped children in integrated preschools. Types of play observed include "social" forms, such as parallel or cooperative play, or nonsocial forms, such as independent or isolate play. Devoney *et al.* (1974) found a substantial increase in the quantity and quality of play of handicapped children when they participated in structured play situations with nonhandicapped peers; however, without both direct teacher intervention in structuring the situation and the participation of nonhandicapped children, there were no substantial effects on the social play of the handicapped children. Other analyses of play behavior and social interaction in the integrated preschool setting indicated that non-handicapped children play with each other slightly more than they play with handicapped children. Handicapped children exhibit more social play when nonhandicapped playmates were the only ones available; otherwise, they generally played by themselves (Peterson & Haralick, 1977).

In addition to direct structuring or teaching, reciprocal peer imitation may also promote positive social interactions (Apolloni & Cooke, 1978). Peterson *et al.* (1977) showed that both handicapped and nonhandicapped preschoolers who can imitate peers as part of an experimental task are more *likely* to imitate a nonhandicapped peer than a handicapped peer. Sociometric measures included in the study indicated that the developmental handicap did not appear to interfere with the popularity of the children. These results favor the integrated preschool environment, in which the handicapped child has the chance of benefitting from imitation of nonhandicapped peers. Furthermore, imitation of retarded children by nonretarded children in such settings is unlikely to occur unless it is directly reinforced (Cooke *et al.*, 1977). Nevertheless, Nord-quist (1978) cautions that the effects of integration on the nonhandicapped child need to be carefully studied as well. Guralnick (1978a), too, cautions that although the evidence appears to be strongly in favor of integration (with benefits for the nonhandicapped as well as the handicapped children), there are a number of factors that are likely to limit the outcome of child–child interactions (e.g., the developmental levels of the children involved, the so-cial–personality characteristics of the children, the resources available, and the type of intervention model employed).

It is clear that more normative data on social interaction in integrated pre-school settings is needed. Apolloni and Cooke (1978) cite the need for finding the optimal "skill blend" of handicapped and nonhandicapped children that will maximize positive interactions between children of varying developmental levels. There is some data to suggest that nonhandicapped preschool children adjust their speech (in terms of productivity and complexity) to the develop-mental level of similar-aged handicapped peers (Guralnick & Paul-Brown, 1977). The optimal ratio of handicapped to nonhandicapped children that would facilitate positive interactions also needs to be researched. For example, most of the literature mentioned thus far in this section refers to a ratio of retarded to nonretarded children of 1:2 or 1:4; it might be more realistic to investigate the interactions of retarded children who are mainstreamed into a much larger group of nonretarded children. Some research has shown that nonretarded children matched to the chronological age, as opposed to the mental age, of the retarded children serve as better models and peer reinforcers in the mainstreamed setting (Knapczyk & Peterson, 1977). Finally, since main-streaming is an attempt to find the most appropriate social context for the education of handicapped and nonhandicapped children, Hartup (1978) strongly urges researchers to focus on peer relationships and intergroup contacts.

How much are the interactions of preschoolers affected by attitudes toward the handicapped? In addition to the inclusion of measures or ratings in studies of peer interactions or child outcomes, there is some literature that directly pertains to the attitudes of preschoolers. Although no articles on preschool children's perceptions of disability were readily available a decade ago (Jones & Sisk, 1967), more recent research suggests the following:

1. Nonhandicapped children first become aware of physical handicaps at about age 4, but their awareness of less obvious handicaps occurs at later ages.
2. Nonhandicapped children have a negative view of the handicapped.
3. Younger nonhandicapped children have a less negative attitude than older ones.
4. Mere contact with handicapped children does not necessarily reduce negative attitudes (Levitt & Cohen, 1976).

Research by Asher (Note 10) showed a clear age-related shift from a lack of understanding of disability to understanding. Furthermore, knowledge about disability had no effect on children's willingness to share, liking of others, etc. Gerber (1977) found that nonhandicapped preschoolers were aware of the handicaps of their peers and exhibited more rejection than acceptance toward them. Most of these studies use some type of sociometric measure, such as indicating preferences between pictures of handicapped and nonhandicapped children.

Attitudes of preschoolers are important when considering the advocacy role that nonhandicapped children may learn to assume. If it could be demonstrated that one child outcome of preschool mainstreaming is that nonhandicapped children learn to serve as a buddy or helper of handicapped children, a strong case in favor of preschool mainstreaming could be made in regard to advocacy.

Teacher Variables

There is considerable discrepancy as to which teacher variables are most important to successful mainstreaming. For example, is teacher training critical or are teacher attitudes?

With regard to general preschool programming, Karnes and Teska (1975) suggest that the pattern of staff functioning may be as important as the curriculum for successful educational intervention. The need for teacher skills to facilitate planning and positive social interactions in the integrated preschool classroom has been highlighted in a number of sources (Cleary, 1976; Gorelick, 1973; Meisels, 1977). Fredericks, Baldwin, Grave, Moore, Riggs, and Lyons (1978) have identified careful training as a crucial ingredient in the integration of moderately and severely handicapped preschoolers, while at the same time they have questioned the practicality of this notion: "Whether or not it is feasible to adequately train staff and conduct the programming necessary, however, is a serious concern [p. 205]."

The other significant teacher variable affecting the success of preschool mainstreaming is that of teacher or staff attitudes. Wynne *et al.* (1975), however, cite both the ability and attitude of the teacher as most important to the successful outcome of the integrated preschool. Some of the data on attitudes comes from studies of preschools' willingness to mainstream handicapped children. Two such studies (Abelson, 1976; Gorelick, 1973) yielding slightly different results will be reported here. On the basis of information gathered through on-site observation, interviews with the project directors, and written questionnaires, Abelson found that of all of the 45 preschools surveyed, none expressed an unwillingness to accept a handicapped child. Blindness and wheelchair confinement were found to be least desirable. Gorelick (1973), however, found that of 72 preschools surveyed, 44 were already serving children with some kind of physical or mental handicap, and 60 were agreeable about accepting referrals of handicapped children. In this survey, severely mentally retarded children were least preferred, while partially deaf children were most preferred.

The need for positive attitudes among teachers of handicapped children is a consistently stressed factor in reports of Head Start mainstreaming efforts. Positive teacher attitudes appear to be critical for encouraging acceptance of the handicapped child by the nonhandicapped peer group (Klein, 1975), for understanding and accepting children's individual differences (Mayer, 1974), and for maximizing success in preschool mainstreaming (Christopherson, 1972). A study of attitudes of teachers who were previously untrained in special education but had mentally or physically handicapped preschoolers placed into their classroom showed that attitudes changed in a realistic direction following mainstreaming (Clark, 1976). For example, after mainstreaming teachers indicated general agreement on items such as the following:

1. Modification of class routines is necessary for integration.
2. Similar instructional competencies are effective with both normal and exceptional children.
3. All exceptional children will not necessarily respond similarly to a particular educational methodology.

4. Physically impaired children are not necessarily easier to mainstream than mentally impaired children.

Effects on Parents and Family

Previous sections of this review have emphasized repeatedly the important contribution of parental involvement and participation to preschool program and child success. Mainstreaming represents a substantial change for children in the nature of preschool service delivery. However, limited attention has been paid to the effect of mainstreaming on the parents of the handicapped children who are being placed in less restrictive settings. The quantity of the current literature related to parental satisfaction with preschool mainstreaming is limited (D'Audney, 1976; Dunst, 1976; Garrett & Stovall, 1972; Morton & Hull, 1976; Stern, 1969; Cansler, Note 4; Grossi *et al.*, Note 5), especially in consideration of the accelerated rate at which mainstreaming is being implemented. Also, most of the literature in this area consists of position papers written by parents that include personal insight on such issues as views of mainstreaming, obstacles to overcome, and recommendations (Garrett & Stovall, 1972). Although data-based research on the effects of preschool mainstreaming on parents and family is practically nonexistent, this area may ultimately prove to be critical in determining mainstreaming success.

Related to the area of parental satisfaction is the study of attitudes of parents toward preschool mainstreaming. Just as some parents have expressed satisfaction with the mainstreaming placements of their handicapped child (Garrett & Stovall, 1972; Stern, 1969), other parents are skeptical of some of the premises of the educational community about this placement alternative. Bennett (1978), the parent of a 15-year-old mentally retarded daughter states, "Mainstreaming, currently fashionable, simply means that *all* kids have an equal shot at mediocre schooling. . . . Bringing retarded children into a regular classroom does not necessarily end segregation and discrimination—it may only camouflage it [p. 164]." In discussing segregated versus mainstreamed placements for handicapped children, Cansler (Note 4) reported on an interview with two deaf adults who advocated that parents make placement choices for their child to maximize options and to allow the child to move back and forth between the "handicapped world" and "mainstreamed world." These handicapped adults stated the need of handicapped individuals to spend time with people who share similar problems and also with people who do not. A study (Dunst, 1976) of attitudes of parents with children in either integrated or segregated early education classes illustrates the point that the opinions of parents may differ widely on the appropriateness of mainstreamed settings. On the basis of their response to questionnaire items, parents of handicapped children enrolled in an integrated classroom and parents of the nonhandicapped children enrolled in the same classroom believed that integration had beneficial effects for the handicapped children and little or no negative effects on the other children. On the other hand, parents whose handicapped children were enrolled in a segregated program and parents whose nonhandicapped children were also enrolled in a nonintegrated program had significantly less positive attitudes toward mainstreaming.

Although the placement of young handicapped children in mainstreaming settings has largely been approached from the point of view of child effects, the important implications for parents of placing their handicapped child in a mainstreamed setting warrant careful consideration. Does the placement of a handicapped child in a program that also serves nonhandicapped children create additional stress for the parents of handicapped children, as they are exposed to the normal developmental growth of their child's peers? Under these circumstances, do parents have different needs requiring alternative opportunities for involvement in program activities than in situations in which the handicapped child is placed in a segregated setting? The fact that the parents of mainstreamed preschoolers have special needs, too, has been highlighted in reports of Head Start (Final Report, 1974a, 1974b). What effect does the mainstreaming placement have on the parents' evaluation of their child's developmental progress? What factors contribute to a parent's positive view of mainstreaming? What is the nature of the parental involvement models that will most effectively contribute to parental satisfaction with mainstreaming programs? Research to date has not addressed such questions; however, information from such research has the strong potential of improving the education of handicapped children.

Recent interviews with 29 university students, all handicapped since their preschool years (Raper, Mesibov, & Turnbull, Note 11) highlighted the key role parents play in the success of their handicapped child. Sixty-one percent of these young adults identified their parents as the most important influence in helping them deal with their special needs. They described their parents as especially helpful when they encouraged independence, recognized strengths, and reinforced confidence, determination, and participation in social life. Forty-six percent of the handicapped individuals complained that their parents were either overprotective because of the handicap or overeager for them to demonstrate their strengths and compensate for their weaknesses. Based on these reports, the attitudes and perceptions of parents toward mainstreaming would be expected to influence the handicapped child's success in the mainstreamed setting.

Documenting parental attitudes and perceptions is a necessary prerequisite to developing intervention programs aimed directly at assisting parents in their own adjustment and development of their child. For example, one position paper (Turnbull & Blacher-Dixon, Note 12) focuses on conceptual issues related to the effects of mainstreaming on parents and highlights the need to evaluate preschool mainstreaming in terms of its effect on the family and parents, rather than merely in terms of its educational efficacy for the child. Particularly during preschool years, when parents are in the midst of adjusting to the fact that their own child is handicapped, sensitivity to parental effects is viewed as essential for the later positive adjustment of both the child and family.

The roles and responsibilities of fathers and family members other than parents in preschool mainstreaming are not clearly differentiated in the literature. Some programs encourage the involvement of both parents of each child by conveniently locating the setting of school programs or events or by including special father involvement sessions (Luterman, 1967; Strattner, 1974). Garrett and Stovall (1972) recognize the problem of family and sibling resentment that might develop when parents become overinvolved with the mainstreaming process. Such problems may be eliminated with innovative programming such as that described by Stack (1973), which takes the teacher into the home in order to involve the entire family in integrating the child.

The Head Start Network actually focuses on serving handicapped children *and their families* (Final Report, 1974a; Grossi *et al.*, Note 5). Many Head Start centers offer supportive services and counseling for parents and report positive effects in increasing involvement and efforts with families.

Although some integrated preschool programs have adopted a family approach, no programs found to date stress the role of siblings in preschool mainstreaming. Further research is needed to explore the extent to which handicapped children who have nonhandicapped siblings live in a mainstreamed home environment. Furthermore, it may be useful to examine how the development and educational progress of a handicapped child is affected by the presence or absence of a nonhandicapping sibling (i.e., the mainstreamed home environment versus the nonmainstreamed home environment). The role of siblings in preparing nonhandicapped peers to interact socially with their handicapped brother or sister needs to be explored, along with the accompanying stress factors that may or may not be present for the nonhandicapped sibling. Such data on the behavior of both handicapped children and their siblings may contribute to further understanding of both the role of the family in mainstreaming and the effects of preschool mainstreaming on the family.

Conclusions

It is difficult to draw broad-based conclusions from the heterogeneous body of literature reviewed here. One fundamental problem is the lack of a common, operational definition of preschool mainstreaming by which programs or models can be grouped for comparison. Preschool mainstreaming *at the very least* is the placement of handicapped and nonhandicapped children in the same educational setting. *At the most*, however, mainstreaming is a form of early intervention that has the potential of producing many social as well as educational benefits for both handicapped and nonhandicapped children. The implications of preschool mainstreaming for children, families, and educators apply to several domains.

IMPLICATIONS FOR PRACTICE

Although a number of researchers and educators have suggested variables or parameters that contribute to successful preschool mainstreaming (e.g., Guralnick, 1975; Nix, 1977), no model of integration has been shown empirically to be consistently preferable. Linking a strong research component to preschool mainstreaming intervention, as advocated by Guralnick (1973), should provide data relevant to both theory and practice. For example, Guralnick recommends intensive analysis of each child's behavior by applying multiple baseline procedures to most aspects of program development.

One major, still unanswered question is under what conditions and for what type of children is the segregated versus the integrated preschool setting more successful. The research on preschool mainstreaming has not directly approached this issue, most likely because of the lack of comparability between programs mentioned previously. It seems that Wynne *et al.* (1975) offered a reasonable suggestion, that is, only when primary goals are met as successfully in an integrated setting as in a segregated setting does the inclusion of both handicapped and nonhandicapped children in the same classroom become desirable.

IMPLICATIONS FOR THEORY

Just as no one set of variables provides a formula for implementing mainstreaming at the preschool level, there is no one theoretical framework guiding preschool mainstreaming efforts. A number of projects might ascribe to some general theoretical orientation, for example, cognitive developmental, behavioral, and cognitive learning (Anastasiow, 1978) or to a particular curriculum approach, such as programmed, open framework, child-centered, or custodial (Weikart, 1974). Much of the research on the processes involved in social interactions in the integrated preschool setting has been couched within the frameworks of behaviorism or social learning theory. This can be seen in the peer model approach, the reinforcing agent approach, and the imitation approach (Guralnick, 1978a; Snyder *et al.*, 1977), which have been used to foster positive social interactions among preschoolers.

IMPLICATIONS FOR RESEARCH

The relative paucity of data-based articles on preschool mainstreaming, as compared to the number of descriptive articles, highlights the need for further research in this area. The development of an operational definition of preschool mainstreaming and the delineation of preschool mainstreaming models based on such a definition should provide a useful starting point for researchers.

Research on the "efficacy" of preschool mainstreaming from an educational or academic point of view may not prove to be as fruitful as further investigations of peer interactions and social effects, a point made clearly by Hartup (1978). Additionally, the assumption that preschool mainstreaming does more good than harm and is beneficial to *all* handicapped children has not been empirically tested (Blacher-Dixon & Turnbull, Note 3). Continued observational research of handicapped and nonhandicapped children in the classroom is needed to verify empirically the social and emotional gains that parents and others attribute to preschool mainstreaming (Bricker, 1978; Guralnick, 1976; Hennon, 1977; Morton & Hull, 1976).

Finally, in recognition of the critical role that parents have played in preschool programs for the handicapped and that they will now play in shared decision making, as implied by P.L. 94–142, research on the effects of preschool mainstreaming on parents and the family will clearly be in order.

Reference Notes

1. Birch, J. *Mainstreaming definitions.* Paper presented at the annual meet of the Council for Exceptional Children, Kansas City, April, 1978.
2. Stedman, D. J., Anastasiow, N. J., Dokecki, P. R., Gordon, I. J., & Parker, R. K. *How can effective early intervention programs be delivered to potentially retarded children?* A report for the Office of the Secretary of the Department of Health, Education, and Welfare, 1972.
3. Blacher-Dixon, J., & Turnbull, A. P. *Is mainstreaming at the preschool level a conumdrum? . . . The WHAT, WHY and HOW of preschool mainstreaming.* Manuscript in preparation, 1978.
4. Cansler, D. Parents and the gifted–handicapped child. In J. E. Leonard (Ed.), *Chapel Hill services to the gifted-handicapped. A project summary.* Chapel Hill, N.C.: Chapel Hill Training–Outreach Project, 1977.
5. Grossi, J. A., Pinkstaff, D., Henley, S., & Sanford, A. R. *The Chapel Hill study of the impact of mainstreaming handicapped children in Region IV Head Start.* Chapel Hill, N.C.: The Chapel Hill Training–Outreach Project, 1975.
6. *Responding to individual needs in Head Start: A Head Start series on needs assessment. Part*

I: Working with the individual child. Washington, D.C.: Child Development Services Bureau (DHEW/OCD), Head Start Project, 1974.
7. The status of handicapped children in Head Start programs. Washington, D.C.: Fourth Annual Report of the U.S. Department of Health, Education, and Welfare to the Congress of the United States on Services Provided to Handicapped Children in Project Head Start, 1976.
8. Head Start is for the handicapped, too! Update of Region IV effort. Chapel Hill, N.C.: Chapel Hill Training–Outreach Project, 1975.
9. Sanford, A. R., Henley, H. C., Fabrizio, J. J., & Watkins, S. The Chapel Hill study of services to the handicapped in Region IV Head Start. Chapel Hill, N.C.: The Chapel Hill Training–Outreach Project, 1977.
10. Asher, N. W. An examination of pre-school children's attitudes toward the physically handicapped. Paper presented at the biennial meeting of the Society for Research in Child Development, Denver, April 1975.
11. Raper, A., Mesibov, G., & Turnbull, A. Education and the gifted–handicapped child. In J. E. Leonard (Ed.), Chapel Hill Services to the gifted–handicapped. A project summary. Chapel Hill, N.C.: Chapel Hill Training–Outreach Project, 1977.
12. Turnbull, A. P., & Blacher-Dixon, J. Preschool mainstreaming: Possible parental dilemmas. Manuscript in preparation, 1978.

References

Abelson, G. A. Measuring preschools' readiness to mainstream handicapped children. Child Welfare, 1976, 50, 216–220.

Ackerman, P., & Moore, M. G. Delivery of educational services to preschool handicapped children. In T. D. Tjossem (Ed.), Intervention strategies for high risk infants and young children. Baltimore: University Park Press, 1976.

Anastasiow, N. J. Strategies and models for early childhood intervention programs in integrated settings. In M. J. Guralnick (Ed.), Early intervention and the integration of handicapped and nonhandicapped children. Baltimore: University Park Press, 1978.

Aniello, V. A. Educational specifications pertinent to the design of an educational complex for preschool trainable mentally retarded children. Dissertation Abstracts International, 1974, 34A(9), 5749. (University Microfilms No. 74–6389)

Apolloni, T., & Cooke, T. P. Integrated programming at the infant, toddler, and preschool levels. In M. J. Guralnick (Ed.), Early intervention and the integration of handicapped and nonhandicapped children. Baltimore: University Park Press, 1978.

Assessment of the handicapped effort in experimental Head Start and selected other exemplary preschool programs serving the handicapped: Final Report (Vol. 1, Chap. 1–7). Syracuse University: Division of Special Education and Rehabilitation, 1974. (ERIC Document Reproduction Service No. ED 108 441)

Bennett, J. M. Company, halt! In A. P. Turnbull & H. R. Turnbull (Eds.), Parents speak out: Views from the other side of the two-way mirror. Columbus, Ohio: Charles E. Merrill, 1978.

Bricker, D. D. A rationale for the integration of handicapped and nonhandicapped preschool children. In M. J. Guralnick (Ed.), Early intervention and the integration of handicapped and nonhandicapped children. Baltimore: University Park Press, 1978.

Bricker, D. D., & Bricker, W. A. Non-categorical education for the preschool child. Nashville, Tennessee: George Peabody College, 1975. (ERIC Document Reproduction Service No. ED 073 745)

Brill, R. G. Mainstreaming: Format or quality? American Annals of the Deaf, 1975, 120(4), 377–381.

Bronfenbrenner, U. Is early intervention effective? In M. Guttentag & E. L. Struening (Eds.), *Handbook of evaluation research*, Beverly Hills: Sage, 1975.

Buchanan, R., & Mullins, J. B. Integration of a spina bifida child in a kindergarten for normal children. *Young Children*, September 1968, 23, 339–344.

Christopherson, J. The special child in the "regular" preschool: Some administrative notes. *Childhood Education*, 1972, 49(3), 138–140.

Clark, E. A. Teacher attitudes toward integration of children with handicaps. *Education and Training of the Mentally Retarded*, 1976, 11(4), 333–335.

Cleary, M. E. Helping children understand the child with special needs. *Children Today*, 1976, 5(4), 6–10.

Cohen, S. Integrating children with handicaps into early childhood programs. *Children Today*, January–February 1975, pp. 15–17.

Cooke, T. P., Apolloni, T., & Cooke, S. A. Normal preschool children as behavior models for retarded peers. *Exceptional Children*, 1977, 43(8), 531–532.

D'Audney, W. (Ed.). *Giving a head start to parents of the handicapped*. Omaha: University of Nebraska Medical Center, Meyer Children's Rehabilitation Institute, 1976. (ERIC document Reproduction Service No. ED 119 434)

Devoney, C., Guralnick, M., & Rabin, H. Integrating handicapped and nonhandicapped preschool children: Effects of social play. *Childhood Education*, 1974, 50(6), 360–364.

DeWeerd, J. Introduction. In J. B. Jordan, A. H. Hayden, M. B. Karnes, & M. M. Wood (Eds.), *Early childhood education for exceptional children: A handbook of ideas and exemplary practices*. Reston: The Council for Exceptional Children, 1977.

Dunst, C. J. Attitudes of parents with children in contrasting family education programs. *Mental Retardation Bulletin*, 1976, 4(3), 120–132.

Estes, J. Children develop language to relate to the hearing world. *Volta Review*, 1974, 76(9), 559–561.

Evans, J. *Identification and supplementary instruction for handicapped children in a regular bilingual program*. Paper presented at the annual meeting of the American Educational Research Association, San Francisco, April 1976. (ERIC Document Reproduction Service No. ED 123 891)

Fallis, J. R. The key to integrated learning for children who are hearing impaired. *Volta Review*, 1975, 77(6), 373–376.

Federal Register, August 23, 1977.

Feldman, B. Hospital Head Start university affiliated program for handicapped and non-handicapped. Master's thesis, Pacific Oaks College, 1974. (ERIC Document Reproduction Service No. ED 104 101)

Final report on assessment of the handicapped effort in experimental regular Head Start and selected other exemplary pre-school programs serving the handicapped (Vol. 1). Syracuse University: Division of Special Education and Rehabilitation, 1974. (ERIC Document Reproduction Service No. Ed 108 440)

Final report on assessment of the handicapped effort in experimental regular Head Start and selected other exemplary pre-school programs serving the handicapped (Vol. 2). Syracuse University: Division of Special Education and Rehabilitation, 1974. (ERIC Document Reproduction Service No. ED 108 441)

Final report on costs in serving handicapped children in Head Start: An analysis of methods and cost estimates. Syracuse University: Division of Special Education and Rehabilitation, 1974. (ERIC Document Reproduction Service No. ED 108 443)

Fine, S. A high proportion of maladjusted preschool children in a group of normal preschoolers: Results and implications. *Canada's Mental Health*, 1974, 22(4), 3–4.

Fredericks, H. D. B., Baldwin, V., Grave, D., Moore, W., Riggs, C., & Lyons, B. Integrating the moderately and severely handicapped preschool child into a normal day care setting. In M.

J. Guralnick (Ed.), *Early intervention and the integration of handicapped and nonhandicapped children*. Baltimore: University Park Press, 1978.

Gallagher, J. J., Ramey, C. T., Haskins, R., & Finkelstein, N. W. Use of longitudinal research in the study of child development. In T. Tjossem (Ed.), *Intervention strategies for high-risk infants and young children*. Baltimore: University Park Press, 1976.

Galloway, C., & Chandler, P. The marriage of special and generic early education services. In M. J. Guralnick (Ed.), *Early intervention and the integration of handicapped and nonhandicapped children*. Baltimore: University Park Press, 1978.

Garrett, C., & Stovall, E. M. A parent's views on integration. *Volta Review*, 1972, 74(6), 338–344.

Gerber, P. J. Awareness of handicapping conditions and sociometric status in an integrated preschool setting. *Mental Retardation*, 1977, 15(3), 24–25.

Gorelick, M. C. *Are preschools willing to integrate children with handicaps? Careers in integrated early childhood programs*. California State University, Northridge: Preschool Laboratory, Home Economics Department, Social and Rehabilitation Service, 1973. (ERIC Document Reproduction Service No. ED 097 794)

Guralnick, M. A research-service model for support of handicapped children. *Exceptional Children*, 1973, 39, 277–282.

Guralnick, M. Early classroom based intervention and the role of organized structure. *Exceptional Children*, 1975, 42, 25–31.

Guralnick, M. J. The value of integrating handicapped and nonhandicapped preschool children. *American Journal of Orthopsychiatry*, 1976, 46(2), 236–245.

Guralnick, M. J. (Ed.). *Early intervention and the integration of handicapped and nonhandicapped children*. Baltimore: University Park Press, 1978. (a)

Guralnick, M. J. Integrated preschools as educational and therapeutic environments: Concepts, design, and analysis. In M. J. Guralnick (Ed.), *Early intervention and the integration of handicapped and nonhandicapped children*. Baltimore: University Park Press, 1978. (b)

Guralnick, M. J., & Paul-Brown, D. The nature of verbal interactions among handicapped and non-handicapped preschool children. *Child Development*, 1977, 48, 254–260.

Hartup, W. W. Peer interaction and the processes of socialization. In M. J. Guralnick (Ed.), *Early intervention and the integration of handicapped and nonhandicapped children*. Baltimore: University Park Press, 1978.

Haskins, R., Finkelstein, N. W., & Stedman, D. J. Infant-stimulation programs and their effects. *Pediatric Annals*, 1978, 7(2), 123–128.

Hennon, M. L. *Identifying handicapped children for child development programs*. Atlanta, Ga.: Humanics Press, 1977.

Hobbs, N. *The futures of children.*San Francisco: Jossey-Bass, 1975.

How to integrate hearing-impaired children in regular classrooms. *The special education report*, 1976, Issue No. 510, 1–9.

Howard, N. K. *Regular class placement of the exceptional child: An abstract bibliography*. Urbana, Ill.: ERIC Clearinghouse on Early Childhood Education, 1974.

Hull, W. A., & McCarthy, D. G. Supplementary program for pre-school visually handicapped children: Utilization of vision/increased readiness. *Education of the Visually Handicapped*, 1973, 5(4), 97–104.

Ipsa, J., & Matz, R. D. Integrating handicapped preschool children within a cognitively oriented program. In M. J. Guralnick (Ed.), *Early intervention and the integration of handicapped and nonhandicapped children*. Baltimore: University Park Press, 1978.

Jones, R. L., & Sisk, D. A. Early perceptions of orthopedic disability. *Exceptional Children*, 1967, 34, 42–43.

Justice, W. P. Serendipity-integrated summer preschool program. *Deficience Mentale/Mental Retardation*, 1974, 24(3), 4–9.

Karnes, M. B., & Teska, J. A. Children's response to intervention programs. In J. J. Gallagher

(Ed.), *The application of child development research to exceptional children*. Reston, Va.: The Council for Exceptional Children, 1975.

Karnes, M. B., & Zehrbach, R. R. Alternative models for delivering services to young handi-capped children. In J. B. Jordan, A. H. Hayden, M. B. Karnes, & M. M. Wood (Eds.), *Early childhood education for exceptional children*. Reston, Va.: The Council for Exceptional Children, 1977.

Kaufman, M. J., Gottlieb, J., Agard, J. A., & Kukic, M. B. Mainstreaming: Toward an explication of the construct. *Focus on Exceptional Children*, 1975, 7(3), 1–12.

Kennedy, A. E. C. Operation chatterbox. *Hearing and Speech Action*, 1975, 43(3), 24–25.

Kennedy, P. K., Northcott, W., McCauley, R., & Williams, S. M. Longitudinal sociometric and cross-sectional data on mainstreaming hearing impaired children. *The Volta Review*, 1976, 78(2), 71–78.

Klein, J. W. Mainstreaming the preschooler. *Young Children*, 1975, 30(5), 317–326.

Knapczyk, D. R., & Peterson, N. L. Social play interaction of retarded children in an integrated classroom environment. *Research and the Retarded*, 1977, 3(4), 104–112.

Korn, M. The integration of handicapped children in a municipal day care center. *Deficience Mentale/Mental Retardation*, 1974, 24(3), 26–30.

Lapides, J. *Exceptional children in Head Start. Characteristics of preschool handicapped children.* College Park, Md.: Head Start Regional Resource and Training Center, 1973. (ERIC Repro-duction Service No. Ed 089 8440)

Layman, E. Children who hear aid the hearing impaired. *Volta Review*, 1974, 76(1), 36–41.

Levitt, E., & Cohen, S. Attitudes of children towards their handicapped peers. *Childhood Edu-cation*, 1976, 52(3), 171–173.

Lewis, E. G. The case for "special" children. *Young children*, 1973, 28(6), 269–374.

Lillie, D. L. *Early childhood education*. Chicago: Science Research Associates, 1975.

Luterman, D. M. A parent-oriented nursery program for preschool deaf children. *The Volta Review*, 1967, 69(8), 515–520.

MacMillan, D. L., & Semmel, M. I. Evaluation of mainstreaming programs. *Focus on Exceptional Children*, 1977, 9(4), 1–14.

Mayer, C. A. *Understanding young children. The handicapped child in the normal preschool class.* Urbana, Ill.: ERIC Clearinghouse on Early Childhood Education, 1974.

McCay, V. Integration or mainstreaming. *American Annals of the Deaf*, 1975, 120, 15–16.

Meisels, S. J. First steps in mainstreaming. Some questions and answers. *Young Children*, 1977, 33(1), 4–13.

Morton, K. A., & Hull, K. Parents and the mainstream. In R. L. Jones (Ed.), *Mainstreaming and the minority child*. Minneapolis, Minn.: University of Minnesota. Leadership Training Institute Publication, The Council for Exceptional Children, 1976.

Neisworth, J. T., & Madle, R. A. Normalized day care: A philosophy and approach to integrating exceptional and normal children. *Child Care Quarterly*, 1975, 4(3), 163–171.

Nix, G. W. Mainstream placement. Question/check list. *Volta Review*, 1977, 79, 345–346.

Nordquist, V. M. A behavioral approach to the analysis of peer interactions. In M. J. Guralnick (Ed.), *Early intervention and the integration of handicapped and nonhandicapped children*. Baltimore: University Park Press, 1978.

Northcott, W. H. Candidate for integration: A hearing-impaired child in a regular nursery school. *Young Children*, 1970, 5(6), 367–380.

Northcott, W. H. The integration of young deaf children into ordinary educational programs. *Exceptional Children*, 1971, 38(1), 29–33.

Northcott, W. H. Reading list on integration. *The Volta Review*, 1973, 75(1), 33–35.

Northcott, W. H. Integrating the preprimary hearing-impaired child: An examination of the process, product, and rationale. In M. J. Guralnick (Ed.), *Early intervention and the integration of handicapped and nonhandicapped children*. Baltimore: University Park Press, 1978.

100   3. *Preschool Mainstreaming*

Painter, M. *The Santa Cruz eleven: A comprehensive plan for the education of autistic and seriously emotionally disturbed children.* Washington, D. C.: Bureau of Education for the Handicapped (DHEW/OE), 1914. (ERIC Document Reproduction Service No. Ed 112 531)

Peterson, N. L., & Haralick, J. G. Integration of handicapped and nonhandicapped preschoolers: An analysis of play behavior and social interaction. *Education and Training of the Mentally Retarded,* 1977, *12,* 235–245.

Peterson, C., Peterson, J., & Scriven, G. Peer imitation by nonhandicapped preschoolers. *Exceptional Children,* 1977, *43*(4), 223–225.

Podell, S. M. The effectiveness of developmental training. *Optometric Weekly,* 1976, *67*(40), 1074–1076.

Pollack, D., & Ernst, M. Learning to listen in an integrated preschool. *The Volta Review,* 1973, *75*(7), 416–422.

Providing for the preschool child with problems. Ferguson, Mo.: Ferguson–Florissant School District, 1975. (ERIC Document Reproduction Service No. ED 013 371)

Ray, J. R. *Behavior of developmentally delayed and nondelayed toddler-age children: An ethological study.* Doctoral dissertation, George Peabody College, 1974.

Rister, A. Deaf children in mainstream education. *Volta Review,* 1975, *77*(5), 279–290.

Sauer, R. B. *Handicapped children and day care* (Rev. 2nd ed.). New York: Bank Street College of Education, 1975. (ERIC Document Reproduction Service No. ED 119 808)

Schramm, B. J. *Case studies of two Down's syndrome children functioning in a Montessori environment: Research project.* Dayton, Ohio: University of Dayton, School of Education, 1974. (ERIC Document Reproduction Service No. ED 111 120)

Snyder, L., Apolloni, T., & Cooke, T. P. Integrated settings at the early childhood level: The role of nonretarded peers. *Exceptional Children,* 1977, *43*(5), 262–266.

Special educational early childhood project in Fort Worth Independent School District, Title VI, ESEA. Final report. Washington, D. C.: Bureau of Elementary and Secondary Education, 1971. (ERIC Document Reproduction Service No. Ed 052 550)

Stack, P. M. In our program—Everyone gets into the act. *The Volta Review,* 1973, *75*(7), 425–430.

Stern, V. W. Finger paint on the hearing aid. *The Volta Review,* 1969, *71*(3), 149–154.

Strattner, M. J. Deaf and hearing children learn together: An Australian model. *Young Children,* 1974, *29*(4), 231–234.

Tait, P. E. Believing without seeing: Teaching the blind child in a "regular" kindergarten. *Childhood Education,* 1974, *50*(5), 285–291.

Turnbull, H. R. Legal implications. In A. J. Pappanikow & J. L. Paul (Eds.), *Mainstreaming emotionally disturbed children.* Syracuse, N.Y.: University Press, 1977.

Weikart, D. P. Curriculum for early childhood special education. *Focus on Exceptional Children,* 1974, *6*(1), 1–8.

Winkelstein, E., Shapiro, B. J., Tucker, D. G., & Shapiro, P. P. Early childhood educational objectives for normal and retarded children. *Mental Retardation,* 1974, *12*(5), 41–45.

Wynne, S., Brown, J. K., Dakof, G., & Ulfelder, L. S. *Mainstreaming and early childhood education for handicapped children: A guide for teachers and parents.* Final Report. Washington, D.C.: Bureau of Education for the Handicapped, 1975. (ERIC Document Reproduction Service No. ED 119 445)

Peer Social Behavior in Integrated Preschool Settings: Developmental and Instructional Potentials

4

Introduction

One of the more active areas of integrated programming for handicapped and nonhandicapped children has involved preschool settings. During the 1960s and 1970s a vast amount of applied research, systematic educational programming, and federal dollars were devoted to intensive and, on some occasions, longitudinal intervention into the lives of handicapped preschool children and their families. Although many evaluation efforts suffered from an array of methodological deficiencies (e.g., culturally biased assessment indices, minimal specification of teachers' behaviors, inadequate control tactics, small sample size, global description of target population), it has been generally accepted that systematic, structured programming can lead to substantial changes in handicapped preschool children's behavioral development, particularly in terms of social interaction skills (Apolloni & Cooke, 1977; Stedman, 1977).

The vast majority of this programmatic research was conducted in nonintegrated settings with teachers as the principal intervention agents. Moreover, the educational procedures employed required a one-to-one instructional format. In situations in which the opportunities for tutorial-like instruction is limited, it is necessary to develop other instructional resources. In developmentally integrated settings, normal or less-handicapped peers offer one typically unused resource for social behavior training.

In this chapter, the utilization of three mechanisms of peer influence are discussed in terms of their potential as intervention strategies for withdrawn children. Specifically, peer social initiations, peer reinforcement, and peer

101

modeling are described. In this review, particular attention is paid to clinical application issues associated with each intervention strategy.

Peer Relations and Behavioral Development

For many decades, psychologists and educators have emphasized the importance of parent–child interaction to later behavioral development. While child–child interactions have been the subject of naturalistic and manipulative study for many years, very few investigators have considered the function of peer relations on human development.

˜ Hartup (1977) proposes that children are developmentally "at risk" when they do not experience successful encounters with peers. Indeed, evidence shows that socially isolate children have problems acquiring appropriate language behaviors, moral values, and acceptable methods of expressing sexual and aggressive feelings (Harlow, 1969; Piaget, 1932; Strain, Cooke, & Apolloni, 1976; Whitman, Mercurio, & Caponigri, 1970). Moreover, socially isolate children show less exploratory behaviors than socially competent youngsters.

Longitudinal and retrospective studies indicate that childhood social isolation is associated with later-appearing behavior disorders. Children described as "loners" during the early school years are represented disproportionately in groups of juvenile delinquents, school dropouts during adolescence, and adults who experience adjustment problems (Roff, Sells, & Golden, 1972). Other longitudinal research (Michael, Morris, & Sorokes, 1957; Robins, 1966) reveals that children identified as socially withdrawn are more susceptible than socially competent youngsters to be referred to psychiatric services as adults. Similarly, Rolf (1972) presents data that indicates a negative correlation between adult psychopathology and sociometrically evaluated peer acceptance. A series of retrospective studies (Birren, 1944; Frazee, 1953; O'Neal & Robins, 1958) show that a large percentage of adults demonstrating psychopathology were described by caregivers and teachers as withdrawn as young children. Strain *et al.* (1976) have pointed out that both longitudinal and retrospective paradigms are methodologically suspect. •Yet, the preponderance of evidence does suggest that social withdrawal in childhood can become a persistent pattern for later interaction, and that such interaction can contribute to behavioral deviancy in adulthood (Ferster, 1965).

The classic work of Harlow and his associates with rhesus monkeys suggests that peer contact can reverse deviant and delayed social behaviors exhibited by animals initially reared in isolation. Prior to employing young monkeys to correct deviant social behavior patterns, research evidence indicated that the social pathology of monkeys reared in isolation was irreversible. The precise therapeutic procedure involved physically pairing 6-month-old isolate monkeys with 3-month-old "therapist" monkeys. Almost immediately, the isolate animals began to engage in reciprocal play, and their repetitious, timid, and occasional aggressive activity diminished.

ASSESSMENT OF PEER RELATIONS

Although few would argue that early peer interactions are vital for children's overall behavioral development, there is considerable debate regarding the most appropriate indices of social interaction–withdrawal. One group of scientists has considered social interaction–withdrawal in terms of the frequency or rate at which children engage in specific categories of behavior in a social context (Kirby & Toler, 1970; Milby, 1970; O'Connor, 1969, 1972; Walker & Hops, 1973). Thus, social competency and social isolation are considered in terms of the number of times a child engages in activity such as passing a ball to a peer, smiling at a peer, or playing a cooperative game. Frequency and rate measures have been found to be particularly valuable in the assessment of clinical interventions (see Cooke & Apolloni, 1976; Strain & Timm, 1974); however, extreme caution should be taken in using these indices in a diagnostic process of determining who is or is not socially withdrawn. Since measures of frequency or rate of behavior are extremely sensitive to nonprogrammed and often subtle stimuli in preschool environments, comparisons between normative data collected in one setting and diagnostic or screening data in another may be spurious. A brief list of stimuli known to alter significantly the rate or frequency of interaction includes number and kinds of toys available (Quilitch, Christophersen, & Risley, 1977), sex of children available for interaction (Fagot & Patterson, 1969), physical arrangement of space (Risley, 1975), and suggestions for activity made by teachers (Shores, Hester, & Strain, 1976).

A second group of scientists has considered issues of popularity, rejection, and friendship formations via sociometric instruments administered to members of a particular child's peer group (Amidon, 1961; Bonney, 1971; Gottman, Gonso, & Rasmussen, 1975; Gottman, Gonso, & Schuler, 1976). Thus, children who receive low-status scores from their peers are considered developmentally at risk (Greenwood, Walker, & Hops, 1977). In support of this position, several studies have shown that adults with adjustment problems are more likely than normal peers to have had low acceptance or high rejection scores as children (Kohn & Clausen, 1955; Stengel, 1971). A limitation of sociometric indices is the persistent problem of poor test–retest reliability. Reported correlations cover a range from .32 (Hartup, Glazer, & Charlesworth, 1967) to .78 (Moore & Updegraff, 1964). Coefficients in this range *insure* considerable error in clinical judgments of who is and who is not socially withdrawn.

In a discussion of assessment instruments used in social interaction–withdrawal research, Greenwood *et al.* (1977) have offered several characteristics of ideal indices, including:

1. Instruments should be applicable to both screening and treatment evaluation needs.
2. Instruments should offer normative data that are obtained in the same stimulus settings as screening and treatment evaluation information.
3. Instruments should show adequate reliability across time and presentations.
4. Instruments should be cost- and time-effective in their administration.

SUMMARY

The literature on early peer relations indicates that successful interactions with one's age-mates is a necessity for normal growth and development (Hartup, 1977). Without such contact, children are prone to developmental delay in their language, cognitive, and social functioning. Moreover, social isolation may result in overt pathology throughout the life span. In integrated settings, the challenge is one of measuring accurately and then employing most effectively the powerful influence of nonhandicapped children to develop appropriate social behaviors in their handicapped classmates.

Behavioral Processes of Peer Influence

Interactions between preschool children are remarkably regularized. They are not random, but rather quite predictable with respect to timing and content (Hartup, 1977). The observed reciprocity that characterizes preschool children's interactions can be traced to newborns' first social encounters. An increasing amount of naturalistic and experimental data points to the human newborn's "predisposition" to respond positively to social stimuli. For example, social consequences operate as a powerful reinforcer for infants' vocal behavior (Rheingold, Gewirtz, & Ross, 1959), interaction patterns within visual and vocal modes are quite reciprocal between infants and caregivers (Strain, 1975), and infants clearly prefer the human voice and face over inanimate stimuli (Stone, Smith, & Murphy, 1973).

Although there has been little research conducted to date, studies of infant–infant interaction also point to the regularity and predictability of social encounters. Buhler (1931) provided an early documentation of reciprocal interaction patterns between children under 18 months of age who were placed together in daily play sessions. At 6 months of age the infants were found to engage in frequent interaction with each other. These interactions occurred most often when the children were mutually occupied with play materials.

Bridges (1933) conducted a cross-sectional study of the interaction patterns between infants in dyads and triads of 9–12, 12–15, and 15–24 months of age. It was noted that both aggressive and positive interactions were greatest among the older groups. In a similar study, Maudry and Nekula (1939) observed dyads of age-peers from 6- to 25-months-old. Infants of 6–8 months spent most of their time together engaged in solitary behaviors with toys. These behaviors included "looking at," "smiling at," and "grasping." Dyads of children 9–13 months often engaged in quarrels that were usually the result of attempts to acquire or maintain a favorite play object. Children from 19–25 months began to focus their attention from toys and materials to each other. The majority of interactions at this age level were positive.

In summary, research on the early interaction behavior of infants and toddlers points to the regularity and predictability of these behaviors (Apolloni & Cooke, 1975). It is most likely that the same behavioral processes that promote the reciprocity of interaction between adults also function at the infant, toddler, and preschool level (Hartup, 1977; Nordquist, 1977). These processes include the reciprocal exchange of positive social bids, social reinforcement delivered by peers, and peer modeling. Each of these processes will be considered in terms of its applicability as a social behavior intervention procedure in integrated settings.

RECIPROCITY OF INTERACTION AND
PEER BEHAVIOR CHANGE

Reciprocity of interaction may be described as the equitable exchange of positive social behaviors between interactants. Although this definition is limited to the analysis of social dyads, the concept of reciprocity has its roots in sociological theory. Merton (1956), for example, argued that the survival of capricious political machines could be understood by the exchange of political favors between constituents and party bosses. Similarly, Gouldner (1960) proposed that reciprocity is an ethical norm found in all cultures. Gouldner (1960) stated:

> Specifically, I suggest that a norm of reciprocity in its universal form makes two inter-related, minimal demands: (1) people should help those who have helped them, and (2) people should not injure those who have helped them [p. 162].

Observational Research on Reciprocity

Social psychologists also have considered reciprocity as a significant influence during interaction between adults. Rosenfeld (1967) demonstrated that the frequency of nonverbal expressions of similar topography between unacquainted interactants was significantly intercorrelated. Kendon (1967) studied unacquainted interactants as well, and reported that members of particular dyads exchanged gazes on an equal basis.

Expanding these correlational findings, Pruitt (1968) demonstrated that adults who give positive responses tend to receive an equal number of positive responses at a later time from their peers. Within a structured game situation, Pruitt found that:

1. The level of reward received by an individual was related directly to the level of reward that person had given.
2. All parties consistently rewarded individuals who had provided a standard level of reward to their peers.
3. Reward was often given with the expectation that the recipient would reciprocate at a later time.

An extensive observational study of family interaction patterns by Reid (1967) revealed that the greatest amount of social reinforcement was provided to that family member who consistently offered the greatest amount of social reinforcement. Moreover, the family member offering the least amount of social reinforcement was also the recipient of the least amount of social reinforcement.

Observational research has been conducted also on the reciprocal quality of child–child interaction. Lee (Note 1) observed that babies who responded contingently to their peers' social bids were sought out more frequently than babies who did not. A series of observational studies by Hartup and his colleagues has revealed the reciprocal exchange of positive social behaviors between preschool children (Charlesworth & Hartup, 1967; Hartup & Coates, 1967; Hartup *et al.*, 1967). These investigators observed four categories of behavior: (*a*) giving positive attention and approval; (*b*) giving affection and personal acceptance; (*c*) submission; and (*d*) token giving. Although these categories are identical to those described by Skinner (1953) as potentially reinforcing, no functional assessment was made of the precise relationship between these events and other child behaviors. In each study it was observed that the number of positive events emitted toward peers was positively related to the amount of positive contact received from peers. Specifically, there was a .79 correlation between the frequency with which a child gave and received positive social events.

In a recent, large-scale study by Greenwood, Walker, Todd, and Hops (Note 2) continuous observation procedures were employed to assess the social contacts of preschool children. Results indicated a .90 correlation between initiated positive behaviors and positive behaviors emitted in response to these overtures.

The results of these observational studies indicate that preschool children's behavior helps shape their own social environment. Specifically, youngsters' behavior patterns tend to set the occasion for that kind of social reaction by peers that validates their own approach to peers. For example, the shy, withdrawn child is seldom the recipient of positive social behavior from peers, whereas the child who initiates positive social bids toward peers tends to receive many positive social responses from age-mates. It seems reasonable to suspect that positive social initiations by nonhandicapped children could be employed to increase the positive social behavior of withdrawn, handicapped classmates. Recent behavioral research confirms this proposition (Ragland, Kerr, & Strain, 1978; Strain, 1977; Strain, Shores, & Timm, 1977).

Functional Analysis Research on Reciprocity

In an initial study, Strain *et al.* (1977) trained two nonhandicapped preschool boys to initiate positive social contact with six withdrawn, behaviorally disordered age-peers. The handicapped children, all males, were selected from an integrated preschool program. All of the subjects were selected on the basis of observational data that confirmed their infrequent interaction with any other children, handicapped or not, in the class. In this case, the simple integration of nonhandicapped with handicapped children in a play setting did not produce positive behavior outcomes. Both nonhandicapped boys were given four 20-min training sessions in which they practiced specific behaviors that could be used to initiate social play with their handicapped peers. Verbal behaviors such as "Come play," "Let's play school," and "Throw the ball" and motor responses such as passing a toy were taught. A role-playing strategy was used in which the trainer assumed the typical social behavior pattern of the target children. Every other appropriate social initiation by the peer was either praised by the trainer or ignored. After 5 sec of ignoring, the trainer explained to the children that many attempts to play might well be ignored by the handicapped children, but they were to continue initiating play. This procedure of "training to expect rejection" seems essential to prevent the social behaviors of nonhandicapped children from being punished and eventually extinguished by initial peer opposition and rejection. Employing a withdrawal-of-treatment design, the peer "therapists" made few social approaches to handicapped peers during the initial baseline phase. Peers greatly increased the level of initiations during intervention, reduced initiations during a second baseline phase, and again increased the level of initiations in a final intervention phase. During no phase in the study did adults prompt or reinforce any child's positive social behavior. For each target subject, positive social behavior greatly increased in response to increased levels of initiations. For five of the subjects, an increase was observed also in their social initiations toward each other and their nonhandicapped peers. The amount of behavior change resulting from the peer-mediated tactic was related directly to the subjects' initial social repertoire. That is, children who engaged in the most social activity during the initial baseline phase were most affected by this intervention.

In the second study in this series, Strain (1977), attempted to replicate this peer-mediated tactic and assess generalization of behavior change across time and settings. One triad of behaviorally disordered preschool boys and one nonhandicapped peer participated. These subjects were enrolled in the same integrated setting as that described previously. The peer therapist also participated in training sessions identical to those employed in Strain *et al.* (1977).

All intervention sessions during the withdrawal-of-treatment design took place in a small playroom equipped with gross- and fine-motor toys, dress-up clothes, and kitchen area items. The generalization sessions took place in the subjects' own classroom. On 25 of the 40 days of the study, generalization assessment took place shortly after training. On the other days, there was a 23-hr time lapse between training and generalization assessment. Intervention data from this study closely replicated results reported by Strain et al. (1977). For one handicapped child whose baseline of interaction was nearly zero, the intervention tactic was not effective. Generalization data indicated that positive behaviors exhibited during training maintained across time and settings. It is important to note, however, that the level of positive behavior in generalization sessions was approximately one-half the level observed during training.

The results of these two studies on preschool handicapped children and their nonhandicapped peer therapists indicate that the reciprocity or occasion-setting function of social stimuli may be employed to increase the social behaviors of withdrawn children. Additionally, the peer therapists were remarkably consistent in their adherence to initial training and instructions across phase changes. Data on children with extremely limited social repertoires suggest that more intensive training tactics, such as prompting and reinforcement, are required to produce positive social interaction.

A third study in this series, Ragland et al. (1978), was concerned with promoting positive social behavior in school-age autistic children. Although this study was not conducted in an integrated setting, and the target subjects were 9- and 10-years-old, the results are nonetheless applicable to preschool integrated programming. Initially, these subjects' developmental skills were similar to those of preschool-level children. Also, the subjects were observed to engage in active social withdrawal and physical aggression toward peers. In previous studies, children were more "passive" in their social withdrawal. Again, an age-peer was trained to emit specific social initiations toward handicapped children. Prebaseline observations on the target subjects indicated that they would physically isolate themselves during free play periods and occasionally engage in brief tantrums if approached by a peer. The intervention sessions in the withdrawal-of-treatment design were conducted in a small playroom equipped with toys that promote cooperative play (e.g., telephones, balls, trucks, cooking utensils, puppets). Unlike earlier studies, the peer therapist began intervention at different points in time for each subject. This experimental procedure was employed to determine whether a high level of social initiations directed toward one child would produce an increase in the positive behavior by children not currently under intervention procedures. One might suspect that intervention applied to one subject would provide other handicapped children the opportunity to imitate appropriate social behavior being modeled by the peer therapist and the handicapped child who was receiving the intervention.

An increased level of peer initiations resulted in an immediate acceleration in the frequency of all subjects' positive social behavior. For two of the subjects who were most oppositional to social initiations, negative behaviors also showed a slight increase during intervention conditions. In no instance did intervention applied to one child result in a "spillover" of treatment effect on the behavior of children not under intervention at that time.

In the final study of this series, Strain, Kerr, and Ragland (1979) compared the relative effectiveness of the social initiation tactic with typical prompting and reinforcement procedures. One peer was trained to administer both the intervention tactics. The target subjects were four autistic-like children with developmental ages between 3 and 5 years. During an initial baseline phase the peer trainer made few social approaches toward the subjects and did not prompt or reinforce their social play with each other. In the initial intervention phase two of the subjects were randomly selected to receive the social initiation tactic while the other two children were prompted and verbally praised for play with each other and the trainer. Following a return to baseline phase, the interventions were implemented again, this time with subjects who had not received a particular intervention during the first treatment phase. The results showed that the two intervention tactics produced quite similar results across all four children.

Clinical Application Issues

In summary, research on this peer-mediated tactic offers a promising approach to promoting positive interaction between handicapped and nonhandicapped children. The successful implementation of such a strategy requires that a number of issues be addressed by the practitioner. First, research to date has indicated that children must display some positive behaviors prior to treatment if the strategy is to be successful. Exactly what behaviors and their frequency of occurrence are yet to be determined (Strain & Carr, 1975). It would seem that socially appropriate verbal behavior is necessary for reciprocal interaction (Hester & Hendrickson, Note 3). In those studies conducted by Strain and his colleagues, the most successful initiations (those followed by a positive peer response) were vocal–verbal. Unfortunately, the data collection system did not provide a fine-grain assessment of the precise verbal topographies involved. Since vocal–verbal behaviors occur infrequently between handicapped preschool children (Guralnick & Paul-Brown, 1977), some stimulus novelty effect could account for the responsiveness of the handicapped subjects to vocal–verbal initiations (Cantor & Cantor, 1964; King, 1966; Strain & Cooke, 1976). In a related study, Mueller (1972) identified several behaviors that were predictive of successful social initiations between children of $3\frac{1}{2}$- and $5\frac{1}{2}$-years-old. Data indicated that 62% of all utterances were successful (i.e., they obtained a verbal response from the partners). Another 23% were followed by visual orientation by the partner to the speaker. The most powerful predictor of reciprocal interaction was visual attention of the partner prior to speaking.

Other behaviors may also set the occasion for reciprocal interaction. For example, Cooke and Apolloni (1976) taught school-age, mildly handicapped children to smile at each other, share toys, make appropriate physical contacts, and engage in complimentary comments. Using imitation training, these behaviors were developed successfully in a classroom setting. In a free play period that immediately followed training, the target subjects and other mildly handicapped children were observed. Newly trained positive behaviors of target subjects were maintained, and untrained children also began to display these same behaviors. One interpretation is that the target responses set the occasion for reciprocal responding by peers. However, the data collection system did not permit an analysis of reciprocal behavior patterns. Clearly, research at this point is needed to determine the response topographies having a high probability of setting the occasion for and maintaining interaction. With such data in hand, intervention strategies could then be applied to teach these responses to handicapped children.

A second issue critical to the successful implementation of peer-mediated tactics concerns the appropriateness of data collected. Most observational studies of social interaction development have focused on the singular behavior categories of individual target children (Buell, Stoddard, Harris, & Baer, 1968; Kirby & Toler, 1970; O'Connor, 1969, 1972). In his classic commentary on social psychological research, Sears (1951) stated:

> In spite of their long prepossession with social influences on the individual, psychologists think monadically. For them the universe is composed of individuals. The individuals are acted upon by external events, to be sure, and in turn the external world is modified by the individual's behavior. But the universal laws sought by the psychologist almost always relate to a single body. They are monadic laws, and they are stated with reference to a monadic unit of behavior [p. 478].

By its very nature, the most profitable study of social interaction requires the use of observational systems that answer the questions: Who gives what to whom, when, and with what effect (Strain & Shores, 1977)? A number of observational systems that meet these criteria are available (see Greenwood *et al.*, 1976; Strain & Timm, 1974), and practitioners should clearly seek to employ assessment devices that maximize the feedback on intervention outcomes.

A final issue related to the successful use of the social initiation tactic concerns the generalization or maintenance of positive social behavior in less-controlled settings. Research evidence to date indicates that positive social behaviors developed by this tactic do generalize to nontreatment settings; however, the magnitude of behavior change has been considerably less than that observed during training sessions.

The precise level of behavior generalization observed at any one time is a product of complex interactions between a number of factors. The first factor concerns the degree of behavioral handicap exhibited by target children. In peer- and adult-mediated studies, the level of generalization appears, in part, to be a function of subjects' overall behavioral repertoire (Gable, Hendrickson, & Strain, 1978). For example, studies employing severely or profoundly retarded and autistic children have evidenced minimal success in promoting generalized behavior change. Recent research on the mechanisms of behavior generalization indicates that severely handicapped children's lack of behavior change across time and settings may be the result of their responding (simultaneously) to the presence of irrelevant as well as relevant stimuli (Rincover & Koegel, 1975).

A second factor related to generalized behavior change relates to the difference between *behavior generalization* and the *maintenance* of behavior in the generalization setting(s) (Koegel & Rincover, 1977). Behavior generalization refers to the initial level of responding in nontreatment environment(s). Maintenance of behavior, on the other hand, refers to the level of posttreatment responding over an extended time or several trials. In efforts involving social initiation tactics, it appears that generalization, as defined above, can be expected to occur. However, the maintenance of behavior, which is controlled by a separate set of variables, is less certain. Research by Koegel and Rincover (1977) indicates that maintenance of treatment effects can be enhanced by reducing the discrepancy between training and generalization settings. For example, practitioners might consider the systematic, response-dependent leaning of social initiations, training across settings and peer "therapists," and/or controlling the social behaviors of nontrained peers in the generalization setting(s) (Strain & Hill, 1979).

A final factor affecting generalized behavior change, and the total study of social interaction, is the level of conceptual and methodological sophistication applied to the analysis of social behavior interventions. Observational data on the phenomena of concern would suggest that a useful conceptualization of social interaction development must promote a reciprocal or dyadic unit of measurement (Strain *et al.*, 1976). By and large, reciprocal notions of social behavior have been promoted by developmental psychologists (Bell, 1968; Cairns, 1972). The variables of concern to these scientists have included birth order, sex, age, intelligence, and personality factors. Since teachers and other practitioners have no direct control over these variables, this literature basically advises one what to expect. However, when faced with a withdrawn, handicapped child, the question is how can positive behaviors be developed (Nordquist, 1977)?

In contrast, many intervention tactics have been examined by behavioral scientists who advocate an operant conceptualization of social behavior. However, these tactics have been evaluated with observational systems that focus solely on individuals rather than the behavioral exchange between children (Strain & Timm, 1974). A more complete approach to the study of social behavior in general and posttreatment responding in particular would incorporate dyadic, exhaustive recording systems in the assessment of operant procedures. Wahler, Berland, Coe, and Leske (1977) suggest that such an analytical approach might well produce data that do not support a strict operant or reinforcement interpretation of social interaction. This complete descriptive approach would, of course, be of great value in identifying physical, spatial, and behavioral stimuli associated with various levels of social interaction across settings.

PEER REINFORCEMENT AND SOCIAL BEHAVIOR CHANGE

A central, although seldom expressed, operating principle of peer reinforcement research is that liking, interpersonal attraction, and friendships are determined by an individual's history of reward in the presence of particular individuals (Strain & Hill, 1979). There are several conditions by which the condition of reward in the presence of another person can be met (Lott & Lott, 1974). First, by the quality of one's characteristics (e.g., beauty, family relationship) another person may be provided with pleasure simply by being in the same place at the same time. Second, an individual can offer direct reinforcement to a peer in the form of smiles, positive personal comments, or offers of valued items. Third, a person may be instrumental in providing another with access to primary or secondary reinforcers. For example, a person's skillful behavior may attain success in a game or access to favored items. Finally, a person may become liked or attractive through a pairing process with events totally independent of that person's behavior. For example, Lott and Lott (1974) maintain that an individual's temporal association with potentially reinforcing settings like a holiday party or vacation can lead to an increased level of attraction. In integrated preschool settings, any or all of these processes may be employed to increase the amount of social interaction between handicapped and nonhandicapped children.

Correlational Studies of Peer Reinforcement

As was noted earlier, Charlesworth and Hartup (1967) have reported that preschool children exchange, on an equitable basis, behaviors that are thought to be reinforcing. Other observational data are also available that support this view of preschool children's social behaviors (Hartup et al., 1967; Kohn, 1966; Marshall & McCandless, 1957).

A number of investigators have sought to correlate the occurrence of particular child behaviors (potential reinforcing or punishing events) with the behavior of interacting peers. For example, Patterson, Littman, and Bricker (1967) studied the consequences for aggressive behavior in two nursery school settings. Six categories of children's responses to peer aggression were observed: passive, cries, defensive postures, telling the teacher, recovering property, and retaliation. Short-term, temporal analyses revealed that crying, passivity, and defensive behaviors were the most frequent consequences of aggression. When these behaviors occurred, additional acts of aggression toward the original victim increased. Patterson *et al.* (1967) suggest that aggressive acts are reinforced by these behaviors. When the original aggressor was met with threats of or actual aggression by the intended victim, additional acts of aggression toward these victims rarely occurred. Thus, aggressive acts may also be punished by victims' acts of counteraggression. Longitudinal data revealed similar reinforcement–punishment processes in operation. Children who were initially nonaggressive, but who successfully punished aggressive initiations by peers, became more active aggressors across time. It was also found that children who were not regular victims or who did not successfully punish aggression from peers showed no increase in aggressive behavior across time.

Kopstein (1972) employed a similar methodology to examine the effects of aggressive, negative reactions to both positive and negative social initiations. Interaction data were obtained during free-play periods in which two groups of elementary-age, trainable mentally retarded children were engaged in self-selected activities. Results discordant with a strict reinforcement–punishment conceptualization of aggression were obtained. Aggressive responses to positive social bids reduced the probability of later instances of positive contact. However, aggressive responses to aggressive overtures resulted in an increased level of aggressive interaction. It would appear that some of the negative responses by peers operated as "punishers" of positive interaction whereas others served to set the occasion for additional hostile interaction. The conflict in results between this study and that of Patterson *et al.* (1967) may have been due to unspecified differences in the topography, temporal relationship, intensity, and/ or duration of specific behaviors labeled as aggression. On a similar conceptual issue, it is important to recall that behavior categories such as positive interactions or aggression only represent a topographical description of behavior. They do not imply nor can they be interpreted as functional categories of behavior that have predictable reinforcing or punishing effects on the activity that precedes them. The functional properties of behaviors can only be determined by their systematic manipulation across time (Strain *et al.*, 1977). Even then, the functional effects of specific behaviors will vary across time and individuals (Bijou & Baer, 1963).

Experimental Analyses of Peer Reinforcement

Expanding upon observational research, a number of investigators have provided an experimental analysis of peer reinforcement in preschool classes. In his now classic study, Wahler (1967) collected baseline data on a number of social behaviors exhibited by five preschool children. For three subjects, behaviors associated with frequent positive consequences by peers were determined. For the other two children, behaviors associated with infrequent positive consequences by peers were identified. In an initial intervention condition, Wahler instructed peers who had frequently reinforced certain behaviors to now ignore their three classmates when they engaged in these designated behaviors. Similarly, the peers were instructed to reinforce their two classmates' behaviors that they had ignored previously. Results indicated that members of the peer group responded in strict compliance to the experimenter's instructions. Additionally, behaviors that were reinforced by peers increased significantly and behaviors that were ignored decreased accordingly. These differential effects were replicated during a subsequent reinstatement of baseline and intervention contingencies.

Johnston and Johnston (1972) provided evidence that peer- as opposed to adult-mediated reinforcement is associated with greater treatment generalization effects. Three contingency arrangements for producing correct articulation were evaluated in treatment and free-play settings. The first arrangement included the provision of contingent teacher attention and tokens for correct utterances. The second procedure required both correct responding and self-recording of these behaviors before attention and tokens were provided. In the third procedure, two children were taught to attend to each other's correct responses and ignore incorrects. All procedures resulted in increased levels of correct responding; but only differential peer reinforcement resulted in behavior change during the free play period.

In a study of peer reinforcement effects in an integrated setting, Guralnick (1976) further demonstrated the influence of classmates' behavior on social interaction. Using role rehearsal tactics, Guralnick trained nonhandicapped preschool children to model, prompt, and reinforce social behaviors by their handicapped peers. Baseline data indicated that few positive interactions occurred between handicapped and nonhandicapped children. When handicapped children were given the opportunity to observe two nonhandicapped peers playing cooperatively, no behavior change occured. However, a combined peer-modeling, prompting, and reinforcement strategy produced a substantial change in the social play and verbal interaction between handicapped and nonhandicapped children. The results of this study are most intriguing, although it is not possible to determine which or what combination of intervention procedures (modeling, prompting, reinforcement) was responsible for the increase in handicapped children's social interactions with normal age-peers.

A number of studies have shown that friendships between preschool and school-age children are related to the exchange of rewarding events (Drabman, Spitalnik, & Spitalnik, 1974; Karen, 1965; Kirby & Toler, 1970). For example, Kirby and Toler employed a stimulus-pairing technique in which a 5-year-old isolate boy offered choices of candies to his playmates just prior to a daily free play period. The child was instructed to ask each peer which of several kinds of candy he or she would like. Prior to this procedure, the target child was observed to engage in positive interaction during 13% of the free play time. As long as the subject engaged in the candy-offering activity, his level of positive interaction was above 60% during free play.

In further work on the relationship between exposure to positive consequences and positive social interaction, Strain (1981) attempted to alter the behavioral rejection of three mildly handicapped, school-age boys enrolled in a regular classroom. During a 5-day baseline period the three target subjects engaged in only four episodes of positive interaction with nonhandicapped peers during a 20-min recess period. On each of these occasions, the target subjects had initiated the interaction. During the first intervention phase, each of the target subjects was assigned by the experimenter to one of three teams of children. The teams participated in a 15-min competition game prior to the daily recess time. On each day, members of the teams took turns playing a bean bag toss game. All members of a team would earn a reward if the team's total point score exceeded a designated criterion. The game was arranged physically such that children tossed across a large barrier and were therefore unable to see the actual score they earned. After each toss, the experimenter would call out a score. On each team, the target subject had the last toss on each day, and the experimenter would always announce a score sufficient for the team members to earn their reward. Observational data collected during recess indicated that the intervention procedure resulted in approximately 20 times the amount of positive social interaction as that observed during baseline. Moreover, target subjects and their peers initiated episodes of interaction on an equal basis.

Haskett (Note 4) provided particularly unambiguous data regarding the relationship between children's social responsiveness and the maintenance of social encounters. More than 20 infants and preschool youngsters were introduced individually into a play setting with two age-peer confederates and familiar toys. Four social behaviors were examined: verbalizations, visual regard, onlooking, and mutual play. The peer confederates alternated being either verbally responsive or nonresponsive to subjects' play initiations. Subjects invariably directed most of their social initiations toward the verbally responsive confederate.

Research on the delivery of peer reinforcement demonstrates that these events can be programmed successfully to increase the positive social behavior of withdrawn handicapped children. Although minimal data are available, it is possible that peer-mediated reinforcement may result in more generalized responding than adult-mediated reinforcement (Johnston & Johnston, 1972). In fact, there is some evidence that adults' behavior may distract children from ongoing interaction (O'Connor, 1972). For example, Shores *et al.* (1976) analyzed social interaction between preschool behaviorally disordered children under three experimental conditions: (a) active teacher prompting and rein-forcement; (b) no teacher involvement; (c) teacher structured free play, with no active prompting and reinforcement. When teachers initially structured play by suggesting activities for children, then withdrew from the setting, the level of social interaction between subjects increased significantly over baseline, no teacher involvement, and active prompting and reinforcement conditions. Since behavioral generalization to natural environmental contingencies should be the terminal goal of all intervention efforts, it is probably more efficient to utilize peers at the onset of training (Guralnick, 1977).

A number of important conceptual and applied questions concerning peer reinforcement of social interaction remain unanswered. For example, who are the most powerful reinforcers in integrated preschool settings? There is some observational evidence to indicate that same-sex children are more effective reinforcing agents than opposite-sex youngsters (Fagot & Patterson, 1969). It is certainly possible that some handicapped preschool children would not be reinforced by attention from peers (or adults). In such cases, the stimulus pairing technique as applied by Kirby and Toler (1970) and Strain (1981) to increase interaction between handicapped and nonhandicapped children might be ap-plied to increase the reinforcement value of social attention.

Another important question concerns the long-term effects of peer reinforce-ment on handicapped and nonhandicapped children. What alternations, if any, occur in the interaction patterns between agents of reinforcement and nontarget children? Do handicapped children begin to interact more positively with non-handicapped peers with whom they have no reinforcement history? What, if any, collateral behavior changes take place for nonhandicapped and handi-capped children during and following peer reinforcement? It would be partic-ularly beneficial if, for example, nonhandicapped children become more ef-fective behavioral models because of their reinforcement history with handicapped peers (Hartup & Coates, 1967). These and many other issues demand thorough experimental study.

PEER MODELING AND SOCIAL BEHAVIOR CHANGE

An extensive body of research points to the importance of modeling processes during early childhood (Bandura & Walters, 1963). Observational learning includes both informal and programmed interactions between children whereby new behaviors are learned and existing response patterns undergo modification as a direct result of observing another's behaviors and consequences for them. The availability of appropriate behavioral models is an often heard rationale for integrated programming, and several studies are available that support the efficacy of peer modeling as a social behavior intervention for withdrawn children.

Film-Mediated Models

O'Connor (1969, 1972) has employed film-mediated models to increase positive interaction among preschool children. In his initial study, one group of youngsters saw a film portraying peer interaction. A comparison group saw a nature film of equal length. Social interaction between members of the two groups was observed in a free play class period that followed their viewing of the film. Statistical analyses revealed that positive interaction between experimental subjects significantly surpassed the level observed prior to viewing the film and the postviewing level demonstrated by comparison subjects. Strain *et al.* (1976) have observed, however, that two of the six experimental children primarily were responsible for the positive behavior change. Those subjects who were most isolate during the pretreatment observation were least affected after the intervention. Although no specific data are provided, it is possible that the more isolate of subjects demonstrated other behavioral deficits, including the lack of a generalized imitative repertoire.

O'Connor (1972) replicated and expanded these initial findings in a comparative study of modeling versus direct shaping procedures on social interaction development. In summary, the results indicated that subjects who received the observational learning experience were more socially active than children who had been exposed to direct shaping alone. The largest generalization effect was demonstrated by subjects who had received both observational and direct shaping intervention for positive behavior change.

Walker and Hops (1973) further tested the efficacy of film-mediated models on withdrawn children's social behavior. Two subjects were shown the same training film used by O'Connor (1969) and they were reinforced for positive interaction with peers. A third withdrawn subject's peers were shown the film, but the target child was not. Reinforcement procedures were also implemented. Although the treatment "package" approach used here does not readily lend itself to a clear, component analysis of modeling and reinforcement effects, the data do suggest that the film modeling had a minimal impact on the observed behavior change. First, both laboratory (Bandura, Ross, & Ross, 1963) and applied studies (O'Connor, 1969, 1972) of observational learning have consistently shown immediate (though likely short-term) behavior change following treatment. In this study, however, it was not until the reinforcement had been imposed for several days that consistent behavior change was noted. It seems likely that Walker and Hops' stringent procedures for selecting severely withdrawn children yielded a group of youngsters whose behavior repertoire matched that of the more isolate subjects employed by O'Connor (1969).

More precise information on the interaction between initial behavior repertoire and observational learning effects has been provided by Keller and Carlson (1974). These authors observed the effects of film-mediated models on five categories of positive social behavior: verbalizations, imitation, smiling, token giving, and affection. The categories of verbalizations, imitation, and smiling, which had the highest previewing level, were also the only categories to show statistically significant postviewing change. Across-target comparisons revealed that the least behavior change was demonstrated by the most isolate of the 19 preschool-age subjects.

Language Models

Research has been conducted also on the effects of modeled linguistic utterances on the verbal behavior of handicapped children in an integrated setting (Guralnick, 1976). In this study, a nonhandicapped age-peer was trained to use correct syntactical structures, which were reinforced by an adult. The observing, handicapped child was reinforced for attention to the particular language forms being used by the nonhandicapped peer. The procedure resulted in increased use of appropriate language forms by the target child. It is likely, however, that the use of correct language forms by the handicapped child would not continue in the absence of direct consequences. Kazdin (1973) proposes that such vicarious learning as that demonstrated by Guralnick may be due, in part, to the cue properties of reinforcement delivery. That is, observing youngsters come to emit behaviors reinforced by others with the expectation that these behaviors will bring about positive consequences for them. The importance of reinforcement delivery to observing children has been demonstrated by Strain and Pierce (1977). In this study, one mentally retarded preschool child from each of two dyads was given social reinforcement contingent upon attention-to-task behavior. The other two retarded children never received any reinforcement for their on-task activity. Reinforcement applied to the designated child in each dyad resulted in an immediate increase in the attending behavior of both subjects. However, after a number of days (approximately 10), the attending behavior of observing subjects began to decline, and at the end of 20 days the level of attending behavior paralleled that observed during nonreinforcement conditions.

In a related area of language research, Guralnick and Paul-Brown (1977) have reported that nonhandicapped preschool children regulate the length and complexity of verbalizations toward handicapped children. Nonhandicapped children were observed in verbal interaction with other nonhandicapped, mildly handicapped, moderately handicapped, and severely handicapped peers during instructional and free play periods. Data from each classroom setting indicated that nonhandicapped and mildly handicapped peers received a similar length and complexity of directed verbal behavior. Moderately and severely handicapped children, however, were exposed to much more brief and less complex utterances from their nonhandicapped peers. Although data on preschool children's verbal interactions are extremely limited, these and other reports (Bates, 1975; Shatz & Gelman, 1973) indicate a remarkable similarity to the speech regularization of parents with their children (Broen, 1972; Snow, 1972). It is important to note that many authors (e.g., Mahoney & Seely, 1976; Moerk, 1976) have proposed that parents' speech adjustments to their children's comprehension abilities serve to stimulate language acquisition.

Establishing Imitative Behavior

While the imitation process offers an important contribution to the array of behavioral change tactics available in integrated settings, many handicapped children display minimal levels of generalized imitation. In such cases, direct training is required to establish peer imitation of appropriate behaviors. In an initial series of studies, Apolloni, Cooke, and Cooke (1977) and Cooke, Cooke, and Apolloni (1977) trained developmentally delayed toddlers to imitate motor activity, material use, and verbalizations modeled by nondelayed peers. Training tactics included the use of physical and verbal cues by an adult to imitate peers. Reinforcement was also provided to the handicapped children contingent upon correct imitation. Physical and verbal cues were systematically removed as imitative behavior became more reliable. Results indicated that each subject's level of imitative behavior increased in the training setting. With the exception of verbalizations, the subjects also exhibited an increased level of the modeled behaviors in a free play situation that closely followed training sessions.

In a replication effort (Peck, Apolloni, Cooke, & Cooke, Note 5), this imitation training paradigm was applied directly in free play settings. Here, developmentally delayed preschool children were prompted and reinforced for imitating the ongoing free play behavior of nonhandicapped classmates. The adult trainer was not present during generalization assessment. Again, the procedure resulted in a substantial increase in peer imitation. Increases in imitative behavior were noted also during generalization sessions. Finally, social interaction between delayed and normal children increased concomitant with the initiation of training procedures. In a follow-up study, however, Cooke, Apolloni, and Cooke (Note 6) showed that imitation training did not result in sustained interaction between handicapped and nonhandicapped children when nonhandicapped children had the option to play with either a normal or a handicapped child.

Variables Affecting Imitative Behavior

Given that a child possesses the behavioral prerequisites to reproduce a modeled behavior, a number of variables can affect the performance of imitative behavior at any given time. Important variables include those concerned with the discriminative properties of the modeled response and various personality characteristics of the individual modeling the response.

The discriminative properties of the modeled response appear to be affected primarily by the observation of reinforcement or punishment contingent upon the designated response (Bandura, 1971). Specifically, such consequences function as a discriminative stimulus for observing children because they signal (in the natural classroom environment) the delivery of reinforcement or punishment to these subjects. The cue properties of reinforcement or punishment are made more salient by the delivery of consequences that clearly designate the behavior(s) of concern. For example, Kazdin, Silverman, and Sittler (1975) examined the differential effects of nonverbal approval (patting a child), nonverbal approval paired with a verbal prompt to the nonreinforced child ("Dave, look at Timmy"), and nonverbal approval paired with verbal approval ("That's really good") on the attentive behavior of target subjects and observing peers. The results indicated that nonverbal approval in the form of patting a child altered the attentive behavior of reinforced children only. Vicarious effects were noted when either a prompt or verbal approval accompanied nonverbal reinforcement.

In similar work, Christy (1975) demonstrated that highly specific contingency contracts with individual children resulted in vicarious effects on the in-seat behavior of observing children. Following a baseline period, the teacher addressed the group as follows:

> Everybody listen. I'm going to make a deal with [child's name]. [Child's name], if you are sitting in your seat when the whistle blows, you'll get a goody. A goody is a piece of candy, or raisin, or nut, or marshmallow. The whistle blows from this box. Every time you're sitting in your seat—all the way down and facing front—when the whistle blows, you get a goody [p. 190].

All target and observing children either increased in the desired behavior or decreased variability by the end of the study. Particularly large changes were noted for the children with relatively low rates of sitting during the initial baseline.

Similar results have been recorded in studies involving problem-solving situations. Geshuri (1972), for example, found that imitation of correct responses was demonstrated more often by children who observed descriptive praise for specific behaviors as opposed to those who observed more generalized reinforcement for correct performance.

The effects of vicarious punishment on imitative behavior also has received considerable attention (Bandura, 1971; Morris, Marshall, & Miller, 1973; Walters, Parke, & Cone, 1965). For example, Morris *et al.* (1973) showed 120 first- and second-grade students one of the following filmed sequences:

1. Baseline: Confederate child plays with toys while adult reads a book.
2. Nonsharing, no outcome: Confederate refuses to share candy with a fictitious peer and no consequences are given.
3. Nonsharing, punished: Confederate refuses to share candy and adult says she cannot play any longer and asks her to leave the room.

4. Punishment only: Confederate does not model nonsharing, but adult delivers the same punishments as described above.

Following this viewing, each subject was given a bag of candy and told that there would not be sufficient candy for all the children who were to come and that perhaps the subject would want to leave some candy. Results indicated that simply observing selfish behavior did not affect sharing behavior. Both punishment conditions, however, produced a significant increase in sharing over baseline.

It may also be possible to increase the attention of observing children by providing novel responses to imitate. Parton (1976) reported that infants' imitative behavior was elicited more often by novel as opposed to familiar stimuli. Additionally, novel stimuli may function to set the occasion for interaction between model and observer. In an observational study of social encounters between school-age autistic children, Strain and Cooke (1976) recorded the vocal–verbal, motor–gestural, and initiated–responded dimensions of interaction. Those novel social initiations (i.e., those vocal–verbal behaviors that rarely occurred) were followed by positive peer behaviors significantly more often than frequently occurring, motor–gestural initiations. Haskett (Note 4) also reported that novel stimuli (toys, in this case) may lead to increased peer contact between normal preschool-age children. Target subjects were observed interacting with two confederate children who played with the same materials during baseline. When one of the confederates introduced a new toy, interaction with that youngster increased significantly over the baseline level.

Another set of factors affecting the level of imitative behavior centers on the personal attributes of the model. Generally, research indicates that perceived similarity on various dimensions of personality results in greater peer imitation. For example, imitation has been found to occur more often when model and observer are of the same sex (e.g., Bandura, Ross, & Ross, 1963), when they have shared similar emotional experiences (Aronfreed, 1968), and when they are of similar social status (Rosenkrans, 1967). Of particular importance to integrated programming, Strichart (1974) has noted that children are more likely to imitate models who perform responses competently. Thus, it appears unlikely that normal preschool children would readily imitate less-sophisticated behaviors emitted by handicapped peers.

Summary and Conclusions

Literature reviewed in this chapter documents the critical importance of positive, early peer encounters on children's behavioral development. Both observational and treatment research indicate that linguistic, cognitive and social skills are enhanced by peer interaction. Indeed, limited peer interaction most certainly places young children "at risk" for developmental delay and later-appearing adjustment problems. For handicapped preschool children, segregated settings clearly restrict the interaction available with normal-developing youngsters. Such a situation is particularly detrimental to handicapped children as they are limited in the opportunity to acquire skills that naturally develop in the process of peer interaction.

Given the instructional opportunities for peer-mediated intervention that are available only in integrated settings, a number of behavioral processes may be employed to improve the functioning of handicapped children. Peer social initiations, contingent social reinforcement, and the modeling of appropriate responses are intervention procedures with consistently demonstrated effectiveness in improving a wide variety of behaviors. Moreover, there is increasing evidence that these peer-mediated strategies produce more rapid and durable behavior change than adult-mediated interventions.

Although considerable research remains to be done, a number of tentative conclusions regarding peer-mediated intervention and integrated programming seem warranted:

1. There appears to be an inverse relationship between degree of handicapping condition and the efficacy of currently developed peer interventions (e.g., Keller & Carlson, 1974; Strain, Shores, & Timm, 1977; Walker & Hops, 1973).

2. In part, the social withdrawal demonstrated by many handicapped children may be attributed to the absence of appropriate social stimuli in segregated settings. This conclusion is based upon the dramatic behavior change in handicapped children following the programmed application of peer social initiations (e.g., Ragland et al., 1978; Strain, 1977; Strain, Shores, & Timm, 1977).

3. Nonhandicapped preschool children as well as mildly handicapped youngsters are remarkably consistent in their application of, at times, complex instructional tactics (e.g., Guralnick, 1976; Ragland et al., 1978; Wahler, 1967).

4. Initial social rejection of handicapped children in integrated settings may be ameliorated by peer-mediated interventions (e.g., Peck et al., Note 5; Strain, 1981).

5. Nonhandicapped children's academic and social behaviors often improve as these youngsters assist their handicapped classmates in similar areas of development (e.g., Dineen, Clark, & Risley, 1977; Ragland et al., 1978).

6. Handicapped and nonhandicapped children may benefit from integrated programming beginning as early as the second year of life (Apolloni, Cooke, & Cooke, 1977; Bridges, 1933; Stedman, 1977).

Reference Notes

1. Lee, L. C. *Social encounters of infants: The beginnings of popularity.* Paper presented at the biennial meeting of the International Society for the Study of Behavioral Development, Ann Arbor, Mich., April, 1973.
2. Greenwood, C. R., Walker, H. M., Todd, N. M., & Hops, H. *Preschool teachers' assessments of student social interaction: Predictive success and normative data* (Report No. 26). Eugene: Center at Oregon for Research in the Behavioral Education of the Handicapped, 1976.
3. Hester, P., & Hendrickson, J. M. *Establishing functional expressive language: The acquisition and generalization of five-element syntactic responses.* Unpublished manuscript, George Peabody College, 1976.
4. Haskett, G. J. *The ecology and early organization of children's social relations.* Paper presented at the meeting of the American Psychological Association, New Orleans, September, 1974.
5. Peck, C. A., Apolloni, T., Cooke, T. P., & Cooke, S. A. *Teaching developmentally delayed toddlers and preschoolers to imitate the free-play behavior of nonretarded classmates: Trained and generalized effects.* Unpublished manuscript, Somona State College, 1976.
6. Cooke, T. P., Apolloni, T., & Cooke, S. A. *The effects of a second nondelayed playmate on the free-play imitation and interaction of delayed and nondelayed children.* Unpublished manuscript, Somona State College, 1976.

References

Amidon, E. The isolate in children's groups. *The Journal of Teacher Education*, 1961, *12*, 412–416.

Apolloni, T., & Cooke, T. P. Peer behavior conceptualized as a variable influencing infant and toddler development. *American Journal of Orthopsychiatry*, 1975, *45*, 4–17.

Apolloni, T., & Cooke, T. P. Integrated programming at the infant, toddler, and preschool levels. In M. J. Guralnick (Ed.), *Early intervention and the integration of handicapped and nonhandicapped children.* Baltimore: University Park Press, 1977. Pp. 147–165.

Apolloni, T., Cooke, S. A., & Cooke, T. P. Establishing a normal peer as a behavioral model for delayed toddlers. *Perceptual and Motor Skills*, 1977, *44*, 231–241.

Aronfreed, J. *Conduct and conscience: The socialization of internalized control over behavior.* New York: Academic Press, 1968.

Bandura, A. *Principles of behavior modification.* New York: Holt, Rinehart & Winston 1971.

Bandura, A., Ross, D., & Ross, S. A. Imitation of film-mediated aggressive models. *Journal of Abnormal and Social Psychology*, 1963, *66*, 3–11.

Bandura, A., & Walters, R. H. *Social learning and personality development.* New York: Holt, Rinehart & Winston 1963.

Bates, E. Peer relations and the acquisition of language. In M. Lewis & L. A. Rosenblum (Eds.), *Friendship and peer relations.* New York: Wiley, 1975.

Bell, R. Q. A reinterpretation of the direction of effects in studies of socialization. *Psychological Review*, 1968, *75*, 81–95.

Bijou, S. W., & Baer, D. M. Some methodological contributions from a functional analysis of child development. In L. P. Lipsitt & C. C. Spiker (Eds.), *Advances in child development and behavior* (Vol. 1). New York: Academic Press, 1963. Pp. 197–231.

Birren, J. W. Psychological examinations of children who later became psychotic. *Journal of Abnormal and Social Psychology*, 1944, *39*, 84–96.

Bonney, M. E. Assessment of effort to aid socially isolated elementary school pupils. *The Journal of Educational Research*, 1971, *64*, 359–364.

Bridges, K. M. B. A study of social development in early infancy. *Child Development*, 1933, 4, 36–49.

Broen, P. A. The verbal environment of the language-learning child. *American Speech and Hearing Association Monograph*, 17, 1972.

Buell, J., Stoddard, P., Harris, F. R., & Baer, D. M. Collateral social development accompanying reinforcement of outdoor play in a preschool child. *Journal of Applied Behavior Analysis*, 1968, 1, 167–174.

Buhler, C. The social behavior of children. In C. Murchison (Ed.), *Handbook of child psychology*. Worchester, Mass.: Clark University Press, 1931.

Cairns, R. B. Attachment and dependency: A psychobiological and social-learning synthesis. In J. L. Gewirtz (Ed.), *Attachment and dependency*. Washington, D. C.: V. H. Winston, 1972. Pp. 29–80.

Cantor, J., & Cantor, G. Observing behavior in children as a function of stimulus novelty. *Child Development*, 1964, 35, 110–128.

Charlesworth, R., & Hartup, W. W. Positive social reinforcement in the nursery school peer group. *Child Development*, 1967, 38, 993–1002.

Christy, P. R. Does use of tangible rewards with individual children affect peer observers? *Journal of Applied Behavior Analysis*, 1975, 8, 187–196.

Cooke, T. P., & Apolloni, T. Developing positive emotional behaviors: A study in training and generalization effects. *Journal of Applied Behavior Analysis*, 1976, 9, 65–78.

Cooke, S. A., Cooke,T. P., & Apolloni, T. Developing nonretarded toddlers as verbal models for retarded classmates. *Child Study Journal*, 1977, 8, 1–8.

Dineen, J. P., Clark, H. B., & Risley, T. R. Peer tutoring among elementary students: Educational benefits to the tutor. *Journal of Applied Behavior Analysis*, 1977, 10, 231–238.

Drabman, R. S., Spitalnik, R., & Spitalnik, K. Sociometric and disruptive behavior as a function of four types of token reinforcement programs. *Journal of Applied Behavior Analysis*, 1974, 7, 93–101.

Fagot, B. I., & Patterson, G. R. An in vivo analysis of reinforcing contingencies for sex-role behaviors in the preschool child. *Developmental Psychology*, 1969, 1, 563–568.

Ferster, C. B. The repertoire of the autistic child in relation to principles of reinforcement. In L. Gottschalk (Ed.), *Methods of research in psychotherapy*. New York: Harper, 1965.

Frazee, H. E. Children who later become schizophrenic. *Smith College Studies in Social Work*, 1953, 23, 125–149.

Gable. R. A., Hendrickson, J. M., & Strain, P. S. Assessment, modification, and generalization of social interaction among severly retarded, multihandicapped children. *Education and Training of the Mentally Retarded*, 1978, 13, 279–286.

Geshuri, Y. Observational learning: Effects of observed reward and response patterns. *Journal of Educational Psychology*, 1972, 63, 374–380.

Gottman, J., Gonso, J., & Rasmussen, B. Social interaction, social competence, and friendship in children. *Child Development*, 1975, 46, 709–718.

Gottman, J., Gonso, J., & Schuler, P. Teaching social skills to isolated children. *Journal of Abnormal Child Psychology*, 1976, 4, 179–197.

Gouldner, A. W. The norm of reciprocity: A preliminary statement. *American Sociological Review*, 1960, 25, 161–179.

Greenwood, C. R., Walker, H. M., & Hops, H. Issues in social interaction/withdrawal assessment. *Exceptional Children*, 1977, 43, 490–499.

Guralnick, M. J. The value of integrating handicapped and nonhandicapped preschool children. *American Journal of Orthopsychiatry*, 1976, 46, 236–245.

Guralnick, M. J. Integrated preschools as educational and therapeutic environments. In M. J. Guralnick (Ed.), *Early intervention and the integration of handicapped and nonhandicapped children*. Baltimore: University Park Press, 1977. Pp. 115–145.

Guralnick, M. J., & Paul-Brown, D. The nature of verbal interactions among handicapped and nonhandicapped preschool children. *Child Development*, 1977, 48, 254–260.

Harlow, H. F. Age-mate or peer affectional system. In D. S. Lehman, R. A. Hinde, & E. Shaw (Eds.), *Advances in the study of behavior* (Vol. 2). New York: Academic Press, 1969.

Hartup, W. W. Peer interaction and the processes of socialization. In M. J. Guralnick (Ed.), *Early intervention and the integration of handicapped and nonhandicapped children*. Baltimore: University Park Press, 1977. Pp. 27–51.

Hartup, W. W., & Coates, B. Imitation of a peer as a function of reinforcement from the peer group and rewardingness of the model. *Child Development*, 1967, 38, 1003–1016.

Hartup, W. W., Glazer, J. S., & Charlesworth, R. Peer reinforcement and sociometric status. *Child Development*, 1967, 38, 1017–1024.

Johnston, J. M., & Johnston, G. T. Modification of consonant speech-sound articulation in young children. *Journal of Applied Behavior Analysis*, 1972, 5, 233–246.

Karen, R. L. *Operant conditioning and social preference*. Unpublished doctoral dissertation, Arizona State University, 1965.

Kazdin, A. E. The effect of vicarious reinforcement on attentive behavior in the classroom. *Journal of Applied Behavior Analysis*, 1973, 6, 71–78.

Kazdin, A. E., Silverman, N. A., & Sittler, J. L. The use of prompts to enhance vicarious effects of nonverbal approval. *Journal of Applied Behavior Analysis*, 1975, 8, 279–286.

Keller, M. F., & Carlson, P. M. The use of symbolic modeling to promote social skills in preschool children with low levels of social responsiveness. *Child Development*, 1974, 45, 912–919.

Kendon, A. Some functions of gaze direction in social interaction. *Acta Psychologica*, 1967, 26, 22–63.

King, M. Interpersonal relations in preschool children and average approach distance. *Journal of Genetic Psychology*, 1966, 109, 109–116.

Kirby, F. D., & Toler, H. C. Modification of preschool isolate behavior: A case study. *Journal of Applied Behavior Analysis*, 1970, 3, 309–314.

Koegel, R. L., & Rincover, A. Research on the difference between generalization and maintenance in extratherapy responding. *Journal of Applied Behavior Analysis*, 1977, 10, 1–12.

Kohn, M. The child as a determinant of his peers' approach to him. *The Journal of Genetic Psychology*, 1966, 109, 91–100.

Kohn, M. L., & Clausen, J. A. Social isolation and schizophrenia. *American Sociological Review*, 1955, 20, 265–273.

Kopstein, D. Effects of accelerating and decelerating consequences on the social behavior of trainable retarded children. *Child Development*, 1972, 43, 800–809.

Lott, A. J., & Lott, B. E. The role of reward in the formation of positive interpersonal attitudes. In T. L. Huston (Ed.), *Foundations of interpersonal attraction*. New York: Academic Press, 1974.

Mahoney, G. J., & Seely, P. B. The role of the social agent in language acquisition: Implications for language intervention. In N. R. Ellis (Ed.), *International review of research in mental retardation* (Vol. 8). New York: Academic Press, 1976.

Marshall, H. R., & McCandless, B. R. A study in prediction of social behavior of preschool children. *Child Development*, 1957, 28, 149–159.

Maudry, M., & Nekula, M. Social relations between children of the same age during the first two years of life. *Journal of Genetic Psychology*, 1939, 54, 193–215.

Merton, R. *Social theory and social structure*. New York: Free Press of Glencoe, 1956.

Michael, C. M., Morris, D. P., & Sorokes, E. Follow-up studies of shy, withdrawn children. II. Relative incidence of schizophrenia. *American Journal of Orthopsychiatry*, 1957, 27, 331–337.

Milby, J. C. Modification of extreme social isolation by contingent reinforcement. *Journal of Applied Behavior Analysis*, 1970, 3, 149–152.

Moerk, E. L. Processes of language teaching and training in the interactions of mother–child dyads. *Child Development*, 1976, 47, 1064–1078.

Moore, S., & Updegraff, R. Sociometric status of preschool children related to age, sex, nurturance-giving, and dependency. *Child Development*, 1964, 35, 519–524.

Morris, W. N., Marshall, H. M., & Miller, R. S. The effect of vicarious punishment on prosocial behavior in children. *Journal of Experimental Child Psychology*, 1973, 15, 222–236.

Mueller, E. The maintenance of verbal exchanges between young children. *Child Development*, 1972, 43, 930–938.

Nordquist, V. M. A behavioral approach to the analysis of peer interactions. In M. J. Guralnick (Ed.), *Early intervention and the integration of handicapped and nonhandicapped children.* Baltimore: University Park Press, 1977. Pp. 53–84.

O'Connor, R. D. Modification of social withdrawal through symbolic modeling. *Journal of Applied Behavior Analysis*, 1969, 2, 15–22.

O'Connor, R. D. The relative efficacy of modeling, shaping, and the combined procedures for the modification of social withdrawal. *Journal of Abnormal Psychology*, 1972, 79, 327–334.

O'Neal, P., & Robins, L. N. Childhood patterns predictive of adult schizophrenia: A follow-up study. *American Journal of Psychiatry*, 1958, 115, 385–391.

Parton, D. A. Learning to imitate in infancy. *Child Development*, 1976, 47, 14–31.

Patterson, G. R., Littman, R. A., & Bricker, W. Assertive behavior in children: A step toward a theory of aggression. *Monographs of the Society for Research in Child Development*, 1967, 32(5), (Serial No. 113).

Piaget, J. *The moral judgement of the child.* Glencoe, Ill.: Free Press, 1932.

Pruitt, D. G. Reciprocity and credit building in a laboratory dyad. *Journal of Personality and Social Psychology*, 1968, 8, 143–147.

Quilitch, H. R., Christophersen, E. R., & Risley, T. R. The evaluation of children's play materials. *Journal of Applied Behavior Analysis*, 1977, 10, 501–502.

Ragland, E. U., Kerr, M. M., & Strain, P. S. Effects of peer social initiations on the behavior of withdrawn autistic children. *Behavior Modification*, 1978, 2, 565–578.

Reid, J. B. *Reciprocity in family interaction.* Unpublished doctoral dissertation, University of Oregon, 1967.

Rheingold, H., Gewirtz, J. L., & Ross, H. W. Social conditioning of vocalizations in the infant. *Journal of Comparative and Physiological Psychology*, 1959, 52, 68–73.

Rincover, A., & Koegel, R. L. Setting generality and stimulus control in autistic children. *Journal of Applied Behavior Analysis*, 1975, 3, 235–246.

Risley, T. R. Day care as a strategy in social intervention. In E. Ramp & G. Semb (Eds.), *Behavior analysis: Areas of research and application.* Englewood Cliffs, N.J.: Prentice Hall, 1975.

Robins, L. N. *Deviant children grown up: A sociological and psychiatric study of sociopathic personality.* Baltimore: Williams & Wilkins, 1966.

Roff, M., Sells, S. B., & Golden, M. M. *Social adjustment and personality development in children.* Minneapolis: University of Minnesota Press, 1972.

Rolf, J. E. The social and academic competence of children vulnerable to schizophrenia and other behavior pathologies. *Journal of Abnormal Psychology*, 1972, 80, 225–243.

Rosenfeld, H. Non-verbal reciprocation of approval: An experimental analysis. *Journal of Experimental Social Psychology*, 1967, 3, 102–111.

Rosenkrans, M. A. Imitation in children as a function of perceived similarity to a social model and vicarious reinforcement. *Journal of Personality and Social Psychology*, 1967, 1, 307–315.

Sears, R. R. A theoretical framework for personality and social behavior. *American Psychologist*, 1951, 6, 476–483.

Shatz, M., & Gelman, R. The development of communication skills: Modifications in the speech of young children as a function of listener. *Monographs of the Society for Research in Child Development*, 1973, 38(5), Serial No. 152.

Shores, R. E., Hester, P., & Strain, P. S. The effects of amount and type of teacher–child interaction on child–child interaction during free-play. *Psychology in the Schools*, 1976, *13*, 171–175.

Skinner, B. F. *Science and human behavior*. New York: Free Press, 1953.

Snow, C. E. Mothers' speech to children learning language. *Child Development*, 1972, *43*, 549–565.

Stedman, D. J. Important considerations in the review and evaluation of educational intervention programs. In P. Mittler (Ed.), *Research to practice in mental retardation*. Baltimore: University Park Press, 1977. Pp. 99–108.

Stengel, E. *Suicide and attempted suicide*. Middlesex, England: Penguin, 1971.

Stone, L. J., Smith, H. T., & Murphy, L. B. (Eds.), *The competent infant*. New York: Basic Books, 1973.

Strain, B. A. *Early dialogues: Reciprocity in vocal interaction between mothers and their three month old infants*. Unpublished Doctoral Dissertation, Peabody College, Nashville, Tenn., 1975.

Strain, P. S. Effects of peer social initiations on withdrawn preschool children: Some training and generalization effects. *Journal of Abnormal Child Psychology*, 1977, *5*, 445–455.

Strain, P. S. Modification of sociometric status and social interaction with mainstreamed mild developmentally disabled children. *Analysis and Intervention in Developmental Disabilities*, 1981, *1*.

Strain, P. S., & Carr, T. H. The observational study of social reciprocity: implications for the mentally retarded. *Mental Retardation*, 1975, *13*, 18–19.

Strain, P. S., & Cooke, T. P. An observational investigation of two elementary-age autistic children during free-play. *Psychology in the Schools*, 1976, *13*, 82–91.

Strain, P. S., Cooke, T. P., & Apolloni, T. *Teaching exceptional children: Assessing and modifying social behavior*. New York: Academic Press, 1976.

Strain, P. S., & Hill, A. D. Social interaction. In P. Wehman (Ed.), *Leisure time skills for the severely handicapped*. Baltimore, Md.: University Park Press, 1979.

Strain, P. S., Kerr, M. M., & Ragland, E. U. Effects of peer-mediated initiations and prompting/reinforcement procedures on the social behavior of autistic children. *Journal of Autism and Developmental Disorders*, 1979, *9*, 41–54.

Strain, P. S., & Pierce, J. E. Direct and vicarious effects of social praise on mentally retarded preschool children's attentive behavior. *Psychology in the Schools*, 1977, *14*, 348–353.

Strain, P. S., & Shores, R. E. Social interaction development among behaviorally handicapped preschool children: Research and educational implications. *Psychology in the schools*, 1977, *14*, 493–502.

Strain, P. S., Shores, R. E., & Timm, M. A. Effects of peer social initiations on the behavior of withdrawn preschool children. *Journal of Applied Behavior Analysis*, 1977, *10*, 289–298.

Strain, P. S., & Timm, M. A. An experimental analysis of social interaction between a behaviorally disordered preschool child and her classroom peers. *Journal of Applied Behavior Analysis*, 1974, *7*, 583–590.

Strichart, S. S. Effects of competence and nurturance on imitation of nonretarded peers by retarded adolescents. *American Journal of Mental Deficiency*, 1974, *78*, 665–674.

Wahler, R. G. Child–child interactions in free-field settings: Some experimental analyses. *Journal of Experimental Child Psychology*, 1967, *5*, 278–293.

Wahler, R. G., Berland, R. M., Coe, T. D., & Leske, G. Social systems analysis: Implementing an alternative behavioral model. In A. Rogers-Warren & S. Warren (Eds.), *Ecological perspective in behavior analysis*. Baltimore: University Park Press, 1977.

Walker, H. B., & Hops, H. The use of group and individual reinforcement contingencies in the modification of social withdrawal. In L. A. Hamerlynch, L. C. Handy, & E. J. Marsh (Eds.), *Behavior change: Methodology, concepts, and practice*. Champaign, Ill.: Research Press, 1973. Pp. 269–307.

Walters, R. H., Parke, R. D., & Cone, V. A. Timing of punishment and the observation of consequences to others as determinants of response inhibition. *Journal of Experimental Child Psychology*, 1965, 2, 10–30.

Whitman, T. L., Mercurio, J. R., & Caponigri, V. Development of social responses in two severely retarded children. *Journal of Applied Behavior Analysis*, 1970, 3, 133–138.

Management of Problem Behaviors in Regular Classrooms

5

Introduction

A major concern of teachers in regular as well as special education classrooms is the management of classroom behaviors that disrupt the teaching and learning process. For the past two decades, applied behavior analysts have produced a large body of literature on the management of disruptive classroom behaviors and the development of appropriate behaviors. This literature has focused on students in primary and elementary grades, and many of the studies have taken place in so-called regular classrooms. These studies were designed typically to respond to one or two "problem" students enrolled in a large classroom, thereby providing a corollary to mainstreamed settings. Only a few of the available studies in this area are included in this chapter. An attempt was made to highlight studies that articulate critical issues or provide innovative answers in the group management of handicapped and nonhandicapped students in integrated settings. The reader who wishes to study the literature on classroom behavior management from a broader perspective is referred throughout the chapter to other reviews (see Hanley, 1970; Kazdin & Bootzin, 1972; McLaughlin, 1975).

Teacher Talk: Approval and Disapproval in the Classroom

What teachers say to their students has been of primary interest to applied behavior analysts. To facilitate a greater understanding of the studies on the manipulation of teacher verbal behavior, this section will provide the reader with a review of studies on the naturally occurring rates of teacher approval and disapproval statements. Regrettably, there have been few research efforts in this area.

White (1975) reported interesting but discouraging findings as a result of 16 studies of the natural rates of teacher verbal approval and disapproval in classrooms from grades 1 to 12. In summarizing her observations, White noted the following:

1. Pupils across the 12 grades received more teacher disapproval than teacher approval.
2. When teachers provided students with praise, it nearly always focused on instructional behaviors. There was very little teacher approval for "managerial behaviors." Pupils rarely experienced praise for behaviors such as standing in line, being quiet, or interacting pleasantly with one another.

In an attempt to analyze natural rates of teacher approval and disapproval, Thomas, Presland, Grant, and Glynn (1978) examined teacher verbal behavior in ten seventh-grade classrooms and compared these rates with those described by White (1975). Despite methodological differences between the two investigations, rates of teacher verbal reinforcement and disapproval matched the earlier findings of White (1975). Specifically, Thomas *et al.* (1978) reported a mean approval rate of 0.2 per observed min and an average disapproval rate of 0.58 per min. Ironically, the children to whom negative remarks were addressed were observed as being on-task for at least 66% of the observed intervals. The authors cited a specific example of the lack of positive correlation between teacher disapproval and on-task behavior: One teacher, whose class spent 90% of their time on-task, demonstrated lower than average rates of positive verbal attention to her students.

In examining teacher commands and reprimands in regular classrooms, Madsen, Becker, Thomas, Koser, and Plager (1968) found that children's out-of-seat behaviors increased when the teacher increased her reprimands for these behaviors. O'Leary, Kaufman, Kass, and Drabman (1970) examined the relative effectiveness of loud reprimands versus soft reprimands on disruptive behavior of primary school pupils. The authors noted that during the initial baseline phase of their first experiment, the teacher relied primarily upon the use of loud reprimands (i.e., statements that could be heard across the room). The introduction of soft reprimands, which could be heard only by the target student, produced significant decreases in the level of disruptive behaviors. The use of soft instead of loud reprimands may be preferable for two reasons: A soft reprimand requires that the teacher be in close proximity with the target student, and soft reprimands require less teacher effort than loud ones.

SUMMARY

Studies on the naturally occurring and manipulated rates of teacher verbal statements raise several clinical concerns. First, it appears that some teachers naturally use disapproval statements far more frequently than approval statements, despite the ineffectiveness of the former. Secondly, teachers may tend to use loud reprimands, which publicly ostracize the "problem" student(s). This problem is magnified if one is attempting to integrate a handicapped or behaviorally deviant student with "nonproblem" students. These studies raise the related issue of pupils' modeling of teacher performance, specifically disapproval statements and loud reprimands, further ostracizing students whose behavior is deviant. Finally, the studies by Madsen, Becker, Thomas, Koser, and Plager (1968) and O'Leary *et al.* (1970) underscore the importance of systematic training of teachers in the use of verbal statements. The use of approval statements may not be a "natural act" for many teachers. Teachers must learn also to observe carefully the effects of their verbal statements on student behavior. In two studies (Madsen, Becker, Thomas, Koser, & Plager, 1968; O'Leary *et al.*, 1970), teachers maintained verbal behaviors despite the negative effects on student disruptions (e.g., reprimands increased out-of-seat behaviors).

Standards for Performance: Classroom Rules

All classroom teachers delineate overtly or covertly a set of rules for student behavior. Several studies have sought to examine the effects of rules on student performance, specifically on the reduction of disruptive classroom behaviors. Most often, rules have been examined as one component of an intervention package (e.g., rules, praise, structure, and ignoring), since the use of rules alone has seldom proved efficacious. Madsen, Becker, and Thomas (1968) studied the differential effects of three classroom interventions: rules, ignoring inappropriate behaviors, and approval for appropriate behaviors. Kindergarten and primary classroom teachers nominated target subjects who exhibited a high frequency of disruptive classroom behavior. Three students from each classroom were observed, although the intervention procedures were applied to the whole class. During the first intervention, teachers were trained to develop a set of classroom rules; each teacher then reviewed these rules with the class five times daily. During the second intervention phase, the teachers ignored systematically all inappropriate behaviors. (One teacher used this intervention alone, while the second teacher used it in combination with the rules.) During the third phase of the investigation, teachers implemented an intervention package consisting of rules, ignoring inappropriate behaviors, and praising appropriate behaviors. To teach these skills to the teachers, a weekly seminar was held, and consultation was provided in the classroom. The results of the study were as follows:

1. Rules alone had no effect on child performance in either classroom.
2. No effects were observed as a result of using ignoring as a single strategy.
3. When rules were combined with ignoring in one classroom, the inappropriate behavior increased.
4. The intervention package (i.e., rules, ignoring, and praise) improved behavior dramatically in both classrooms.

This study is interesting for several reasons. First, the necessity for formal training of teachers in behavior modification procedures with follow-up consultation was confirmed. Secondly, the study supported others that showed that rules alone or in combination with ignoring were not effective ways to manage classroom behaviors. Unfortunately, many traditional classrooms rely primarily upon rules and the ignoring of inappropriate behaviors to improve child performance. Finally, the study underscored the importance of teacher praise, since classroom behavior improved only when positive feedback was added to rules and ignoring to form an intervention package.

An investigation of classroom rules in combination with praise, ignoring, and token reinforcement was conducted by O'Leary, Becker, Evans, and Saudargas (1969). The results of this study confirmed the earlier findings of Madsen, Becker, and Thomas (1968) that rules alone did not reduce disruptive classroom behaviors. The combination of using rules as well as educational structure (i.e., teacher-directed sessions in which the total class participated in a discussion) was also ineffective. The most effective combination of procedures resulted when a token economy program was combined with rules, structure, praise, and ignoring strategies. During the token economy condition, children received points four times each afternoon for adhering to classroom rules. These points were exchangeable for small toys and prizes at the end of the day. As stated by Walker (1979), the necessity of incorporating a token economy program into the treatment package may have been in part the result of the kind of students (i.e., severely acting-out) enrolled in the classrooms studied by O'Leary *et al.* (1969). A systematic external reinforcement system may be necessary if one is attempting to modify the behavior of students for whom teacher approval is not an effective reinforcer.

Differential feedback is necessary in order to get students to comply with classroom rules, as demonstrated in a study by Greenwood, Hops, Delquadri, and Guild (1974). The disruptive behavior of students in three primary classrooms was observed under three treatment conditions: rules, rules with feedback, and rules with feedback and reinforcement. The rules condition resulted in no significant behavior change, despite the fact that students were given an extensive initial demonstration and explanation of each rule. When feedback (i.e., signals from a clock light, feedback written on the blackboard, and data charted on a bar graph) was provided in addition to rules, two of the three groups showed significant improvement. The complete intervention package (i.e., rules, feedback, group and individual reinforcement) had the greatest impact on student performance. During this condition, teachers praised students as well as the entire class for appropriate behavior and provided the class with predesignated rewards if they, as a group, met a designated criterion for performance. In order to be able to implement this multifaceted intervention, teachers enrolled in a formal course in classroom management and received several hours of consultation. This arrangement was similar to the training provided by Madsen, Becker, and Thomas (1968). Follow-up observations of students in the three classrooms indicated maintenance of treatment effects over a 3-week period, despite the termination of all treatment procedures.

SUMMARY

Research on rules and feedback justifies several recommendations. First, traditional reliance upon a set of classroom rules is itself a weak behavior modification strategy. Clearly stated, resonable, and enforceable rules should, nevertheless, be developed by classroom teachers (Worell & Nelson, 1974), since classroom rules form an important framework for subsequent feedback and reinforcement to students about their behavior. A second recommendation is that teachers attempt to provide some form of feedback to students on their performance vis-à-vis classroom rules (Greenwood et al., 1974). A third issue raised by the studies is the question of whether or not to reinforce the entire classroom group or to reinforce individual students. The investigation conducted by Greenwood et al. (1974) demonstrated the efficacy of using a group contingency. In a discussion of the use of group contingencies in regular classroom settings, Walker (1979) suggested:

> Such contingencies can be highly effective in regular classrooms if implemented correctly and monitored carefully. It should be noted though that group contingencies of this type are usually not powerful enough to control the behavior of acting-out children effectively. If teachers wish to implement group contingencies, and there is an acting-out child or children in the classroom, it is recommended that a treatment program be applied to a target child's behavior beforehand, followed by implementation of the group contingency. If this is not done, the acting-out child may seriously reduce the potential effectiveness of a group contingency applied to the behavior of the entire class [p. 141].

In the section that follows, a specialized intervention package, "Good Behavior Game," is described. This intervention package incorporates many of the components previously reviewed: rules, feedback, reinforcement of group and individual performance, and response cost.

Good Behavior Game Procedure

The Good Behavior Game was introduced into the research literature by Barrish, Saunders, and Wolf (1969). The Good Behavior Game is a treatment intervention package that consists of four components: rules, feedback, reinforcement, and response cost. The format of the Good Behavior Game is as follows: First, the teacher introduces the game and the classroom rules and divides the class into two teams; second, each receives a mark any time one of its members engages in a predesignated inappropriate behavior; third, the team with the fewer marks, below a predesignated criterion level, is declared the winner for that day and receives some form of reinforcement. The losing team is typically required to do extra work or to forfeit some privilege. In the event that both teams make an identical score, both teams are awarded the reinforcer or privileges.

In the original study of the Good Behavior Game, the general format was investigated during reading and math periods in a fourth-grade regular classroom. The intervention package was effective in reducing talking-out behaviors and out-of-seat behaviors for most of the members of the class. In a subsequent replication study of the Good Behavior Game, Medland and Stachnik (1972) employed 28 fifth graders as subjects. The authors examined the differential effects of two components of the Good Behavior Game: rules and rules plus feedback. Feedback was provided to the students by a light apparatus, which displayed a green signal when students were behaving appropriately and a red signal when someone on a team lost a point. Data from this study indicated that the rules-plus-feedback condition was more effective than the rules-only condition.

In a third study of the Good Behavior Game, Harris and Sherman (1973) used a fifth-grade classroom and a sixth-grade classroom to answer three questions:

1. Is the Good Behavior Game effective in reducing disruptive behavior?
2. Which components of the Good Behavior Game are responsible for behavior change?
3. Will a reduction in disruptive behavior improve the academic performance of the students?

The disruptive behaviors targeted in this study were talking-out behavior and out-of-seat behavior. Academic performance was measured during two separate math periods in the fifth-grade classroom. (Academic performance was not recorded for the sixth-grade classroom.) Four manipulations of the Good Behavior Game procedures were employed to assess the efficacy of different components of the game. In the first manipulation, the consequences for winning a game were eliminated. In the second manipulation, the maximum number of points declared as necessary for winning was altered. In the third manipulation, feedback to students regarding their disruptive behaviors was terminated. In the fourth manipulation, the class, rather than being divided into two teams, was treated as one team. When a team won, its members earned the privilege of leaving school 10 min early at the end of the day. Members of the losing team were required to remain in the classroom. Throughout all conditions, the game was effective in reducing the frequency of disruptive behaviors. The use of a reinforcing consequence and response cost (i.e., leaving school 10 min early and remaining in school for the final 10 min) increased the game's effectiveness. During the nonteam conditions, disruptive behavior occurred at a higher rate, particularly once the group met the criterion number of points for losing. The manipulation of the number of points required for winning resulted in the students' changing their behavior accordingly; that is, "students scored as many marks for disruptive behavior as the criterion for both teams winning allowed [p. 415]." The removal of feedback had no effect on disruptive behavior.

SUMMARY

The Good Behavior Game has been effective in reducing the disruptive behavior of regular classroom students. However, there are several issues that must be considered in using the Good Behavior Game in integrated educational settings. First, two of the studies (Barrish *et al.*, 1969; Harris & Sherman, 1973) reported that one or more students refused to take part in the game. This finding is significant if one is considering the use of the Good Behavior Game procedures in a classroom where a few students produce most of the problems. Second, the Good Behavior Game employs a group contingency based on individual performance. In using a group contingency a teacher must monitor carefully the interactions of team members to insure that scapegoating does not occur. This is especially important in classrooms in which handicapped children already may have difficulty being accepted by their nonhandicapped peers. Third, the Good Behavior Game requires the teacher to observe and give feedback on the designated problem behaviors. In two of the studies (Barrish *et al.*, 1969; Harris & Sherman, 1973) the teacher served as the primary observer. In the third study, trained observers using a light apparatus provided the feedback (Medland & Stachnik, 1972). It is unlikely that additional observers will be provided to most regular classroom teachers. A fourth concern relates to the choice of reinforcers. The very effective reinforcer (i.e., allowing students to leave school 10 min early) described by Harris and Sherman (1973) is not feasible in many public school settings. Finally, the choice of response cost, like the selection of reinforcers, must be evaluated in terms of feasibility in mainstreamed classroom settings.

Peer-Mediated Feedback Strategies

While many studies have incorporated the use of adult feedback, there have been studies that primarily focused on peer feedback or a combination of teacher and peer feedback. The findings of these studies are particularly significant for mainstream settings, since the inclusion of peers in an intervention program for an exceptional child is critical for maintenance of treatment effects (Strain & Kerr, 1981).

Drabman and Lahey (1974) examined a classroom setting in which a 10-year-old child was targeted as being the most disruptive student in the room. The teacher reported that this child, in addition to being disruptive, was frequently teased by others and had no friends. The intervention examined in this ABAB study was the use of private feedback, given by the teacher to the target child about every 10 min during a 45 min classroom period. The use of a kitchen timer facilitated the teacher's providing feedback on the designated schedule. Three measures of behavior change in the target child, her classmates, and her teacher were recorded. First, the level of disruptive behavior exhibited by the target child and her peers was recorded during all four phases. Second, frequent sociometric ratings permitted the investigators to determine whether or not the target child's status changed as a result of the intervention procedure; and third, the verbal comments made to the target child by the classmates and by her teacher were classified as positive or negative.

The authors reported that the private feedback procedure not only decreased the target child's level of inappropriate behavior but also decreased the inappropriate behavior of her classmates. During the first feedback condition, the target child's sociometric status improved. However, the authors reported that the sociometric instrument was inadequate and did not accurately measure changes in the following two conditions. The findings with respect to positive and negative teacher comments to the target child have relevance to those trying to modify the behavior of mainstream teachers: despite the target child's improved behavior, her teacher did not praise her more frequently. The teacher did reduce the number of disapproval statements to the student. The child's classmates spoke more positively to her during treatment phases but continued to make the same number of negative comments as before. The authors pointed out that teachers must be trained to show approval, since the verbal behavior of a child's classmates may be modeled upon the performance of their teacher. (It should be noted that no specific consultation to the teacher about her verbal behavior was provided in this study.)

A recent pair of studies (Kerr, Strain, & Ragland, in press; Ragland, Kerr, & Strain, in press) have examined the use of peer feedback for social behaviors. In the first study, three socially isolate children, ages 10–12 years, were nominated by the teacher for intervention because they seldom played with other children appropriately on the playground. During a daily goal-setting and feedback session, these children and their classmates talked about individual goals and evaluated one another's progress toward those goals. Each student in the group was assigned a behavioral goal by the teacher; daily feedback consisted of a vote and a brief supporting statement of whether or not a classmate had met his goal for that day. The results of this initial study indicated that the goal setting and feedback procedure was a highly successful intervention package for improving the cooperative play of the isolate students during a daily recess period. Anecdotal reports indicated that nontargeted classmates also benefited from the intervention.

The second study in this series (Kerr *et al.*, in press) attempted to delineate the relative contribution of teacher goal setting and peer feedback. Four students were selected as subjects because of their inappropriate behavior on the playground. An initial baseline phase resulted in no recorded cooperative behaviors for any of these students. Instead, they teased, fought physically, and bickered during each recess period. When teacher-established goals were introduced, a slight improvement, albeit variable, was observed in their play. A return-to-baseline phase resulted in a slight decrease in cooperative play. Only when teacher goals and peer feedback were combined did the four students improve and begin playing cooperatively in a consistent pattern.

SUMMARY

Peer-mediated feedback is a powerful intervention strategy, when paired with specific behavioral goals. The group goal setting and peer feedback procedure studied by Kerr *et al.* (in press) can be implemented readily in most classrooms. The following section describes a procedure that also manipulates the feedback or attention a student receives from his or her teacher and peers.

Time Out Procedures

Time out has been described as the most popular form of punishment used for disruptive classroom behaviors (Patterson & White, 1969). The term *time out* refers to the removal of a child from an ongoing reinforcing activity. The intensity of this intervention ranges from extremely mild (e.g., the turning away of an adult) to quite strong (e.g., the placement of the child in a separate time out room).

In an examination of the acceptability of time out, Kazdin (1980) employed a group of undergraduate students to evaluate procedures commonly used in special and regular classrooms. During the first of two experiments, the subjects rated the acceptability of the procedures in this order:

1. Reinforcement of behaviors incompatible with inappropriate classroom behaviors
2. Contingent observation, in which the student was placed in a chair at the side of the room to observe but not interact with others
3. The withdrawal of attention, in which the teacher signaled to classmates that the child was to receive no attention from them for a period of 10 min
4. Isolation, or being placed in a separate time out room across the hall from the classroom

Results of a second experiment indicated the isolation was viewed more favorably when included in a contingency contract. Positive reinforcement of incompatible behavior was rated again as the most acceptable of the treatments; isolation as a singular intervention was least acceptable. Research to date indicates that the less exclusionary forms of time out are effective in reducing many behaviors typically identified as problematic in regular and special education settings. (For a detailed discussion of guidelines for the use of time out in classrooms, the reader is referred to Gast and Nelson, 1977).

Research studies have used time out typically in combination with some reinforcement procedure (e.g., DRO [Differential Reinforcement of Other behaviors]). In a study conducted by Wasik, Senn, Welch, and Cooper (1969), two forms of time out were examined: withdrawal of teacher attention for inappropriate attention-getting behavior by a child, and a 5-min physical isolation, used when a child engaged in aggressive or resistive behaviors. In addition to using the time out procedures, the two teachers were trained to use praise and to provide attention to the students for appropriate classroom behavior. The two subjects in the study were 7-year-old girls in a demonstration school for the culturally deprived. Both students had a history of verbal and physical aggression and were generally disruptive. Results indicated that the treatment package consisting of teacher praise and time out was effective in modifying the inappropriate classroom behavior of the students. A 3-month follow-up observation indicated that long-term effects had been achieved.

An innovative method of nonexclusionary time out was described by Foxx and Shapiro (1978) in a study of five retarded students in a residential special education classroom. A ribbon worn by the students indicated that they were eligible for teacher-dispensed reinforcement and for participation in classroom activities. Time out consisted of the removing of this ribbon. The "ribbon" students received edible and social reinforcers approximately every 3 min. For all students, the level of disruptive behavior was lower during the time out ribbon and reinforcement conditions than during baseline or reinforcement-alone conditions. This intervention seems quite useful for regular classrooms. One must keep in mind, however, the high level of systematic reinforcement also provided to the students.

Two studies have examined the use of time out procedures with preschool children. Porterfield, Herbert-Jackson, and Risley (1976) used contingent observation in a study on the disruptive behavior of children ages 1–3 years. The contingent observation procedure consisted of removing the student from a group activity to "sit and watch" quietly before being returned to the group. Data indicated that the contingent observation procedure was more effective than a traditional redirection procedure in reducing disruptive and aggressive behavior in this day care facility. In the second preschool study, Wilson, Robertson, Herlong, and Haynes (1979) employed 13 kindergarten students as subjects. An ABAB design was used to evaluate the effectiveness of using a small open booth for a 5-min time out period. Observations were recorded on the target student as well as on 12 peers who were not subject to the time out procedure. The contingent social isolation procedure reduced the aggressive behavior of the target child as well as producing some decrease in the aggressive behavior of children who were not targeted for intervention. To determine the nature of this vicarious effect, a post hoc analysis was conducted to determine whether or not a change in the target child's acting-out behavior was responsible for subsequent decreases in the aggressive behavior of his classmates. It appeared that the appropriate behavior of the peer group could not be attributed solely to changes on the part of the target student.

SUMMARY

Mild forms of time out from reinforcement can have a positive effect on the classroom behavior of preschool and elementary school students. In all of the studies cited, time out was combined with a teacher reinforcement procedure. This intervention package is recommended for mainstream teachers, since it has proven effective (Wasik *et al.*, 1968) and is considered highly acceptable as a treatment procedure (Kazdin, 1980). Another set of procedures that is gaining acceptance, self-management, is described next.

Self-Management Procedures

One goal of the educational process is to enable children to control their own behaviors (Lovitt & Curtiss, 1969). A recent body of literature has sought to examine the efficacy of various self-management procedures including the following:

> 1. Self-assessment—the individual may examine his own behavior and decide whether or not he has performed a specific behavior or class of behaviors.
> 2. Self-recording—the individual may objectively record the frequency of his own performance of a given behavior or class of behaviors.
> 3. Self-determination of reinforcement—the individual may determine from all available reinforcers the nature and amount of reinforcement he should receive contingent upon his performance of a given behavior or class of behaviors.
> 4. Self-administration of reinforcement—the individual dispenses his own reinforcers (which may or may not be self-determined) contingent upon his performance of a given behavior or class of behaviors [Glynn, Thomas, & Shee, 1973, p. 105].

Studies that have examined the use of self-management procedures in regular classrooms will be reviewed in this section. Like other studies of classroom behavior, the studies of self-management procedures typically targeted disruptive behaviors for intervention.

SELF-RECORDING

The use of self-recording is among the most popular of the self-management procedures. One of the first studies of self-recording was conducted by Broden, Hall, and Mitts (1971). Two eighth-grade students served as subjects in the two single-case experiments. In the first experiment, a "highly motivated" girl was trained to mark a simple scoring sheet when she was studying and when she felt that she was not studying. Each recording sheet provided the student with 30 opportunities to record the "study" or "not study" behavior during a 40-min history class. An initial baseline period was followed by the first self-recording phase, during which the student was trained to use the self-recording sheet. These two phases were then replicated. Two additional interventions were examined in the last two phases of the study. "Self-recording plus praise" consisted of the basic procedure supplemented with teacher praise given on a variable schedule. "Praise only" consisted of teacher attention without the self-checking procedure. During the final condition of this study, both teacher attention and self-recording were withdrawn.

The results indicated that the initial self-checking had an immediate and dramatic effect on the percent of study behaviors recorded by the experimental observer. During Baseline 2, this effect was reversed. The reintroduction of self-recording once again produced high levels of study behavior. Teacher attention to the student was recorded throughout the study, but no significant differences were observed in the level of teacher attention during the first four conditions. When the teacher was directed to praise the student during the fifth phase of the study, the level of teacher attention increased significantly, as did the level of the study behaviors on the part of the student. When self-recording was withdrawn, the student's study rate dropped slightly but did not resume its original baseline level. Teacher praise remained about the same. During the final baseline phase of the study, the student's level of study behavior (77%) maintained. The level of teacher attention dropped, as directed by the experimenter. The data from the last phase suggest that the effects achieved by the self-recording procedure were durable over time.

The second experiment was quite different from the first: The second student was not as motivated to change his behavior as the first student, but was trained to record only inappropriate behaviors (talk-outs); no praise was provided to this student for improving his behavior. The self-recording procedure reduced slightly the level of talk-outs recorded by the experimental observer during the initial intervention phase, but the final self-recording condition did not produce behavior change.

Data on the reliability between students' observations and those of the outside observer were interesting. Although overall levels of interobserver reliability were fairly high (78–89% for the first study; 84–100% for the second study), there was marked variability between scores of the observer and the students on a day-to-day basis. On some days the first student failed to record any behaviors, suggesting that perhaps the recording sheet itself had become a behavioral cue.

A comparison of the two studies suggests that contingent teacher praise is critical to the success of self-recording programs. The authors suggested that teachers "use it as a procedure for initiating desirable levels of appropriate behavior to a point where the teacher can more easily reinforce the desired behavior with attention, praise, grades, or other reinforcers available in the classroom [Broden *et al.*, 1971, pp. 198–199]." This statement is in direct contrast with the assertion that self-management procedures are particularly useful to maintain the effects of adult-mediated interventions, a recommendation based on studies that have demonstrated that behaviors changed through self-management procedures are more resistant to extinction than those established through externally controlled procedures (Johnson, 1970; Kanfer & Duerfeldt, 1967).

Two studies have challenged the assumption that behavior change produced through self-management procedures is more durable than that produced through externally controlled procedures. A study by Santogrossi, O'Leary, Romanczyk, and Kaufman (1973) was conducted with nine adolescent boys, each of whom had a history of seriously disruptive behavior. Each student learned to self-evaluate his compliance with five classroom rules (e.g., raise your hand to talk, face the front of the room). The students were required also to announce their ratings at the end of each 15 min period. This self-evaluation procedure took place during Phase II, following an initial baseline phase. During Phases III–VI the basic self-evaluation procedure was modified. Only when self-evaluation was replaced with a teacher-determined token reinforcement program did the disruptive behavior decrease significantly. This study confirmed the finding of Broden *et al.* (1971) that self-evaluation in the absence of teacher attention or reinforcement was ineffective.

In a classic study on the use of self-regulation versus external regulation of tokens, Bolstad and Johnson (1972) examined the question of maintenance of effects over time. Thirty-eight students constituted the four experimental groups and the control group. The subjects were selected because they emitted high rates of disruptive behavior in their first- and second-grade classrooms. Pre-baseline screening using direct observational data confirmed these problems. During an initial baseline condition, three disruptive behaviors were observed: talking-out or making inappropriate noises, hitting or physically disturbing others, and leaving the work area without permission. During the first experimental phase, the three treatment classroom groups were exposed to the external regulation condition (i.e., the evaluation of classroom behavior and the dispensing of subsequent reinforcement by the experimenter). Reinforcement consisted of points exchangeable for small school-related prizes (e.g., pencils and paper). During the third phase, two of the three treatment groups were trained in self-regulation procedures (i.e., the use of self-observation cards and the self-administration of reinforcers according to previously designated criteria). Each student compared his recording with that of the observer to determine the level of points to be received. If the student's rating agreed with that of the observer, the student was awarded the same number of points that he received during the second phase of the study. Students whose ratings were beyond the range of 3 marks from the rating of the observer were fined 2 points. During the fourth phase only the self-regulation procedure was in force. Students were awarded points according to their own data, with no comparisons to observers' data. The fifth phase of the study constituted an extinction phase for all groups. Prizes were withdrawn and only one group was asked to continue self-recording. The findings of this study are summarized below:

1. Both external and self-regulation procedures were effective in reducing disruptive behaviors.
2. The self-regulation procedure appeared slightly more effective than the external regulation procedure during three of the experimental phases. During these phases, children in the self-regulation groups exhibited 40% fewer disruptive behaviors than their counterparts in the externally regulated group.
3. The students were capable of accurate self-evaluation, with the exception of seven students whose self-observation data were inaccurate.

4. The data did not support the notion that behaviors developed through self-regulation procedures are more resistant to extinction than those developed by external regulation.
5. A positive effect was observed for control subjects enrolled in classrooms with target subjects. Control group students exhibited lower levels of disruptive behavior during the study than during prebaseline observations.

Self-reinforcement, as well as self-imposed fines, were examined in a study by Humphrey, Karoly, & Kirschenbaum (1978). Subjects were enrolled in a second-grade reading class. Self-reinforcement consisted of self-evaluation of reading performance and self-reward of tokens on a teacher-designated exchange rate. (In addition, the teacher reviewed a list of classroom rules every 30 min.) The self-reward procedure followed an initial baseline phase. After a return to baseline condition, students were assigned to a self-imposed cost condition. Under this condition, students evaluated their work and fined themselves a designated number of tokens for inaccurate responses. Under both self-management conditions, tokens were exchanged 2 hr after class for backup reinforcers consisting of edibles, toys, and special privileges. Data on the number of reading assignments attempted indicated that both self-reward and self-response cost procedures were effective when compared with the baseline procedures. The self-reward condition produced a slightly greater number of assignments attempted. Data on the accuracy of reading assignments indicated that students maintained approximately the same level of accuracy throughout all phases of the study. Disruptive behavior varied considerably during all of the experimental conditions, although there was a slight decrease during the two self-management phases. No attempt was made to determine the maintenance of treatment effects, and data were not provided on the accuracy of the students' self-assessments.

The accuracy of self-recording was examined by McLaughlin and Malaby (1974). This study employed three sixth-grade students who filled out a self-report on task completion. Despite the limited amount of time spent in training, the students demonstrated accurate recordings ranging from 94 to 100% reliability with an outside observer. The authors suggested that the use of a permanent product facilitated accurate self-reporting (McLaughlin, 1976). In addition to this factor, the categories on which the students scored themselves were quite clear and may have made self-recording easier than in other studies. The categories used by McLaughlin and Malaby (1974) were as follows: " 'assignment was complete,' 'assignment was incomplete,' 'no assignment was given,' or 'pupil was absent' [McLaughlin, 1976, p. 651]."

Accuracy in self-recording was facilitated through the use of cue cards in a study conducted by Glynn and Thomas (1974). A cueing system was developed in response to some confusion on the part of the students as to what constituted appropriate and inappropriate behaviors. In describing their study, the authors cited a common classroom phenomenon: The teacher provided a direction (e.g., "Stop what you are doing and look at me"), but failed to provide a subsequent direction to students that they were to return their attention to their individual assignments. Students were confused, therefore, as to whether on-task behavior consisted of continuing to look at the teacher or returning to one's work. This confusion about teacher behavior existed despite the fact that all the students were third graders and had at least 2½ years of previous experience with teachers! The cueing charts consisted of colored posters placed in front of the class. A red poster indicated one set of on-task behaviors (e.g., look at the teacher, remain in your seat, be quiet), whereas a green poster indicated a different set of behaviors (e.g., work on the assignment at your desk). Data presented on individual subjects indicated clearly that self-control procedures were most effective when combined with the cueing procedure.

The maintenance of treatment effects following the use of a self-management program was addressed in a study by Drabman, Spitalnik, and O'Leary (1973). The self-management procedure consisted of students rating themselves on the number of disruptive behaviors in which they engaged in an after-school reading program. Based upon their performance ratings the students earned points, which were exchanged at the end of the day for reinforcers. Students' ratings were compared with the teacher's ratings of their behavior. If the two ratings agreed within one point, students earned the number of points they had assigned to themselves. If the pupil–teacher evaluation was discrepant by more than 1 point, the pupil was fined all of his points for the rating period. Fading of the self-evaluation and teacher-evaluation procedures was accomplished through a random selection of students for the reliability check. During the first segment of the fading procedure, a coin was tossed to determine which of the two classroom groups would be checked for their accuracy. During the next fading segment, students' names were drawn from a pile, resulting in only two reliability checks per day. Subsequent fading procedures resulted in only one student check. The low rates of disruptive behavior maintained during a 12-day follow-up period. In a replication study conducted by Turkewitz, O'Leary, and Ironsmith (Note 1) the fading procedure proved useful in maintaining low levels of disruptive behavior in the absence of external or self-regulated intervention. Generalization to a brief period within the classroom was also noted, although no generalization of treatment effects was observed outside of the students' regular classroom.

SUMMARY

While results are inconclusive with respect to some aspects of self-management interventions (e.g., maintenance over time, generalization to other settings, requirement of teacher reinforcement as an accompanying intervention), the literature on these procedures is developing rapidly and offers promise to teachers who need an efficient way to help students to control their behaviors. Until definitive recommendations can be made, teachers are urged to consider carefully the target student(s), the availability of backup reinforcement and feedback, and the choice of target behaviors in designing self-management interventions. A procedure that involves varying levels of self-control, contingency contracting, is discussed in the next section.

Contingency Contracting

The term *contingency contract* was coined by Homme (1970) to describe a written explanation of contingencies to be used with a student by the teacher or parent. A contingency contract typically consists of (*a*) a written schedule of behaviors that are desired, accompanied by assigned point values; and (*b*) a schedule of designated activities, rewards, or privileges for which points can be exchanged (Cantrell, Cantrell, Huddleston, & Woolridge, 1969). Contingency contracting is described in this chapter, since it has applicability for the mainstreamed classroom setting. Contracting is useful whenever a teacher wishes to modify the behavior of one or a few students in a large classroom group. (These authors have also observed the use of contingency contracting for an entire classroom group, but it is generally recognized that such a procedure would require considerable preparation time on the part of the classroom teacher.) In the studies reviewed in this section contracts typically were used with problem students who were enrolled in regular classrooms.

White-Blackburn, Semb, and Semb (1977) examined the use of good behavior contracts with four sixth-grade students who were indentified as being off-task and disruptive, as well as having difficulties in completing their daily classroom assignments. The contract developed for these students not only included a list of rewards, but also included a list of penalties. These consequations were based upon existing school facilities and standard classroom privileges. At the end of the project, the experimental students' behavior compared favorably with the performance of model students. Cantrell and his colleagues (1969) also reported favorable results using contingency contracting with public school children in grades 1 through 11. This examination of the use of the contingency contracting procedure was a nonexperimental one, but did result in a number of excellent clinical guidelines. These procedures, which appear to be confirmed by subsequent experimental studies, included the following:

1. Initial screening was used to prevent contingency contracting from being used inappropriately. A specific focus of this initial screening was to

determine whether or not the student could actually perform what was expected of him or her.

2. Adults involved with the student were interviewed as a method of determining their ability to carry out the exigencies of a contract. Adults who appeared unable or unwilling to commit themselves to such a program were eliminated as change agents.

3. Change agents were informed that contracts would likely result in failure if they were not carried out reliably or if they were terminated midway.

4. Contracts were written in a manner that made the conditions, rewards, and measurement procedures clear to both parties.

As Jenkins and Gorrafa (1973) stated, contingency contracting is in fact a special case of what typically occurs in a token economy. In contingency contracting, there is a direct relationship between a certain response and its consequation, whereas in a token economy program, a symbol or token mediates this relationship. Jenkins and Gorrafa (1973) conducted a study in which both procedures were used simultaneously with 12 mildly retarded children. A multiple baseline design across reading and mathematics was employed to examine the relative efficacy of three conditions: no tokens, tokens, and tokens superimposed by a contingency contract. Despite some methodological problems, the results suggested a positive relationship between the use of the combined strategies and increased performance levels in the two curricular areas.

SUMMARY

Contingency contracting is an empirically validated treatment procedure for one or a few children in a classroom setting. The primary application of this procedure has been with students who are disruptive or are frequently off-task. Contingency contracting is closely related to other interventions such as home report cards and token reinforcement procedures.

Home-Based Reporting

If parents will participate in a home-based contract system, teachers gain a valuable resource in reducing disruptive behavior in the classroom. In a daily home report-card system, performance in school is specified for the student in a similar manner to that described for contingency contracting procedures. The primary difference between the two procedures is that reinforcement is provided at home by parents rather than in school. Home report cards vary from traditional report cards in two major ways: First, the home-based report card includes very specific goals for social or academic performance; second, a home-based report is usually sent on a more frequent basis than the traditional report card.

Schumaker, Hovell, and Sherman (1977) conducted an analysis of the effect of daily home report cards on the classroom performance of "problem adolescents." Three experiments were conducted. In the first two experiments, students were identified by school personnel as exhibiting problem classroom behaviors (e.g., truancy, tardiness, failure to complete assignments, interrupting others during classtime). Before initiating either experiment, the investigators interviewed the students' teachers and developed report cards that reflected the conduct rules in the students' classes. During the first experiment, an intial baseline phase provided teachers with the opportunity to monitor students' performance on the items listed on the report card. No discussion of the report cards was held. During the intervention phase of this experiment, parents were trained in a home visit how to praise students for improved performance at school and how to select and provide privileges based on school performance. Two kinds of privileges were developed: basic privileges (e.g., television watching, snacks, late bedtime) and special privileges (e.g., trips, movies, athletic events). Parents were also provided basic training in how to determine point–performance ratios and how to handle the exchange of points for privileges. To insure that parents could carry out the program, a contact was made with each family twice during the first week and once a week thereafter. Data on the number of rules followed in school and the percentage of classroom points earned during the home-report condition indicated that all three students responded well to the program. A survey of teacher satisfaction also indicated that teachers were more pleased with student performance during the report card intervention than during the baseline period. Semester grade point averages for each of the students increased during the treatment conditions.

The second experiment was conducted to determine the necessity of using home-based contingent privileges. The authors reported that the study was motivated by the reluctance of some parents to use reinforcers other than praise. The subjects in the second experiment were two seventh-grade boys whose parents participated voluntarily in the program. Procedures were identical to those described in the first experiment, with one exception. During the first intervention phase, school performance was reinforced with praise only. During the second intervention, the full treatment package (i.e., report card, praise, and privileges) was again used. The results indicated that although initial performance levels improved under the report card and praise-only condition, this improvement did not maintain over time. The report card system was most effective, therefore, when supported with home privileges. During the third experiment, school counselors replaced the experimenters in using the home report-card system. The purpose of this program manipulation was to evaluate whether or not the home report-card system could be used effectively by persons not specifically trained in behavior modification principles. Two eighth-grade students and their families participated in this project. The study indicated that the school counselors were highly successful in implementing the home report-card system, and that the effects of the system were equal to those in the previous two experiments.

In their discussion of the results, Schumaker *et al.* (1977) raised several issues of clinical application. First, they noted that during the final experiment the school counselor spent 1 hr a week on each student's program. Others who used the home report-card system, however, substituted short weekly phone calls for home visits. The authors also suggested the use of parent group meetings instead of individual consultation as a way to make the home report-card system more efficient. A second major consideration was fading out the program. The authors cited the use of a fading procedure in which students used a shortened version of the daily card, then shifted to twice-a-week reports, then weekly reports, and then no reports.

Other studies reported the effectiveness of using home-managed privileges with elementary school students. Todd, Scott, Bostow, and Alexander (1976) used home-based report cards for two elementary school students enrolled in regular classrooms. The daily report card procedure not only used home-based privileges, but also incorporated a response cost clause (i.e., 1-day suspension from school). Home report cards have been used with elementary school students to eliminate discipline problems in school (Ayllon, Barber, & Pisor, 1975), to move a student from school-based to home-based control of classroom behavior (Colman, 1973), and to increase academic performance (Karraker, 1972). Home-based reports might be particularly useful during the first months of the school year to improve an exceptional child's transition into a regular classroom.

SUMMARY

Home report cards, a modified form of contingency contracts, have demonstrated effectiveness in reducing disruptive behavior. Home reports are most effectively used with backup reinforcers provided by parents. This procedure is recommended for teachers who wish to manage the behavior of one or two students in a classroom. The next section describes token reinforcement procedures that are useful for total group management.

Token Reinforcement Systems

Token reinforcement procedures have claimed a permanent place in the special education literature but may be novel to teachers trained in regular education.

Walker and Buckley (1974) outlined the basic components of a token reinforcement system as follows:

1. Tokens which can be easily and quickly given.
2. Backup reinforcers suited to the preferences of the individuals in the program.
3. Rules specifying which behaviors earn how many tokens.
4. Rules specifying how tokens can be spent.
5. Procedures for initiating the program (e.g., making the tokens valuable through pairing with backups; sampling the reinforcers).
6. Procedures for shifting the rules for reinforcement as an improvement occurs to foster maintenance of gains.
7. Procedures for getting off the token system while keeping the gains [pp. 6–7].

Token economy programs have been used in a variety of school and clinical settings including special education classrooms (Broden, Hall, Dunlap, & Clark, 1970); regular classrooms (McLaughlin & Malaby, 1972); the school cafeteria (Muller, Hasazi, Pierce, & Hasazi, 1975) and the school bus (Chiang, Iwata, & Dorsey, 1979). In each published study, token reinforcement programs have proven more effective than baseline procedures (O'Leary & Drabman, 1971).

For token systems to be adopted successfully in regular educational settings they must display the characteristics cited by McLaughlin (1975): (*a*) effectiveness; (*b*) ease of implementation; (*c*) cost effectiveness; (*d*) acceptance by community at large and by pupil consumers. These variables will be highlighted in this review of selected studies on token systems.

McLaughlin and his colleagues reported a series of studies on the use of token reinforcement programs in classrooms. In a study on intrinsic reinforcers in a token economy program, McLaughlin and Malaby (1972) attempted to develop an inexpensive and easily implemented token program for a regular fifth- and sixth-grade classroom. The token program was applied to the entire class of 29 students and was managed by one teacher. This study is particularly important to the present review, as it represents one of the first attempts to apply token reinforcement procedures under typical public school conditions. The purpose of the token economy in this study was to increase assignment completion in spelling, handwriting, language, and math classes. Points could also be earned for appropriate behaviors such as bringing supplies for the classroom pets, writing neatly, taking assignments home, or being quiet during transition periods. A response cost condition provided loss of points for behaviors such as failure to complete assignments and fighting. Points were exchanged for privileges available within the school, including playing with classroom pets, writing on a special blackboard, participating in a game, seeing the grade book, and being on a class committee. Students individually met with the teacher to receive points, which they recorded by themselves on a point sheet. Points were exchanged for activities once a week. One student was assigned the role of banker and he or she managed the bookkeeping for this exchange process. The authors reported that the use of students to maintain the token economy program limited the amount of time spent on the program by the teacher to approximately 25 min per week. The experimental conditions employed to evaluate the effectiveness of these token economy procedures consisted of the following:

Baseline. During the baseline condition the point system was not in effect. Traditional behavior management procedures (e.g., staying after school and teacher reprimands) were used during this condition.

Token I. The token economy procedures were introduced, with a weekly exchange scheduled. These procedures were in effect for 75 days.

Token II. This condition was identical to the Token I condition with the exception that exchanges of points for privileges were scheduled on a variable basis. The mean number of days between exchanges was 4.25.

Quiet behavior. Assignment completion, the primary target behavior, was removed from the list of behaviors that earned points. A new behavior, "quiet behavior," was substituted in its place. The exchange procedure was held on a variable schedule as before. Following this condition, the Token II procedures were again in effect.

Both token procedures were effective in reducing the level of variability in assignment completion by students. The Token II condition was more effective in this regard than the Token I procedure. When the quiet behavior condition was introduced, variability in assignment completion was noted again. The reintroduction of the Token II procedures reduced variability and produced high rates of task completion across all four curricular areas. The majority of students in the class reported favorable reactions to the token program.

In another attempt to develop a token economy program that would be workable in the typical regular classroom, Gallant, Sargeant, and Van Houten (1980) used a preferred curriculum activity as the backup reinforcer for task completion in other areas. The study took place in a regular sixth-grade classroom in which the target student, an 11-year-old gifted child, was enrolled. The student was referred to the study on the basis that he rarely completed daily work assignments, despite his great intellectual ability. A small study area, closed off from the rest of the classroom, housed the science activities, which served as backup reinforcers. In order to gain access to these activities, the student was required to complete a daily assignment within the allotted time and to meet a 95% accuracy criterion. During the final treatment phase of this study, the student was told that he was to determine for himself when he had completed assignments correctly and was therefore eligible to work in the science area. No contingencies were placed on the student's performance during this phase. Follow-up data were recorded for 3 weeks following the final self-determined intervention phase. The introduction of the science contingency raised assignment completion levels to 100% for both reading and math, with the exception of 1 day. Perfect assignment completion was also observed during the self-determined condition and throughout the 3-week follow-up period. Data on the accuracy of assignments were also impressive: Scores on reading during the science contingency condition ranged from 94 to 100%, while assignments in math received scores of 80–100%. This treatment effect also was observed during the self-determination condition and during the postcheck period. In order to spend time in the science area, the target student had to complete his work within the time set aside for the reading or math period. Data on actual time spent in the science area indicated that the student earned about 15 min per day. Taken collectively, these data meet the requirement of effectiveness set forth by McLaughlin (1975) in his discussion of token programs. In regard to the three additional characteristics of a good token economy program (McLaughlin, 1975), the study also received high marks. The classroom teacher involved in the study was easily able to manage and implement the contingency set forth. In fact, the program was simplified to such an extent that it did not require the use of a formal contract or a systematic token exchange system. (To replicate this procedure with more than one student in a regular classroom or with students who are less gifted, a teacher might want to use either a contingency contract procedure or a formal token economy program.) The criterion of cost effectiveness was met, since the materials necessary for this program were available through the science budget within the school. Finally, the use of academic activities as a backup reinforcer is an alternative that appeals to the general community as well as to students who are highly motivated to pursue a particular area of the academic or nonacademic (e.g., music, art, or vocational) program. A final recommendation for this type of program is based upon data collected on the number of assignments completed in nontargeted curricular areas. Before the science contingency was in effect, the targeted student's work completion level averaged 58% in spelling and language. When the science contingency was introduced, this level increased to 93%, suggesting that the effects of this program generalized to nontargeted curricular areas.

The studies by McLaughlin and Malaby (1972) and by Gallant *et al.* (1980) point to critical issues in the implementation of token economy procedures. It is important that teachers identify specific behaviors for reinforcement, if these are the behaviors that they wish to change. In the studies cited previously, task completion was addressed specifically by the reinforcement contingencies, and subsequent improvement was noted for the completion of assignments. In a study conducted by Ferritor, Buckholdt, Hamblin, and Smith (1972), however, the provision of reinforcement for "attending behavior" did not have an effect on arithmetic performance of 14 third graders in an inner-city school. Tokens were provided by the teacher as she rotated throughout the classroom.

If a student was attending (e.g., looking at work, writing, addressing a question to the teacher), the student received a token. Tokens were exchanged approximately once a week for a choice of backup reinforcers. Although this reinforcement condition consistently decreased the number of disruptions in the classroom and increased the level of attending behavior, it did not have an effect on the number of problems correctly worked. Only when contingencies were placed both on attending behavior and on accuracy of work did the number of correct answers increase. It is interesting to note that when tokens were contingent upon accurate performance, the level of disruptions increased and attending behavior dropped slightly. (It is important that the reader understand, however, that the baseline level of attending behavior was 80%, a figure that some regular classroom teachers would deem high.) A second experiment in this study confirmed the results of the first experiment. This study, like a few others (e.g., Haubrich & Shores, 1978), raises questions about the importance of attention to task to academic performance, a relationship that is held nearly sacred by many educators.

All token systems do not succeed. Kuypers, Becker, and O'Leary (1968) reported a study entitled, "How to make a token system fail." (In fact, the token system did have a marginal positive effect on reducing the level of deviant behavior for 12 third- and fourth-grade students.) The author cited that one of the principal drawbacks in the implementation of the token economy program was the failure to train the teacher in the systematic application of differential social reinforcement. Thus, the authors underscored the importance of thoroughly preparing teachers to implement a token system.

SUMMARY

Research on token reinforcement systems constitutes a major portion of the applied behavior analysis literature on classroom management. Without a doubt, token systems are effective in reducing disruptive behavior and, if implemented correctly, can produce marked gains in academic performance. It is possible to develop token systems that meet the criteria of effectiveness, cost efficiency, acceptability, and ease of implementation, making them an appealing behavior management procedure for adoption in mainstreamed settings. The successful implementation of token economy programs requires adequate teacher training, however. Teacher preparation is described in the following section.

Teacher Training: Consultation Programs

In nearly every published study of behavior management procedures, there is a brief section outlining the ways in which the experimenters trained the classroom teachers to carry out reliably the procedures in question. In some studies, this teacher training intervention was minimal; in others, a series of seminars and consultation visits were provided. The purpose of this section is to review consultation efforts that have focused specifically on training teachers in behavior management skills. Consultation programs and procedures highlighted in this section were chosen for their innovative approaches to solving the problems faced by teachers in mainstreaming classrooms.

A study conducted by Cossairt, Hall, and Hopkins (1973) analyzed the important teacher behavior, contingent attention. Training was provided to three elementary school teachers in their classrooms. The teachers volunteered for the study because they were having difficulty managing disruptive classroom behavior. The in-class training was examined as an alternative to formalized behavior modification seminars, which many teachers are unable to attend. An initial baseline condition conducted in each classroom permitted the experimenters to ascertain the level of teacher attention to students, the level of student attention to teachers, and the appropriateness of this interaction. The first treatment condition consisted of a three-part instruction. First, teachers were taught the importance of providing attention to students on a contingent basis; second, teachers were requested to praise students who listened to instructions; and finally, teachers were left with a written reminder: "Teacher praise for attending instructions sometimes increases instruction-attending behavior [p. 92]." This message was written on the mathematics instruction sheet that each teacher read at the beginning of the class session. During the feedback condition two teachers were provided verbal feedback at the end of each lesson. The experimenter relayed to the teacher the number of intervals during which her praise to students was appropriate. During the next treatment condition, teachers received feedback as well as praise from the experimenters for responding appropriately to students' behavior. The order of intervention conditions was altered slightly for the three teachers. The results of baseline observations confirmed findings of other researchers regarding natural rates of teacher approval and disapproval (White, 1975). None of the three teachers emitted any praise statements for appropriate student attending behaviors during baseline conditions. Data from the instructions condition revealed no behavior change. In describing these results the author stated, "What occurred in the instructions condition of this experiment may be what happens when teachers receive instructions from principals and consultants who are attempting to change teacher behavior with infrequent visits to the classroom [p. 99]." Inconclusive results were obtained during the feedback condition. Results of the feedback-plus-social-praise intervention emphasized the importance of social praise in changing the behavior of teachers. Significant increases in appropriate teacher praise were noted for all three teachers when they began receiving social praise from the experimenter. As expected, the level of students' attending behaviors increased concomitantly with the level of appropriate praise the students received from their teachers. This result indicates the effectiveness of what might be considered a minimal level of teacher training.

Consultation was limited by uncontrollable circumstances in a study reported by Bornstein, Hamilton, and Quevillon (1977). In this study, the consultant was charged with assisting a teacher in a rural community whose only contact with the consultant was through telephone calls and correspondence. The subject of this consultation was a 9-year-old student in a regular classroom whose out-of-seat behavior triggered a series of noncompliant and aggressive behaviors toward other students. Moreover, the student's relationships with other children and academic standing in his class were declining. Through telephone calls and correspondence, the teacher was successfully trained to carry out a positive practice procedure with the target student. Data collected at a 6-month follow-up check indicated that the treatment gains maintained over time. In describing this long-distance form of consultation, the authors cited issues to be considered before engaging in such a format. First, is the target behavior being accurately reported? Second, have safeguards been taken to avoid "impropriety and the impersonalization of services [p. 378]?"

A combination of in-classroom consultation and observation with formal coursework was the procedure employed by Jones and his colleagues in a series of studies on training teachers in classroom management skills (Burka & Jones, 1979; Jones & Eimers, 1975; Jones, Fremouw, & Carples, 1977). In the first of these studies, two third-grade teachers were trained through role playing to use a social skills intervention procedure designed to reduce disruptive student behavior. Total time spent in training was 9 hr, divided into six class sessions. In addition, the experimenter observed each teacher at least once a week to determine whether or not the teachers were implementing reliably the procedures taught in that week's class. Feedback was not provided to teachers during these weekly visits but was incorporated into class discussions during the next meeting. The primary activity of the class meetings was role playing designed to provide teachers with an opportunity to practice group behavior management skills and to receive feedback on their performance. Teachers took turns assuming the roles of disruptive and nondisruptive students, as well as the role of a teacher. (For a specific discussion of the topics addressed during these sessions, the reader is referred to Jones and Eimers, 1975, pp. 425–427). Data on student performance indicated that the teacher training procedure was effective in enabling teachers to reduce disruptive behavior and to increase the arithmetic performance of their students. In a subsequent study, Jones and his colleagues (Jones *et al.*, 1977) trained three teachers, who in turn each trained three additional teachers in the skill package described by Jones and Eimers (1975). The latter study promotes a cost-effective procedure for teachers to assist their colleagues without the additional expense of outside consultants.

Like the model developed by Jones and his colleagues (1977), a combination of class meetings with site visits formed the consultation procedure reported by Greenwood, Hops, Walker, Guild, Stokes, Young, Keleman, and Willardson (1979). The latter authors reported the use of a standardized behavior management program that was validated in two sites. Consultation was based on a standardized behavior intervention package entitled Program for Academic Survival Skills (PASS). The PASS program is one of a series of exemplary behavior management and instructional packages that was developed at the Center at Oregon for Research in Behavioral Education of the Handicapped. A companion volume produced at this center, Contingencies for Learning Academic and Social Skills (CLASS), focused on the management of acting-out students in regular classrooms (Hops, Beicke, & Walker, 1974).

The PASS program was validated in two school systems, one in Utah and one in Oregon. Twenty-five consultants and 50 regular classroom teachers participated in the study. Approximately 1144 students in grades 1–3 were represented in this study. Roughly one-half of the classrooms were designated as control classrooms, while the others were selected to participate in the experimental procedures. Twelve students in each classroom were targeted for observation; this included one mainstreamed student in each classroom. Observations were conducted during reading and/or mathematics classes. A covariance repeated-measures design was used to evaluate the effects of the PASS consultation program in the two sites. Analyses were conducted on direct observational data collected prior to teacher training, during the consultation program, and at the end of the school year. In addition, achievement tests and behavior ratings were administered at the beginning of the school year and at the end of the year. The consumer satisfaction with the program was evaluated through four questionnaires: a student evaluation of the program, a teacher evaluation of the program, a consultant evaluation, and a follow-up questionaire sent to consultants and teachers during the next academic year.

Training of the consultants for this program took place during a 2-day workshop conducted by two of the authors. During this workshop, the consultants reviewed material in the PASS Consultation Manual, listened to lectures on the material, and took turns role playing specific behavior management procedures. Additional training of these consultants during the year was limited to supervision they received by on-site project coordinators. Each consultant was responsible for training one regular classroom teacher in six sessions and in follow-up visits to the teacher's classroom. The meetings were designed to impart specific skills to the elementary school teachers (e.g., use of the clock light, behavioral observation skills, group reinforcement procedures, and systematic use of teacher approval). The purpose of the classroom site visits was to assure that the teachers were implementing the material learned in the previous class session and to provide the teachers with feedback and praise. An analysis of the data collected during the study indicated that the consultants were successful in training the teachers to use the specific behavior management skills. Teachers in both sites increased their use of approval as compared to the control groups. Students of the experimental teachers also demonstrated consistently improved performance. Data collected on the experimental group during the program and at a posttest indicated that students were engaging in appropriate behavior approximately 80% of the time. Finally, all program participants indicated satisfaction with the program. Results of the follow-up survey of teachers and consultants indicated that the program was still in use 1 year later. Unlike many consultation programs, the PASS project had a clearly delineated set of skills for both the consultant and the classroom teacher, as reflected in the two program manuals. (A third manual outlines in detail the procedures to be followed by classroom observers.)

A regular kindergarten teacher enrolling an autistic child received didactic and consultative training in a study reported by Russo and Koegel (1977). The purpose of this study was to examine the feasibility of integrating an autistic youngster into a regular kindergarten classroom with normal children. The first phase of this integration process was conducted by a behavior therapist who worked with the child during three 1-hr training sessions for the purpose of establishing tokens as reinforcers. These sessions took place after school during the first baseline condition. Following these sessions, held outside of the class-room, the therapist moved into the classroom with the student and continued the pairing of tokens with appropriate verbal feedback. Approximately 2 hr per week for 6 weeks were spent in this training. During the final phase of this training, the therapist targeted two additional behaviors, self-stimulation and responding to commands, for modification. Two weeks were spent in training the kindergarten teacher to manage the student's behavior following the pro-cedures previously developed by the therapist. Throughout this 2-week period, the teacher received didactic information on behavioral techniques during three 1-hr after-school sessions. Following this training, the teacher was totally re-sponsible for the student's school program. Supervision of the teacher then consisted of telephone or personal discussions of specific problems. The therapist visited the classroom at least once a week to provide feedback to the teacher. Data collected throughout the study indicated that the kindergarten teacher was successful in increasing the number of social behaviors, reducing the level of self-stimulation, and increasing the level of appropriate responding to instruc-tions by the autistic youngster. At the end of the school year, the student was recommended for a regular first-grade placement.

The second experiment in this study evaluated the training of the first-grade teacher by the therapist. Again, the teacher was capable of modifying the three targeted behaviors. In describing the results of the two experiments, the authors stated:

> Autistic children have previously been excluded from public-school programs, or in some
> cases are given only the option of a "special" autism class. The significance of this study

> lies in its suggestion that school teachers can easily learn to teach at least some autistic children in regular classrooms. Although much research is still necessary, we expect that a fairly large number of autistic children may be able to benefit from the treatment described here [Russo & Koegel, 1977, pp. 588–589].

The authors also described four additional cases in which similar teacher training procedures were used to integrate an autistic youngster into a regular kindergarten or elementary school class.

The maintenance of exceptional children in regular educational settings was also the goal of a consultation program, the Prevention–Intervention Project (PIP), described by Cantrell and Cantrell (1976). This consultation project "was designed to solve children's problems prior to referral for formalized services which would demand labeling and possibly exclusion from the opportunities normally available to non-problem children [p. 381]." Support to regular public school teachers was provided by consultants who were trained during a 6-week intensive summer program. In the 1976 report on the PIP program, data were presented on pupils of first-grade teachers who received assistance from the PIP consultants. Pre- and posttest achievement scores for this group of students indicated greater gains than did the scores for a comparable control group. Data on the total number of referrals of students for psychological services during the following year indicated that the experimental group teachers referred significantly fewer students than did the control group teachers. This suggests that the work of the consulting teacher may have prevented some students from needing further services and subsequently from being identified as "problems." Gains in achievement of students whose teachers were receiving support services were also reported by Knight (1978) in a report on the Vermont Consulting Teacher model. This program, like the PIP program, was designed to assist regular classroom teachers with students without regard for categorical labels. Assistance to elementary school students on a noncategorical basis has also been reported by Nelson and his colleagues (Marotz-Sprague & Nelson, 1979; Nelson & Stevens, in press). A team of five consultants provided support services to the staff of a regular elementary school over a 2-year period. Records on the amount of consultation time provided to the school staff indicated that 237.9 hr were provided during the first year of the study, while 266.5 hr were provided during the second year. The majority of this consultation focused on the development of intervention programs for individual children referred informally by their teachers. Documentation on each referral consisted of a written program plan to be implemented by the teacher, a log entry of the amount and type of service provided for the case, and an evaluation as to the success or failure of the intervention program. The latter evaluation was based upon three types of information: the child's mastery or nonmastery of the terminal objectives stated in the program plan, an analysis of the data collected for each case, and the teacher's evaluation of the program's success. Data on 53 cases suggested that the majority of the cases could be classified as treatment successes. While the majority of these cases dealt with an individual child of concern, six cases involved an entire class. This study provided valuable information on the types of referrals that one is likely to receive as a consultant to regular teachers. The further accumulation of time log data by consultants would assist administrators in making decisions about the number of consulting personnel necessary to maintain exceptional students in regular classrooms. It would appear that many cases can be managed with a minimal amount of consultation time (Marotz-Sprague & Nelson, 1979).

SUMMARY

Even a brief review of some of the consultation programs available to regular classroom teachers reveals the diversity with which experimenters have addressed the issue of providing assistance to teachers. In some programs, teachers enrolled in a regular course on behavior management principles, while in others, no formal training was involved. Some authors reported pupil data on pre- and posttest measures alone, whereas others conducted meticulous direct observations of both pupil and teacher performance. Still others focused their evaluation efforts on the specific behaviors of consultants (see Deno & Mirkin, 1977). In summarizing the state of the art in school consultation, Meyers, Martin, and Hyman (1977) stated:

> Perhaps the greatest single weakness which is found in the literature is an inadequate description of procedures for changing the consultee's behavior. . . . While many articles discuss techniques which teachers can be encouraged to implement, there is virtually no detailed discussion of the techniques and process variables which help the consultant influence the teacher so that he is willing to implement suggested changes. Future work in practice, training, and research regarding consultation will have to attend to this problem and specific consultation procedures will have to be delineated more clearly.

> Finally, the current state of the consultation literature indicates generally inadequate research for . . . approaches to consultation. If school consultation is to become a viable area for practitioners, and if the related skills are expected to have an opportunity to develop and improve, then research and evaluation is essential. It is encumbent upon practitioners, trainers, and researchers in the field of consultation to contribute to an increase in the sophistication and quality of consultation research in the future [pp. 11–12].

Concluding Remarks

As indicated in the preface, one of the issues raised by leading professionals in special education regarding critical issues in mainstreaming was the concern that teachers would not have the skills necessary to manage disruptive classroom behaviors. Indeed, a major emphasis in the applied behavior analysis literature on classroom behaviors has been the reduction of so-called disruptive behaviors. In a classic review of behavior modification studies in classroom settings, Winett and Winkler (1972) expressed their concern that too much emphasis was placed in the research literature on reducing inappropriate behaviors and creating "quiet, docile, and obedient 'young adults' [p. 500]." The issue of target behavior selection must be explored sensitively, not only by researchers, but by mainstream teachers and their consultants. Standards for social behavior functioning may require significant alteration if exceptional children are to be integrated with their nonhandicapped classmates.

While many applied behavior analysis studies have been conducted in regular classrooms, further studies must take place in classrooms that qualify as "mainstream educational settings." These settings not only include so-called regular classrooms, but other settings within the school environment in which handicapped children are integrated with normal or less severely handicapped peers. Few studies have examined children's social behavior in other than classroom settings (e.g., playground, cafeteria, physical education program). Studies that take place in nontraditional educational settings (e.g., resource room, parent-implemented educational program, residential program) are indeed rare.

Finally, a more concerted effort must be made in examining truly exceptional students who are enrolled in classrooms with normal students. Few researchers have addressed the special problems raised when severely handicapped students or highly talented students are integrated with students whose performance falls within the normal range. The studies by Russo and Koegel (1977) and by Gallant *et al.* (1980), are exceptions to traditional research practice.

In conclusion, the technology documented in the applied behavior analysis literature on the modification of children's classroom behaviors is impressive. While most of these studies were conducted prior to the advent of formal mainstreaming arrangements, they nevertheless offer practitioners a set of invaluable skills for managing children in large instructional groups.

Reference Note

1. Turkewitz, H., O'Leary, K. D., & Ironsmith, M. *Producing generalization and maintenance of appropriate behavior through self-control.* Unpublished manuscript, State University of New York at Stony Brook, 1974.

References

Ayllon, T., Barber, S., & Pisor, K. The elimination of discipline problems through a combined school–home motivational system. *Behavior Therapy*, 1975, 6, 616–626.
Barrish, H. H., Saunders, M., & Wolf, M. M. Good behavior game: Effects of individual

contingencies for group consequences on disruptive behavior in a classroom. *Journal of Applied Behavior Analysis*, 1969, 2, 119–124.

Bolstad, O. D., & Johnson, S. M. Self-regulation in the modification of disruptive behavior. *Journal of Applied Behavior Analysis*, 1972,5, 443–454.

Bornstein, P. H., Hamilton, S. B., & Quevillon, R. P. Behavior modification by long distance: Demonstration of functional control over disruptive behavior in a rural classroom setting. *Behavior Modification*, 1977, 1, 369–380.

Broden, M., Hall, R. B., Dunlap, A., & Clark, R. Effects of teacher attention and a token reinforcement system in a junior high special education class. *Exceptional Children*, 1970, 36, 341–349.

Broden, M., Hall, R. V., & Mitts, B. The effect of self-recording on the classroom behavior of two eighth-grade students. *Journal of Applied Behavior Analysis*, 1971, 4, 191–199.

Burka, A. A., & Jones, F. H. Procedures for increasing appropriate verbal participation in special elementary classrooms. *Behavior Modification*, 1979, 3, 27–48.

Cantrell, R. P., Cantrell, M. L., Huddleston, C. M., & Woolridge, R. L. Contingency contracting with school problems. *Journal of Applied Behavior Analysis*, 1969, 2, 215–220.

Cantrell, R. P., & Cantrell, M. L. Preventive mainstreaming: Impact of a supportive services program on pupils. *Exceptional Children*, 1976, 42, 381–386.

Chiang, S. J., Iwata, B. A., & Dorsey, M. F. Elimination of disruptive bus riding behavior via token reinforcement on a "distance-based" schedule. *Education and Treatment of Children*, 1979, 2, 101–109.

Colman, R. G. A procedure for fading from experimenter–school-based to parent–home-based control of classroom behavior. *Journal of School Psychology*, 1973, 11, 71–79.

Cossairt, A., Hall, R. V., & Hopkins, B. L. The effects of experimenter's instructions, feedback, and praise on teacher praise and student attending behavior. *Journal of Applied Behavior Analysis*, 1973, 6, 89–100.

Deno, S. L., & Mirkin, P. K. *Data-based program modification: A manual*. Reston, Va.: Council for Exceptional Children, 1977.

Drabman, R. S., & Lahey, B. B. Feedback in classroom behavior modification: Effects on the target and her classmates. *Journal of Applied Behavior Analysis*, 1974, 7, 591–598.

Drabman, R. S., Spitalnik, R., & O'Leary, K. D. Teaching self-control to disruptive children. *Journal of Abnormal Psychology*, 1973, 82, 10–16.

Ferritor, D. E., Buckholdt, D., Hamblin, R. L., & Smith, L. The noneffects of contingent reinforcement for attending behavior on work accomplished. *Journal of Applied Behavior Analysis*, 1972, 5, 7–17.

Foxx, R. M., & Shapiro, S. T. The time out ribbon: A non-exclusionary time out procedure. *Journal of Applied Behavior Analysis*, 1978, 11, 125–136.

Gallant, J., Sargeant, M., & Van Houten, R. Teacher determined and self-determined access to science activities as a reinforcer for task completion in other curriculum areas. *Education and Treatment of Children*, 1980, 3, 101–111.

Gast, D. L., & Nelson, C. M. Time out in the classroom: Implications for special education. *Exceptional Children*, 1977, 44, 461–464.

Glynn, E. L., & Thomas, J. D. Effects of cueing on self-control of classroom behavior. *Journal of Applied Behavior Analysis*, 1974, 7, 299–306.

Glynn, E. L., Thomas, J. D., & Shee, S. N. Behavioral self-control of on-task behavior in an elementary classroom. *Journal of Applied Behavior Analysis*, 1973, 6, 105–113.

Greenwood, C. R., Hops, H., Delquadri, J., & Guild, J. J. Group contingencies for group consequences in classroom management: A further analysis. *Journal of Applied Behavior Analysis*, 1974, 7, 413–425.

Greenwood, C. R., Hops, H., Walker, H. M., Guild, J. J., Stokes, J., Young, K. R., Keleman,

K. S., & Willardson, M. Standardized classroom management programs: Social validation and replication studies in Utah and Oregon. *Journal of Applied Behavior Analysis*, 1979, *12*, 235–253.

Hanley, E. M. Review of research involving applied behavior analysis in the classroom. *Review of Educational Research*, 1970, *40*, 597–625.

Harris, V. W., & Sherman, J. A. Use and analysis of the "good behavior game" to reduce disruptive classroom behavior. *Journal of Applied Behavior Analysis*, 1973, *6*, 405–417.

Homme, L. How to use contingency contracting in the classroom. Champaign, Ill.: Research Press, 1970.

Hops, H., Beicke, S., & Walker, H. M. *Contingencies for Learning Academic and Social Skills (CLASS): Manual for consultants*. Eugene, Ore.: Center at Oregon for Research in the Behavioral Education of the Handicapped, University of Oregon, 1974.

Humphrey, L. L., Karoly, P., & Kirschenbaum, D. S. Self-management in the classroom: Self-imposed response cost versus self-reward. *Behavior Therapy*, 1978, *9*, 592–601.

Jenkins, J. R., & Gorrafa, S. Superimposing contracts upon a token economy. In G. Semb (Ed.), *Behavior analysis and education—1973*. Lawrence: University of Kansas Support and Development Center for Follow-Through, Department of Human Development, 1973.

Johnson, S. M. Self-reinforcement versus external reinforcement in behavior modification with children. *Developmental Psychology*, 1970, *3*, 147–148.

Jones, F. H., & Eimers, R. C. Role playing to train elementary teachers to use a classroom management "skill package." *Journal of Applied Behavior Analysis*, 1975, *8*, 421–433.

Jones, F. H., Fremouw, W., & Carples, S. Pyramid training of elementary school teachers to use a classroom management "skill package." *Journal of Applied Behavior Analysis*, 1977, *10*, 239–253.

Kanfer, F., & Duerfeldt, P. H. Effects on retention of externally or self-reinforced rehearsal trials following acquisition. *Psychological Reports*, 1967, *21*, 194–196.

Karraker, R. J. Increasing academic performance through home managed contingency program. *Journal of School Psychology*, 1972, *10*, 173–179.

Kazdin, A. E. Acceptability of time out from reinforcement procedures for disruptive child behavior. *Behavior Therapy*, 1980, *11*, 329–344.

Kazdin, A. E., & Bootzin, R. R. The token economy: An evaluative review. *Journal of Applied Behavior Analysis*, 1972, *5*, 343–372.

Kerr, M. M., & Ragland, E. U. Pow Wow: A group procedure for reducing classroom behavior problems. *The Pointer*, 1979, *24*, 92–96.

Kerr, M. M., Strain, P. S., & Ragland, E. U. Component analysis of a teacher-mediated peer feedback treatment package: Effects on positive and negative interactions of behaviorally handicapped children. *Behavior Modification*, in press.

Knight, M. F. Vermont's consulting teacher model of inservice training of educational personnel. In C. M. Nelson (Ed.), *Field-based teacher training: Applications in special education*. Minneapolis: University of Minnesota, 1978.

Kuypers, D. S., Becker, W. C., & O'Leary, K. D. How to make a token system fail. *Exceptional Children*, 1968, *35*, 101–109.

Lovitt, T. C., & Curtiss, K. A. Academic response rate as a function of teacher and self-imposed contingencies. *Journal of Applied Behavior Analysis*, 1969, *2*, 49–54.

Madsen, C. H., Becker, W. C., & Thomas, D. R. Rules, praise, and ignoring: Elements of elementary classroom control. *Journal of Applied Behavior Analysis*, 1968, *1*, 139–150.

Madsen, C. H., Becker, W. C., Thomas, D. R., Koser, L., & Plager, E. An analysis of the reinforcing function of sit-down commands. In R. K. Parker (Ed.), *Readings in educational psychology*. Boston: Allyn & Bacon, 1968.

Marotz-Sprague, B., & Nelson, C. M. The inservice consultant: A role for teacher trainers working with behavior disorders in the schools. *Monograph in Behavioral Disorders*, 1979, *2*, 24–37.

McLaughlin, T. F. The applicability of token reinforcement systems in public school systems. *Psychology in the Schools*, 1975, *12*, 85–89.

McLaughlin, T. F. Self-control in the classroom. *Review of Educational Research*, 1976, *46*, 631–663.

McLaughlin, T. F., & Malaby, J. E. Intrinsic reinforcers in a classroom token economy. *Journal of Applied Behavior Analysis*, 1972, *5*, 263–270.

McLaughlin, T. F., & Malaby, J. E. Increasing and maintaining assignment completion with teacher and pupil controlled individual contingency programs: Three case studies. *Psychology*, 1974, *11*, 45–51.

Medland, M. B., & Stachnik, T. J. Good-behavior game: A replication and systematic analysis. *Journal of Applied Behavior Analysis*, 1972, *5*, 45–51.

Meyers, J., Martin, R., & Hyman, I. *School consultation*. Springfield, Ill.: Charles C. Thomas, 1977.

Muller, A. J., Hasazi, S. E., Pierce, M. M., & Hasazi, J. E. Modification of disruptive behavior in a large group of elementary school students. In E. Ramp & G. Semb (Eds.), *Behavior analysis: Areas of research and application*. Englewood Cliffs, N.J.: Prentice-Hall, 1975.

Nelson, C. M., & Stevens, K. B. An accountable consultation model for mainstreaming behaviorally disordered children. *Behavior Disorders*, in press.

O'Leary, K. D., Becker, W. C., Evans, M. B., & Saudargas, R. A. A token reinforcement program in a public school: A replication and systematic analysis. *Journal of Applied Behavior Analysis*, 1969, *2*, 3–13.

O'Leary, K. D., Kaufman, K. F., Kass, R. E., & Drabman, R. S. The effects of loud and soft reprimands on the behavior of disruptive students. *Exceptional Children*, 1970, *37*, 145–55.

Patterson, G. R., & White, G. P. It's a small world: The application of "time out from positive reinforcement." OPA (Oregon Psychological Association) Newsletter, February, 1969.

Porterfield, J. K., Herbert-Jackson, E., & Risley, T. R. Contingent observation: An effective and acceptable procedure for reducing disruptive behavior of young children in a group setting. *Journal of Applied Behavior Analysis*, 1976, *9*, 55–64.

Russo, D. C., & Koegel, R. L. A method for integrating an autistic child into a normal public-school classroom. *Journal of Applied Behavior Analysis*, 1977, *10*, 579–590.

Santogrossi, D. A., O'Leary, K. D., Romanczyk, R. G., & Kaufman, K. F. Self-evaluation by adolescents in a psychiatric hospital school token program. *Journal of Applied Behavior Analysis*, 1973, *6*, 277–287.

Schumaker, J. B., Hovell, M. F., & Sherman, J. A. An analysis of daily report card and parent-managed privileges in the improvement of adolescents' classroom performance. *Journal of Applied Behavior Analysis*, 1977, *10*, 449–464.

Strain, P. S., & Kerr, M. M. Modifying children's social withdrawal: Issues in assessment and clinical intervention. In M. Hersen, R. M. Eisler, & P. M. Miller (Eds.), *Progress in behavior modification*. New York: Academic Press, 1981.

Thomas, J. D., Presland, I. E., Grant, M. D., & Glynn, T. L. Natural rates of teacher approval and disapproval in grade-seven classrooms. *Journal of Applied Behavior Analysis*, 1978, *11*, 91–94.

Todd, D. D., Scott, R. B., Bostow, D. E., & Alexander, S. B. Modifications of the excessive inappropriate classroom behavior of two elementary school students using home-based consequences and daily report-card procedures. *Journal of Applied Behavior Analysis*, 1976, *9*, 106.

Walker, H. M. The acting-out child: *Coping with classroom disruption*. Boston: Allyn & Bacon, 1979.

Walker, H. M., & Buckley, N. J. *Token reinforcement techniques*. Eugene, Ore.: E-B Press, 1974.

Wasik, B. H., Senn, K., Welch, R. H., & Cooper, B. R. Behavior modification with culturally deprived school children: Two case studies. *Journal of Applied Behavior Analysis*, 1969, *2*, 181–194.

White, M. A. Natural rates of teacher approval and disapproval in the classroom. *Journal of Applied Behavior Analysis*, 1975, 8, 367–372.

White-Blackburn, G., Semb, S., & Semb, G. The effects of a good-behavior contract on the classroom behaviors of sixth-grade students. *Journal of Applied Behavior Analysis*, 1977, 10, 312.

Wilson, C. C., Robertson, S. J., Herlong, L. H., & Haynes, S. N. Vicarious effects of time out in the modification of aggression in the classroom. *Behavior Modification*, 1979, 3, 97–111.

Winett, R. A., & Winkler, R. C. Current behavior modification in the classroom. *Journal of Applied Behavior Analysis*, 1972, 5, 499–504.

Worell, J., & Nelson, C.M. *Managing instructional problems: A case study workbook.* New York: McGraw-Hill, 1974.

Academic Instruction of Children in Mainstream Classes

6

Introduction

This chapter represents a view of applied behavior analysis research in five major curriculum areas: arithmetic, reading, spelling, handwriting, and creative writing. Particular emphasis was placed on studies in which the intervention procedures were described in enough detail to provide the reader with an understanding of how they might be used in mainstream classrooms. An attempt was made to highlight studies that had special relevance to mainstream settings (e.g., studies that were conducted in regular classrooms and studies that were conducted with mildly handicapped students).

The modification of traditional curricular approaches to include less highly skilled students with normal students in regular classrooms is a major problem facing mainstream teachers. This chapter, therefore, is organized according to instructional modifications within each curricular area. Assessment, planning, antecedent teaching procedures, consequation (i.e., the use of feedback, contingent modeling, and praise), peer-mediated programs, and self-management approaches are reviewed. Within each section, recommendations for mainstream teachers are presented.

Following the literature review, final comments are presented about the applied behavior analysis literature in academics. This discussion focuses on issues of target behavior selection, subject description, research settings, and evaluation of treatment outcomes.

The instructional technology reflected in the applied literature on academic interventions offers great promise to both special education and regular education teachers. It is hoped that this review will facilitate the use of this valuable research literature by educators who wish to improve the performance of their handicapped and nonhandicapped students.

Arithmetic

In the initial section of this chapter, studies on the instruction of arithmetic are reviewed. These studies focus on arithmetic computation skills, since there are few published studies on other aspects of mathematics in the applied behavior analysis literature. In discussing the importance of basic computational skills, Cox (1975) reported that 5% of the errors found in children's addition papers and 13% of children's subtraction errors were identified as systematic errors of computation. In citing the importance of remedying these computation errors, Cox (1975) stated, "Without instructional intervention systematic errors will continue for long periods of time [p. 151]." Fortunately, computational systematic errors can be remedied, using one of the strategies outlined in the following sections.

ASSESSMENT AND PLANNING

Little work has been done in the area of applied behavior analytic studies of arithmetic assessment. Yet, as mentioned earlier, systematic computation errors can be remedied through careful error analysis (Cox, 1975). This error analysis was 1 of 10 planning skills taught to teachers of mentally retarded pupils in a study by Burney and Shores (1979).

Three teachers of trainable mentally retarded students volunteered to serve as subjects in this study. Each teacher in turn selected three students whose performance on mathematics was recorded by the experimenter. A multiple-baseline design across teachers and students permitted the authors to evaluate the effectiveness of training teachers in precision planning techniques. These precision planning techniques included counting of correct and error problems, timing of student performance, analysis of attack skills used by students, graphing data, analyzing graphs for trends, and formal error analysis. The results of this teacher planning study indicated that two of the three teachers implemented the precision planning techniques. Methodological difficulties prevented the authors from stating with confidence that the use of planning behaviors resulted in improved pupil performance. Yet, one teacher's students clearly improved in their mathematics performance when she began using planning strategies.

In a subsequent study on teachers' use of precision planning techniques, Kerr and Strain (1978) reported results similar to those of Burney and Shores

(1979). Pupils of all three teachers improved significantly in their performance as measured by the completion of arithmetic worksheets consisting of computation problems. In combination, therefore, these investigations underlined the importance of precise error analysis and planning of instruction in arithmetic.

ANTECEDENT TEACHING STRATEGIES

A growing body of literature has addressed the issue of antecedent manipulation of instructional events in arithmetic. These investigations can be categorized as follows: (a) manipulation of setting variables (e.g., use of a timer); (b) manipulation of instructional materials (e.g., aids); (c) manipulation of teacher variables (e.g., modeling).

Two studies in the first category have examined the effects of timing on children's math performance (Rainwater & Ayllon, 1976; Van Houten & Thompson, 1976). In the latter, Van Houten extended to mathematics previous investigations of timing and its effects on academic performance (e.g., Van Houten, Hill, & Parsons, 1975; Van Houten, Morrison, Jarvis, & McDonald, 1974). Twenty second graders, eight of whom had repeated a grade, were employed as subjects. The teacher carried out the experimental procedure, which consisted of an announced 1-min timing of the pupils' completion of addition and subtraction facts worksheets. Approximately 30 min per day were devoted to 1-min timings during the intervention phases of this ABAB-design study. Results indicated that the pupils whose Baseline$_1$ average rate was 3.5 correctly answered problems per minute increased these rates (problems worked during timed periods) during the Intervention$_1$ and Intervention$_2$ phases, respectively. Overall correct rates (for the entire 30-min period, regardless of timed segments) were 3.5, 6.8, 5.5, and 8.2 correctly answered problems per minute.

The effectiveness of this extremely simple procedure was again documented by Rainwater and Ayllon (1976) in a report of four low-achieving first graders in a public school classroom. One-digit addition and subtraction problems, as well as phonics workbook pages, were the targeted responses. A multiple-baseline design (across academic areas) was used to evaluate the students' performance during the Baseline$_1$ and Intervention$_1$ conditions. During baseline sessions, the pupils reportedly engaged in disruptive behaviors (e.g., breaking pencils, poking one another, wandering around); the mean performance for this phase was .85 arithmetic problems correct per minute. During the intervention phase, pupils were allowed the group's average baseline time (14 min) to complete problems. At the end of this interval, the teacher announced "Time's up" and scored the papers. Each pupil received subsequent feedback on his or her correct rate. Pupil performance was positively influenced by the timimg: The baseline average correct rate of .85 increased to a mean of 2.03 during the timed work sessions. (Collateral increases were noted in reading performance.) While it is necessary to withold firm conclusions in the light of such limited data, the effectiveness of timing of children's performance in arithmetic appears promising under the following conditions:

1. Pupils are engaged in "drill" type problems such as simple addition and subtraction facts.
2. Pupils have received sufficient prior instruction in these arithmetic operations.
3. The teacher explicity announces the timing of lessons.
4. Pupils receive some feedback as to their performance.

In an investigation subsumed under the second category of antecedent manipulation, Smith, Lovitt, and Kidder (1973) studied the effects of three instructional aids: paper clips, abacus, and cuisenaire rods. The 10-year-old subject was referred to his special classroom because of academic difficulty. Throughout the study the pupil worked two pages of subtraction problems; these problems were divided into three classes, according to the number of digits and the presence or absence of regrouping. During Phase 1, the pupil was asked to work the problems on the two arithmetic sheets. No other instructions or feedback were provided. Phase 2 allowed for the use of paper clips as counting objects. Prior to starting work, the pupil was shown how to use these. Phase 3 was a return to the baseline conditions. An abacus and a new set of math problems were introduced in the fourth phase. As before, the teacher demonstrated the use of the abacus on a sample problem taken from the new group. Following Phase 5, in which the abacus was removed, the pupil was given assistance in the form of instructions on a sample problem. These directions addressed the specific discrimination of when to and when not to borrow. This assistance was removed for Phase 7. Phase 8 allowed the pupil, following a demonstration, to use cuisenaire rods on problems of the third type. Removal of this assistance and reapplication of the use of the abacus for the Class 2 problems took place during the ninth phase. In the final two phases, the pupil received no assistance (Phase 10) and instructions (Phase 11). Results of this single-subject case study were summarized as follows:

1. All three teaching aids (i.e., abacus, cuisenaire rods, paper clips) were effective in producing improved scores on the targeted class of problems. The cuisenaire rods were not as effective, however, as the other two aids.
2. All three aids produced within-class generalization of improved performance. Again, cuisenaire rods were less effective in producing generalized gains.

3. Across-class gains were not observed as the result of any of the forms of instructional assistance previously cited.

Methodological problems within the study prevent one from drawing any conclusions regarding the use of instructions on a sample problem. More work is needed to determine the differential effects of common instructional aids. However, these forms of assistance do appear to hold promise, as demonstrated with one pupil.

A new third type of antecedent manipulation procedure, demonstration plus permanent model, was the focus of a series of applied experiments conducted by Smith and Lovitt (1975a). Seven male pupils, ages 8–11, participated in the studies, which took place at the Experimental Education Unit of the University of Washington. All shared the diagnostic label *learning disabled* and were below grade level in arithmetic. Each investigation employed as ABA design. Reported reliabilities on timing of work, accuracy of scoring, and accuracy of plotting scores were high. Instructional materials consisted of arithmetic worksheets containing different examples of a similar type of problem each day. Thus each set of problem types was represented by five pages, each with different specific problems to be worked. Instructional materials arranged in this way facilitate the diagnosis of systemic computational errors as suggested by Cox (1975). The demonstration-plus-permanent-model procedure was under study in the first experiment of this series. Specific arithmetic problems were those with three digits requiring borrowing from a zero in the ones column (for Pupils 1, 2, and 3), multiplication with two digits and no carrying (Pupils 4 and 5), and one-digit multiplication facts (Pupil 6). Each pupil received worksheets containing his specific problem type without teacher assistance during the initial 3-day baseline period. The demonstration-plus-permanent-model condition provided each pupil with a teacher demonstration of the solution procedure required by the problems on his worksheet. The teacher also verbalized the process, as she worked the problem. *Permanent model* referred to the fact that the sample problem and its answer remained at the top of the child's paper throughout his lesson time. Following the intervention period, a return-to-baseline condition was employed to determine maintenance of effects in the absence of teacher assistance. Results were reported as follows:

Baseline$_1$ *condition*: 0% correct for all six pupils

Demonstration-plus-permanent-model condition: 100%, 91%, 100%, 90%, 100%, and 100% median correct scores, respectively

Baseline$_2$ *(Maintenance condition)*: 100%, 100%, 93%. 100%, 84%, and 100% median correct scores, respectively

In addition, four of the pupils maintained median correct levels of 100% on subsequent weekly follow up checks during the school year.

The purpose of the second experiment was to determine the relative effectiveness of a feedback procedure and the demonstration-plus-permanent-model procedure. The former consisted of the experimenter's correcting the child's paper (i.e., noting correct answers with C, incorrects with a slash and verbal reminder) in his presence. This tactic was used alone during the second phase of the ABA study. Phase 3 employed the previously described modeling procedure. Results of this study indicated the ineffectiveness of the traditional checking procedure: Baseline levels of zero correct were unchanged during this condition. However, the demonstration–modeling strategy resulted in dramatic changes: All pupils' median scores rose to 100% within 2 days. The final maintenance phase reflected these same high scores.

The third of these experiments was an attempt at component analysis of the demonstration–modeling tactic. To accomplish this, four pupils worked various kinds of problems (e.g., two-digit multiplication with carrying) during baseline, permanent model, demonstration, and maintenance conditions. The demonstration intervention required the teacher to work a sample problem on an index card, which she then removed. The permanent-model condition provided the child with one sample problem that had been worked in his absence. The authors concluded that both interventions were necessary to achieve gains in the arithmetic performance of the pupils. The permanent model provided to one child resulted in gains over baseline of 91%; however, this pupil had previously been exposed to a feedback procedure for 7 days. (The authors did not offer an explanation for this change from the proposed design.) The remaining pupils did not achieve mastery of their problems until the demonstration condition was scheduled for them. Maintenance checks on all pupils indicated that the four pupils retained these gains.

In a related series of studies Smith and Lovitt (1975b) reported the within-class and across-class generalization of performance by these pupils. (*Class* refers to arithmetic problems of one type, such as one-digit times one-digit multiplication). To determine the extent of generalization, pupils received additional worksheets containing (*a*) different problems of the same general type; and (*b*) problems of a different class or type. Results of this series of studies on generalization indicated consistent generalization within a class of problems across all pupils during each of the interventions (i.e., demonstration plus permanent model, and feedback; demonstration, and permanent model, respectively). The studies also considered across-class generalization. However, the generalized gains previously noted were not found in this study. Across-class generalization did not occur in multiplication problems. In most of the subtraction experiments, generalization to other types of problems was noted. To summarize the findings of Smith and Lovitt (1975b):

1. A traditionally used procedure, demonstrating to pupils how to solve an arithmetic problem while verbalizing each step, was deemed effective,

particularly when used in combination with a permanent display of this demonstration.

2. Neither tactic alone appeared as effective as they were in combination.
3. The use of standard correction procedures was ineffective in increasing correct scores.
4. Generalization to other problems of the same category resulted from the use of the modeling procedures.
5. Generalization to other types of arithmetic problems resulted in most of the subtraction studies, but was not observed in studies on multiplication.
6. Gains noted in all studies using the modeling tactics were maintained at high levels for an extended period of time subsequent to the removal of the intervention.

The reader is advised to consider these findings with some caution, due to the pilot nature of the studies (i.e., lack of experiment control, use of clinical designs, lack of specificity in reporting performance scores). However, the studies played an important role in attempting to delineate the powerful aspect of instruction that lies in the manipulation of antecedent events.

FEEDBACK

Teachers respond to their pupils' performance in various ways: praise, disapproval, correction, feedback, or a combination of these. Because there are limited opportunities to respond individually to pupils in the regular classroom, it is critical that a teacher plan her consequation carefully. The misapplication of teacher attention has been cited in several investigations (Hasazi & Hasazi, 1972; Zimmerman & Zimmerman, 1962). The purpose of this section is to examine consequation strategies that have proved successful when attempted by adults.

Immediate correctness feedback and praise were examined by Kirby and Shields (1972) in an investigation employing a 13-year-old boy described as a poor arithmetic student whose attention to work was limited. The study was conducted daily in the student's regular seventh-grade classroom. Work-sheets consisting of 20 multiplication problems (i.e., single-digit advancing to three-digit problems) were assigned during the 24 days of the study. An initial baseline condition of 1 school week revealed that the pupil was working an average of 0.47 problems correctly per minute while attending to his work for approximately 51% of the session. An adjusting fixed ratio (FR) of feedback and praise constituted the 8-day Treatment I phase. This ratio schedule shifted from FR1 to FR16, with schedule changes occurring every third day. The student received feedback and praise by going to the teacher's desk—a practice common in regular classrooms. The results of using this Intervention₁ package were as follows: mean correct rate, 1.36 per minute; attention to task, 97%. Similar results were noted in the Intervention$_2$ condition, which followed a 5-day reversal phase. Thus a relatively simple intervention was effective in improving arithmetic performance with a collateral positive effect on attending behavior. As the authors noted, a teacher, volunteer, or even a peer could provide the praise and feedback with very little effort. It also seems likely that this procedure might enhance pupil performance (and attention) in a number of other academic areas.

Feedback proved again to be a useful teaching technique in a study conducted by Fink and Carnine (1975). The 23 first-grade pupils also learned to graph their own arithmetic performance. An ABAB design was used to evaluate the effectiveness of feedback (Phases 1 and 3), and feedback plus graphing (Phases 2 and 4). It is interesting to note that the pupils were trained to graph errors, instead of correct responses. The combined intervention appeared to be more effective than the feedback (i.e., written number of errors at the top of the pupil's paper) alone in reducing errors. Blankenship and Lovitt (1976) reported positive results in a study of one pupil who was provided immediate feedback regarding the number of correct *and* incorrect responses on his arithmetic worksheets.

In summarizing the applicability of these findings to an integrated setting, several points are clearly supported:

1. Immediate feedback, in the form of corrections or performance scores, improves a pupil's performance in arithmetic.
2. Feedback combined with self-graphing and/or praise may have more treatment strength than feedback alone.
3. Feedback is effective when provided upon completion of an entire set of problems (e.g., FR16, FR10). However, pupils with attending and task completion problems may be more effectively taught through the use of an adjusting schedule (e.g., FR1 advancing to FR10).
4. Positive collateral effects on attending behaviors may result as a function of improved academic performance.

Taken together, these findings point to a useful and relatively simple intervention, which has applicability in large classrooms.

PEER-MEDIATED STRATEGIES

Using pupils to teach each other is a useful strategy for the classroom teacher attempting to individualize instruction. This section will highlight studies involving peers as tutors in arithmetic. In some instances, peers have demonstrated their teaching skills without prior instructions from adults. In a study by Harris and Sherman (1973), members of an entire fourth-grade classroom simply were told to assist each other if they desired during a daily 15-min period. The only teacher involvement during the session was to praise students who were working together on the two-page basal text assignment. As the authors pointed out, the increases in subsequent arithmetic performance were indicative of the notion that many children may possess successful tutoring skills without specific training. Hamblin, Hathaway, and Wodarski (1971) also reported the use of untrained peer tutors in a study of two fifth-grade classes, but they did not report as dramatic gains as those described by Harris and Sherman (1973). Nevertheless, the simplicity of unstructured peer tutoring programs has great appeal for the teacher of a large, multilevel classroom.

Four behaviorally disordered adolescents were observed by McCarty and his colleagues (McCarty, Griffin, Apolloni, & Shores, 1977) to engage spontaneously in increased antecedent peer teaching as a result of a group contingency procedure. The students provided classmates with correct answers and redirected each other to continue working during study sessions occurring under the group contingency conditions. Increases in arithmetic performance were noted during these conditions, which were described as follows: (a) a cumulative contingency, under which subjects received a nickel for each correctly solved problem submitted; and (b) a mixed contingency, under which each subject was required to answer three problems before the group could receive any money. No tangible rewards were employed in a peer-mediated program described by Conlon, Hall, and Hanley (1972). Rather, an elementary school child timed and scored the arithmetic worksheets of two of his classmates. The peer corrector was told how to operate a stopwatch and to mark worksheets; no formal training of this child took place. The peer corrector's arithmetic performance remained at a high level throughout the study, while accuracy scores of his tutees increased during experimental conditions.

These three studies employed peer tutors who were essentially untrained. It would seem wise to attempt this kind of tutoring program if (a) the teacher's time is severely limited; (b) most pupils in a classroom are experiencing similar problems; (c) pupils are allowed a choice of whether to participate; and (d) the target responses can be taught through a simple format (e.g., dictating a problem, showing a flash card).

Some peer tutoring programs have provided their young teachers with rather extensive training. For example, Greenwood and his colleagues (Greenwood, Sloane, & Baskin, 1974) prepared elementary-school-aged children to serve as behavior managers of classmates labeled "unmanageable" during a Sullivan programmed math workbook session each day. These behavior managers, also considered as behaviorally disordered, learned to give out praise, to issue points, and to remove and record points from their classmates. For three of the four managers, a training program produced dramatic increases in the number of appropriate management behaviors exhibited. This would suggest that classroom teachers desiring to use children as behavior managers to improve their own as well as their classmates' behaviors may consider a formally structured training program such as the one described in detail by Greenwood and his colleagues.

Academic tutoring was the goal of three training sessions developed for regular fifth graders by Johnson and Bailey (1974). These students subsequently taught basic arithmetic skills to kindergarten children. Tutor training was accomplished through role playing, in which tutors practiced appropriate teaching skills (e.g., praising correct answers, ignoring misbehavior, modeling the correct answers and correcting errors). Five kindergarten pupils identified as deficient in counting skills received tutoring in daily 20-min sessions. At the end of the study, these children showed greater pre–post gains than a control group.

Training packages originally designed for use by parents were field tested by peers in a project by Reavis and Rice (1978). Twenty primary and elementary school pupils identified as deficient in math or reading were selected to receive instruction from tutors, who were typically one grade ahead of their tutees. The month-long instruction centered around highly structured materials. Gains were made by the tutees and were of a level similar to those achieved by children in the previous parent training project.

The use of peer tutoring in arithmetic instruction is an extremely useful strategy for mainstream classroom teachers, since it permits students to review with each other many of the aspects of arithmetic instruction in the elementary grades (e.g., addition, subtraction, multiplication, and division facts; identification of numerals). In most studies, the training of the peer tutor and the monitoring of the instructional program required little teacher effort or time. Three studies (Hamblin *et al.*, 1971; Harris & Sherman, 1973; McCarty *et al.*, 1977) demonstrated that students could assist one another without any formal training. This model is very appealing for teachers who wish to supplement the instruction received by students in a large group. Peer tutoring, whether it is formal or informal, may promote social interactions between handicapped and nonhandicapped pupils.

SELF-MEDIATED PROCEDURES

Children have, in some instances, been trained to manage one or more aspects of their own instruction in arithmetic. Reports of self-instruction (Lovitt & Curtiss, 1968), self-recording or self-evaluation (Hundert & Bucher, 1978; Rieth, Polsgrove, McLeskey, Payne, & Anderson, 1978), and self-reinforcement (Felixbrod & O'Leary, 1973; Lovitt & Curtiss, 1969) appear in the applied research literature.

One of the earliest such applied studies in arithmetic was conducted by Lovitt

& Curtiss (1968). The student, an 11-year-old boy enrolled at the Experimental Education Unit of the University of Washington, was referred on the basis of behavioral problems. Rates (correct and error) of arithmetic performance were measured throughout the three experiments of this study. During the first experiment, the pupil was requested to say the problems aloud as he worked them. Problems were of the type, one digit minus one digit. This intervention phase was preceded and followed by baseline conditions. (The return to baseline condition provided the pupil with the direction "Don't say the problems aloud." Of course, one could not ascertain whether or not the pupil persisted in verbalizing the problems to himself.) The second and third experiments followed the same basic procedure with one modification. Problems in Experiment 2 were of the type, two digit minus two digit; Experiment 3 used subtraction equations (e.g., $4 - 3 = 9 - ?$). Results of the three investigations supported the effectiveness of the self-verbalization procedure, which produced higher correct rates and dramatically lower error rates than those observed at baseline. However, the highest correct rates for all experiments were recorded during Phase 3, during which the pupil was directed not to verbalize. Slight increases in error rates (over the self-verbalization phases) were noted in all three experiments. The authors concluded that verbalizations reduced the overall variability of responding, but they were unable to establish specific causality for this effect. The correct rates in Phase 3 may have been attributable to the pupil's increased speed in verbalizing the problems silently. Reading aloud may have required more time and thus resulted in lower correct rates and increased accuracy.

Self-recording was the intervention employed by Rieth *et al.* (1978) to improve the arithmetic performance of four severely disturbed boys, ages 11–13 years. In the first of two studies, three boys were trained to graph their own daily math scores. A multiple-baseline (across pupils) design was used to evaluate the effectiveness of the self-recording. Baseline arithmetic performances of the three students were quite variable; the average percent correct scores were 43, 37, and 35, respectively. The self-recording procedure served to reduce each student's variability of scores, as well as to increase average daily scores to 92% correct, 69% correct, and 91% correct, respectively. In the second study reported by Rieth and his colleagues (1978), a single student was trained to graph his daily arithmetic scores. An ABAB design was used to determine the efficacy of this intervention, which resulted in an increase of 40% over the baseline conditions.

In two related studies, Hundert and Bucher (1978) reported the usefulness of a self-scoring procedure implemented by two special education classes. The self-rating was not significant in improving pupil performance, but did reduce both teachers' time spent in correcting assignments. Both studies indicated that pupils tended to exaggerate their scores when tokens were provided according to self-reported performance. Infrequent accuracy checks by the teacher appeared effective in reducing this inaccurate reporting.

Investigations of self-management procedures offer promise to teachers who are incorporating handicapped pupils into regular, large-group settings. The following guidelines might assist the regular or special educator in applying these empirically validated procedures:

1. Three facets of arithmetic instruction that have yielded successfully to self-management are self-verbalization, self-scoring, and self-graphing. Practitioners might attempt to replicate prior successful efforts by choosing one of these for both handicapped and nonhandicapped students.
2. Use of self-management strategies by students has been reported for elementary and junior high classes. However, further study is likely to indicate success at both lower and higher grade levels.
3. It has been noted that checks on student accuracy are important in the reduction of exaggerated scores, particularly when reinforcement is issued contingent upon such scores.
4. The use of self-scoring may not improve performance, but is likely to reduce significantly the amount of teacher time involved in monitoring progress. On the other hand, *self-graphing* has been demonstrated to have a positive effect on arithmetic performance, in one study.

SUMMARY

A number of strategies for instructing students in arithmetic have been described in this section, including teacher-mediated procedures, peer-mediated procedures, and self-mediated procedures. Regrettably, the research on these procedures has been limited to studies of computation skills, excluding other important aspects of mathematics instruction. Hopefully, future research efforts will address other important aspects.

Reading

The norm in regular classrooms is to rely on the basal text adopted by a school system. Various problems have been identified with this use of basals, however. These difficulties seem particularly relevant to the situation of the handicapped youngster in the regular classroom. Smith (1963) has summarized the issues as:

1. Considering the basal program, itself, as the whole program for reading instruction

2. Using one grade level of basal readers with the entire class, regardless of the different instructional levels of the children
3. Requiring children to cover all pages in a certain reader during a semester
4. Insisting that children should not work in a reader higher than the grade represented in their classroom
5. Permitting children to keep their basal readers in their desks or take them home, thus allowing them to become familiar with stories before the teacher is ready to present them
6. Using the teacher's guide as a detailed prescription to be followed exactly or disregarding it entirely
7. Confining instruction to reading stories with no period of skill development
8. Failing to keep records of specific skills on which children need help and not providing extra practice on these skills
9. Using the basal reader as busy work when the children have nothing else to do
10. Using workbooks indiscriminately with all children, failing to check workbooks, and failing to develop supplementary work with children who are not able to work on them independently
11. Requiring purposeless rereading
12. Using the content of the basal readers as the sole basis for the development of study skills needed in the content areas

In an attempt to improve the use of basal texts with handicapped and non-handicapped pupils, Lovitt and Hansen (1976) developed a procedure for appropriate placement of learners in basal reading texts. Seven elementary school pupils enrolled in the Experimental Education Unit at the University of Washington served as subjects. Each pupil was reading from 1 to 3 years below his grade-peers. The placement method relied on two initial assessments; (*a*) a 500-word sample of oral reading in the initial story in seven of the eight readers in the series; (*b*) responses to six comprehension questions (recall, sequence, interpretation, and vocabulary) on each reading sample. These initial assessment procedures required approximately 15 min per pupil per week. These two assessments were scored on three bases: (*a*) oral correct rate of words read per minute; (*b*) error–correct rate of words read per minute; and (*c*) correct percentage of comprehension questions answered. The subsequent determination was to place a student in a basal reader in which the child's average correct rate was between 45 and 65 words per minute (WPM), average error rate was between 4 and 8 WPM, and average comprehension score was from 50 to 75%. Ultimate effectiveness of the placement procedure was measured by a comparison of the initial assessment data with the pupil's performance in reading during the initial days following placement. The authors reported that the three scores were generally higher during the period shortly following placement. In addition, all pupils made significant gains during the following year's reading program, an indication that they were benefiting from appropriate initial placements.

With some minor modifications to simplify the procedure within a large classroom setting (e.g., reduction of number of samples read, use of paraprofessionals, volunteers, and audiotaping to record oral reading performance), this assessment procedure would be very useful to teachers of mainstream classes.

PLANNING STRATEGIES

The basis of all reading lessons is the teaching plan. While this component of instruction appears common to all classrooms, it has been the subject of few systematic investigations.

In one of the initial studies of the effects of teacher planning on reading (word recognition), Kerr and Strain (1978) trained three graduate student teachers to use precision planning tactics as developed by Burney and Shores (1979). These planning skills included the use of correct and error rates, comparison of previous word list performance to present performance, analysis of word attack skills, graphing of daily scores, and trend analysis of data recorded on six-cycle graph paper. Reading performance was measured on sight word lists taken from basal texts used in the elementary level special education classrooms. Results of the multiple-baseline study indicated that all five pupils improved significantly in their sight word reading as a function of their teacher's engaging in the planning tactics. (Similar results were found for arithmetic performance, which was also studied.)

One facet of instructional planning is the selection of stimulus material for the learner. A study to examine the effects of level of difficulty of reading material on the performance of primary school pupils was conducted by Glicking and Armstrong (1978). Measures of the students' task completion and task comprehension were conducted as they encountered more difficult assignments. Supporting the curvilinear relationship between learning and instructional difficulty, the data indicated that academic success and off-task behavior were inversely related.

The importance of systematic planning of stimulus material was again identified in a study by Neef, Iwata, and Page (1977). Six mentally retarded adolescents exhibited faster acquisition of new sight words when known words were interspersed with unknown words as compared with the use of entirely unknown word lists during a baseline condition. In addition, retention of these words appeared greater for those words learned during the interspersal condition. The authors suggested that the presence of known items served to reinforce appropriate behaviors, hence optimizing the learning situation. It would appear that this contingency was also in effect in the study by Glicking and Armstrong (1978).

ANTECEDENT TEACHING STRATEGIES

A variety of antecedent strategies are available to both special and regular educators whose concern is reading instruction. Research has been conducted on the effects of instructions (Lovitt & Hurlburt, 1974), prompting (Knapczyk & Livingston, 1974), and modeling (Haskett & Lenfestey, 1974; Hendrickson, Roberts, & Shores, 1978).

The use of phonics instruction and its relationship to subsequent oral reading performance was the topic of two experiments conducted by Lovitt and Hurlburt (1974). The purpose of the first study was to identify the effects of phonics instruction on the oral reading of a 10-year-old boy labeled "dyslexic." Oral reading performance following the phonics instruction was measured in two readers, one based on a phonics approach and the other not. All sessions took place in the tutor's house. Phonics instruction consisted of a daily 10-min lesson devoted to one of five phonics tasks previously identified as problematic to the pupil. Data from the AB study revealed that phonics instruction was effective in increasing correct rates in five phonics tasks. Moreover, the intervention produced increases in the rate of words read correctly from both books, although oral reading per se was not taught directly. Not surprisingly slightly better performance was observed in the phonics-based reader, Lippincott-2 (McCracken & Walcutt, 1966) than in the Ginn-2 reader (Ousley & Russell, 1961). In the second experiment, two types of phonics instructions were examined: Slingerland (1969) and the Palo Alto reading method (Glim, 1968). Again, all 4 pupils (labeled "dyslexic" and "slow learners") showed improvement in reading during the phonics instruction condition. Again, oral reading was positively affected by the phonics instructions, although it was not the focus of instruction. Additional, more controlled experiments are needed on the topic of phonics instruction.

A different antecedent strategy, prompting, was examined by Knapczyk and Livingston (1974) in their study of question asking and reading comprehension of two junior high students. These educably mentally retarded students were selected from a self-contained special education classroom because of their very low levels of on-task behavior, accuracy of responses, and question asking on SRA reading tasks. During the baseline phase of this study, the two female subjects engaged in their typical reading program. Neither subject was observed to ask the teacher or aide any questions concerning the comprehension tasks. During the intervention phase the teacher and aide began the reading period by verbally prompting the students to ask any questions they might have about the material they read. The number of prompts ranged from 1 to 5 per day for the first few days of this phase. The prompting procedure was effective in increasing the number of comprehension questions asked. A return-to-baseline condition on Subject 1 resulted in a near-zero level of question asking. This finding is not surprising since both prompts and verbal praise formerly offered for questions were dropped, resulting in an extinction period. With the reinstatement of prompting and praise for questions, Subject 1's questioning was restored to a level of approximately 10.3 per 50-min session. (Subject 2 averaged 5.3 questions per session.) A collateral effect was observed in the increased ontask behavior of both students. Measures of accuracy on the reading tasks indicated that both students improved in comprehension, as well.

A different kind of antecedent teaching strategy, prereading, was studied by Lovitt, and his colleagues (Lovitt, Eaton, Kirkwood, & Pelander, 1971). Prereading, or silently reading material before being asked to read it orally, resulted in decreased oral reading error rates for a 7-year-old pupil. [Correct rates did not change significantly.] This strategy is certainly useful for the teacher who must instruct a large group of pupils.

Manipulation of stimulus events in reading instruction consisted of antecedent modeling of basic sight words in a study by Hendrickson and her colleagues (Hendrickson *et al.*, 1978). Training sessions were held in an empty classroom by a graduate student teacher whose pupils were two primary-school-aged boys diagnosed as reading disabled. The antecedent model, "This word is . . .," preceded the question, "What word is this?" This procedure was shown to be effective in producing increases in words read correctly by both pupils. Moreover, the antecedent modeling proved more effective than contingent modeling examined in a subsequent phase.

CONSEQUATION STRATEGIES

This section will review selected studies that have focused on the use of teacher consequation tactics such as feedback, praise, tokens, and administration of other reinforcers. Oral reading as well as reading comprehension have been examined in these studies.

Token Reinforcement

Sight word vocabulary gains were of interest to Lahey and Drabman (1974) in a study involving 16 regular classroom second graders. Three sets of 10 words each were taught in an experimental room adjacent to the classroom during the short-term training program. One group of pupils received tokens for correct answers; the other received no tangible reinforcement. Two performance measures were taken on each word list: trials to criterion during training and the number of words correct on two subsequent retention checks. Results of these observations indicated that pupils in the nontoken condition required approximately twice as many trials to reach criterion as the reinforced pupils. Retention test scores were also significantly lower for the nonreinforced pupils. This discrepancy increased over time. The results of the second retention test were more disparate for the two groups than the results of the first test.

Oral reading and comprehension of textbook passages were examined by Lovitt *et al.*, (1971) in a series of token reinforcement studies. In each of the four series of studies, an elementary school pupil was required to read passages from two readers. The point contingencies were in effect for only one of the texts. In each project, data indicated that the manipulation of reinforcement (points) contingencies resulted in better performance than that noted in the nonintervention texts. While these projects are not experimentally controlled studies, the reader may wish to refer to them for the detailed discussion of various reinforcement contingencies.

Monetary Reinforcement

Two sixth graders served as subjects in a study conducted by Lahey, McNees and Brown (1973) on the effects of reinforcement on reading comprehension. Each student was assessed prior to the study; both read orally on grade level but performed comprehension tasks at 2 years below grade level. During each experimental session, each child was asked to read a passage from the standard sixth-grade basal text, then asked to state the answers to a few factual comprehension questions based on the text. This process was repeated during each session, resulting in data on approximately 30 questions per period. During the initial baseline phase, this procedure was employed without consequation for answers. Phase 2 allowed the children to receive praise and one penny for each correct answer, with no consequation for errors. Phases 3 and 4 replicated the first and second phases, respectively. Results of the study indicated that the two pupils increased their comprehension scores to an average of 90% during intervention conditions. Baseline$_2$ resulted in a significant decrease in these scores for both pupils. Of particular interest to the teacher of a regular, integrated classroom is that no special reading texts or materials were used. The pupils completed all reading in their standard grade level textbooks. Further research using more difficult comprehension questions would be very helpful in assessing the generalizability of these findings to other reading comprehension tasks.

The generalization of reading skills across settings and time was examined by Jenkins, Barksdale, and Clinton (1978). "The worst reading comprehension students in the school [p. 7]" were selected for participation in this study. One fourth-grade and two fifth-grade boys completed reading selections from a high-interest paperback series each day of the program. One section was assigned during the students' regular classroom time. The second was given during the experimental sessions. Twelve recall questions were given to the students for their written answers following each assignment. Reinforcement consisted of small amounts of money (e.g., $.05–.25) distributed by the pupils' parents on a predetermined schedule. The effects of this reinforcement on reading comprehension were evaluated through an across-setting multiple baseline and reversal design. Comprehension was reinforced initially in the experimental sessions, then reinforced only in the regular classroom. The authors also examined the effects of reinforcing comprehension on reading rate and vice versa. This was accomplished by using an across-performance, multiple-baseline design. Major results of the intervention were as follows:

1. When reinforcement was provided in the remedial setting contingent upon correct written answers to comprehension questions, all three students improved their scores above their previous baseline levels. This improvement averaged 25%.
2. When reinforcement was introduced in the classroom setting, an 18% average increase from the nonreinforced period was noted for the students. This level was not as high, however, as that observed in the remedial setting.
3. When upgrades in the reinforcement system were applied to two of the students in the classroom, both improved their performance. (This upgrading required students to attain an increasingly higher minimum correct score in order to receive money.)
4. Positive results in generalization across time were noted in most instances. Removing the reinforcement from the remedial reading session resulted in only minor performance changes for students. All students sustained their comprehension gains, even 2 months after reinforcement for this task was withdrawn. Maintenance effects on classroom comprehension following removal of reinforcement were not as clear-cut.
5. Generalization from the remedial setting to the regular classroom—a common concern of educators—was examined also, with only slightly favorable results. When performance was reinforced in the remedial setting and subsequently increased, collateral gains were not noted in the regular classroom. In fact, two of the students' classroom performance declined. (The authors suggest that interventions should perhaps be attempted initially in the child's regular setting, rather than in a training setting.)

Free Time as Reinforcement

In a departure from research on token reinforcement, Rieth and his colleagues (Rieth, Polsgrove, Raia, Patterson, & Buchman, 1977) examined the use of free time as a reward to three behaviorally disordered pupils aged 7, 10, and 11, respectively. Each of these students served as his own control in a single-subject case study. In the first study, sight words taken from beginning readers were taught, using a variety of remedial reading activities. A weekly exam served to evaluate the student's progress. The ABAB design consisted of a baseline phase, an intervention phase, (i.e., provision of 5 min of free time for each word mastered on the weekly test), and replications of each of these conditions. Data from the Friday tests indicated that the free time contingency was effective in increasing the number of words learned.

Reading in context and reading comprehension were target behaviors for the second study in this series. Results similar to those of the first study were obtained; both targeted behaviors improved when placed under the contingent free time conditions. The final study in this series was used to improve the completion of assignments and the accuracy of those assignments by one subject. An ABAB design similar to those used previously served to evaluate the effects of the free time reinforcement (i.e., free time for completion of assignments, with additional minutes for accuracy). Once more, the free time contingency was effective in producing complete and accurate reading assignments. The ease with which the procedure was implemented suggests applicability for large-group settings.

PEER-MEDIATED STRATEGIES

Children have been trained successfully to assist their teachers in carrying out reading instruction. This section will review studies of peer tutoring, with special emphasis on how these relate to integrated settings.

A concern of educators enlisting the help of capable students to tutor less capable peers is what, if any, negative effects the tutoring process may have on the tutors. In an attempt to answer this question, Davis (1972) enlisted two remedial reading students to teach their classmates in individual sessions. The tutors, 12- and 13-years-old, respectively, taught four younger students, using the Science Research Associates Reading Laboratory Power Builder, a programmed reading series (Parker & Scannel, 1961). All tutoring sessions were tape recorded, so that tutors could be evaluated for the rewarding of points, exchangeable for leisure time activities. Tutoring consisted of providing praise, tokens, and simple directions. The results of the study indicated that tutors as well as tutees improved their performance on the SRA program.

Twenty-three eighth graders were trained as "behavioral engineers" in a study by Willis, Crowder, and Morris (1972). These students were trained in basic behavior modification principles before continuing their training through role plays. Upon completion of this training, they began work with elementary school pupils, each of whom was at least two grade levels beind in reading. The 6-month tutoring program was conducted by the eighth graders in a classroom designated solely for their use. A school counselor did routine observations of the tutoring sessions and completed an evaluation checklist on each tutor. An aide was hired to manage the program. The tutoring procedure (i.e., listening to orally read passages, correcting errors, and requesting the pupil to reread troublesome sentences) was supplemented with simple token reinforcement. Tutors collected data of their pupils' progress by tallying the number of "correct" chips (green) and "error" chips (red). Each tutor was responsible for all aspects of the remedial instruction of two pupils, who were taught together. Evaluation of the program was accomplished by three analyses:

1. The tutored pupils were administered standardized pre- and posttests.
2. The tutees' performance was compared with that of pupils in a Regular Remedial Reading (RRR) Program staffed by a certified teacher.
3. A cost analysis of the two programs was conducted.

The results of these analyses are very encouraging for educators considering the use of peer teaching. Tutored pupils made an average of 1 year's gain on the Slosson Oral Reading Test. A matched sample comparison of RRR pupils and tutees indicated that the latter group did significantly better on the posttest and criterion-referenced performance measure. Finally, the cost of the behavioral engineers' program was $18 a day compared with $45 a day for the RRR program.

In a similar study, Robertson, DeReus, and Drabman (1976) compared fifth-grade tutors with college student tutors. Pupils in a second-grade class were selected to be tutees on the basis of their reading deficits and disruptive behavior. Tutors were trained for their work during four 1 hr sessions, the principal activity of which was role playing. Following this training period, tutors worked with their pupils on Sullivan Readers for two 20-min sessions daily. Results of the study revealed no significant differences in performance gains between pupils tutored by the elementary school students and those tutored by the college students. Reading improvement was noted for both groups. In addition, decreases occurred in disruptive behaviors observed during the tutees' regular classroom time.

On the basis of these studies, it can be assumed that peers are a valuable resource in reading instruction. Students in elementary and junior high school have compared favorably with adults in carrying out structured reading instruction. This instruction has involved modeling, correction, administration of token reinforcement, and collection of data. To prepare for their roles as teachers, students have spent only a few hours, generally in simulated teaching activities. In summary, therefore, peer tutoring offers a cost-efficient and positive alternative to teachers of large groups.

SELF-MEDITATED STRATEGIES

Self-management skills are critical to a student who is to be successful in a large-group setting. The typical teacher–pupil ratio simply does not allow for instruction that is entirely adult-directed. In an effort to explore the potential benefits of self-management, several researchers have conducted studies of self-reward, self-punishment, self-instruction, and self-evaluation. This section highlights some of these investigations.

An interesting series of single-subject projects was described by Lovitt and Curtiss (1969). The purpose of these studies conducted with pupils at the Experimental Education Unit of the University of Washington was to compare self-imposed contingencies with teacher-imposed contingencies. Performance in several academic areas, including reading, was measured. During the first project, a teacher-determined point ratio for performance was compared with the pupils' own points-for-performance ratio. These arrangements were outlined through written performance contracts and were evaluated through an ABCB design. The second project replicated the procedures of the first. The third project was designed to determine whether a pupil was responding to the magnitude of points received (which had been greater during self-reward conditions of the earlier projects than during teacher-reward conditions) or to the self-management aspect of the procedures. To answer this question, three conditions were established: (*a*) teacher-designed ratio of points to performance scores; (*b*) teacher-awarded points of the same ratio that had been previously chosen by a pupil; and (*c*) teacher-designated point ratio. Results of the studies suggest that pupil self-determination of points was more critical to changes in performance than the magnitude of the reward. Pupil performance in the first two studies was greater in self-reward conditions than in teacher-reward conditions. During the third study, the pupil performed at approximately the same level during all three teacher-delivered reward conditions, despite increased points available to him during the second phase (child-determined, teacher-delivered points).

In a continuing look at reading instruction, Lovitt (1973) described a project that involved second graders in several aspects of self-management. The reader is referred to this report for detailed explanations of the way in which students were trained to time their work, to figure their correct and error rates, and to graph these correct and error rates.

SUMMARY

In reviewing the applied behavior analysis literature on reading instruction, one is faced with a variety of different teaching and assessment strategies. Many of these procedures lend themselves to adoption in mainstream classrooms.

Specific recommendations for teachers of regular classrooms are as follows:

1. Traditional reliance upon a basal reading series may present difficulties to the teacher of handicapped students (Smith, 1963). Individualized assessment of both handicapped and nonhandicapped students is mandatory if one is to gain greatest benefit from using a basal text (Lovitt & Hansen, 1976).
2. In order to use basal series or individual reading programs successfully, teachers should be trained in precision planning strategies (Kerr & Strain, 1978).
3. Antecedent teaching strategies, such as prereading and antecedent modeling are effective ways to improve the reading performance of primary school children (Hendrickson *et al.*, 1978; Lovitt *et al.*, 1971).
4. Specific, contingent reinforcement for reading behaviors is an effective method for improving both oral reading as well as reading comprehension skills (Jenkins *et al.*, 1978; Lahey, McNees, & Brown, 1973).
5. Peers may serve as effective reading teachers for their classmates and can be trained for this role in relatively brief sessions (Davis, 1972; Robertson *et al.*, 1976; Willis *et al.*, 1972).
6. Self-reinforcement and self-evaluation strategies are useful in improving students' reading performance (Lovitt, 1973; Lovitt & Curtiss, 1969). This recommendation must be viewed with some caution, as there are few studies on the use of self-management procedures in reading instruction.

Spelling

Spelling is a major problem to many school children (Horn, 1969). Yet no clear consensus exists as to why a word is difficult to spell. Moreover, there appears to be little agreement on how difficult words should be taught (Cahen, Craun, & Johnson, 1971). Some methods that are not useful in spelling instruction have been pinpointed by Haring, Lovitt, Eaton, & Hansen (1978). Regrettably, such procedures are those encountered typically by the handicapped learner in the mainstreamed setting. This section will attempt to delineate remedial strategies that offer hope to the educator who is attempting to improve upon the standardized spelling program.

ASSESSMENT

Few, if any, guidelines are available to educators regarding the selection of appropriate lists of spelling words to be taught. Several approaches have been cited. The "demon" list, comprised of those words frequently misspelled by pupils, is one method (Cahen *et al.*, 1971). Some problems are presented by the use of demon lists. Fitzgerald (1932) noted that pupils frequently use words that are easy to spell; therefore, many types of misspellings may be identified although most children spell these words correctly. Cahen and his colleagues (Cahen *et al.*, 1971) further noted that the demon list method does not reveal why certain words are difficult, nor does it allow a teacher to predict with reliability what additional words will be difficult. In fact, interexpert reliability on establishing demon lists is poor: A mere 20 words constituted the overlap between the lists identified by Jones (1914) and that of Fitzgerald (1932), based on misspellings on over 3000 student papers.

A second approach to the selection of words to teach is to use words that pupils encounter in other curricular areas, such as reading. An obvious problem with this strategy is that other curricula are not designed with spelling as the academic objective. Therefore, there is no assurance that word lists selected from these texts will be sequenced properly for spelling instruction.

A third approach is to select words that share a common phoneme–grapheme pattern. Some data exist for this type of approach (Hanna, Hanna, Hodges, & Rudorf, 1966; Hanna & Moore, 1953; Solomon & MacNeill, 1967). Other researchers have challenged the phoneme–grapheme patterns to predict spelling difficulty (Graham & Rudorf, 1970; Horn, 1957; Roberts, 1967). In summary, controversy surrounds the question, "What makes a word difficult to spell?" As a result, there is no agreement on a body of words that when taught would subsequently enable a student to be a "good" speller.

INSTRUCTIONAL STRATEGIES

Several procedures have been reported for the remediation of poor spelling. These include use of the Good Behavior Game (Axelrod & Paluska, 1975; Barrish, Saunders, & Wolf, 1969), home tutoring (Broden, Beasley, & Hall, 1978), peer tutoring (Dineen, Clark, & Risley, 1977; Harris, Sherman, Henderson, & Harris, 1972), positive practice (Foxx & Jones, 1978), and contingent free time (Kauffman, Hallahan, Hass, Brame, & Boren, 1978). As Lovitt (1975) stated, "Although there have been few studies on spelling, the interventions have been more diverse than in reading [p. 506–507]."

The use of peers as change agents in spelling instruction has been described under two formats: peer tutoring and the Good Behavior Game. The former strategy was first reported by Harris *et al.* (1972), in a study of peers as tutors in a fifth-grade classroom. The class average score on a standardized spelling test was below grade level and most of the class members were earning scores of 75% or less on weekly spelling tests. While this group served as primary subjects, replication studies were carried out in four other classrooms. A weekly pre- and posttest was applied to two 20-word spelling lists given to each student. During the first condition students were encouraged to study one of their lists together for the 10-min period immediately preceding the Friday posttest. No special instructions were provided by the teacher. The second experimental manipulation consisted of a 10 min independent study period, also preceding the posttest. This individual study, therefore, replaced the peer study session during Condition 2. Following this invention, four 1-week conditions evaluated tutoring, independent study, tutoring, and independent study, respectively. Results of this investigation indicated that the peer tutoring was significantly more effective than the independent study procedure. Thus, despite the unstructured nature of the peer tutoring, it produced gains that could not be explained simply by the 10-min study time allowed. While specific components of the tutoring package were not delineated, the study nevertheless introduced the viability of peer tutoring as a spelling instruction strategy. Furthermore, the replication studies indicated that tutoring was effective across classroom settings. Maintenance of the tutoring results was noted in retention checks occurring 2–5 weeks after the study.

If one assumes that all class members took turns tutoring and being tutored in the study by Harris *et al.* (1972), then it can be assumed that both roles served to benefit the students. In an attempt to delineate more specifically the advantages of serving as a tutor, Dineen and his colleagues (1977) conducted a study of three children, aged 9–10 years. Each pupil was described as being 2 years below grade level in reading. Following a pretest on 45 selected words, the three students were trained in the tutoring procedures, which consisted of (*a*) dictating each word from a flash card to the tutee; (*b*) noting and praising each correctly spelled word; (*c*) depositing each word card into a mastery or nonmastery box; and (*d*) providing contingent models for words misspelled. Fifteen words were trained during each daily 20-min session. Following each tutoring session, the tutee was given a posttest on the trained list. The design of the study allowed for each pupil to serve as a tutor for 15 words, to be tutored for another 15-word list, and to receive no training on a third list.

Results for the three children indicated the following pre- to posttest gains: 1% on nontrained words, 47% on tutor words, and 59% on tutee words. Thus, the benefits of being a tutor were similar to those experienced as a tutee.

The use of peers was evaluated in a somewhat different way by Axelrod and Paluska (1975) in a study of the Good Behavior Game (Barrish *et al.*, 1969) applied to spelling instruction. A regular classroom of 22 third and fourth graders served as subjects. (It should be noted that, in contrast to the Harris *et al.* (1972) study, these pupils were performing at grade level.) Daily tests served to measure the number of words each pupil spelled correctly. During the baseline condition, pupils took daily tests on six words announced the previous day by the teacher. The game condition provided pupils membership on one of two classroom teams composed of children of roughly equivalent skills. Following the daily test, the teacher scored all papers and announced as "winners" the team with the higher scores. The members of the winning team were then cheered individually. In the event of a tie, all class members participated in this ceremony. During the third condition, the previous procedures were augmented by the awarding of a small prize to each member of the winning team. The fourth condition replicated the game condition. A return to baseline was the final stage of the investigation. Results were as follows: During baseline, the class average on daily tests was 58% accuracy; the game produced 61% average test scores; the game plus prize condition resulted in the highest class scores, averaging 82.5%. The reinstatement of the game and baseline conditions effected a drop in average class scores to 67% and 58%, respectively. To summarize the findings of Axelrod & Paluska, (*a*) the use of the game did not accomplish significant gains for most of the pupils; and (*b*) the addition of prizes to the game strategy increased significantly the performance of 21 of the 22 pupils. The latter finding corroborates that of Dineen *et al.* (1977), who concluded that reinforcement was critical to the successful tutoring described earlier.

Home-based tutoring sessions conducted by a mother were reported by Broden and her colleagues (1978). In the first study, a 10-year-old child described as being a very poor third-grade student was trained by his mother. The tutoring procedure consisted of (*a*) presentation of each word orally; (*b*) praise of correctly spelled words; and (*c*) modeling those words misspelled by the child. With minor modifications, this basic procedure was carried out on the three nights preceding each weekly test. A withdrawal-of-treatment design was used to evaluate the effectiveness of the mother's tutoring. Results of the nine-phase study indicated that the pupil's performance on the Friday tests was significantly better under the tutoring conditions than when he was not provided assistance. Of additional interest was the finding that the child learned words more quickly as the study elapsed. Relying on the relative ease and high reliability with which the mother had carried out the tutoring steps with one child, the authors then enlisted her help for her second child, a boy of 7. This pupil's spelling had been rated as "satisfactory," but the teacher's comments indicated that he was not performing at his optimal level. As in the first study, this teacher was unaware of the home-based program. A reversal design was employed: General procedures from the first study were followed, with the omission of praise for correct responses. Again, the tutoring produced higher spelling test scores. In summary, the studies supported these conclusions:

1. The systematic tutoring program could be carried out by a mother, with minimal training.
2. The use of praise was not the critical element in the success of the tutoring.
3. Skills in spelling increased throughout the training.

4. There was clear generalization to the school setting, as measured by weekly tests.

Unfortunately a clear statement in support of the retention of words tutored could not be made by the authors.

The use of distributed practice, as reported by Broden *et al.* (1978) was also examined by Rieth and his colleagues (Rieth, Axelrod, Anderson, Hathaway, Wood, & Fitzgerald, 1974), who found that such practice spread over time was superior to massed practice of spelling words. Another look at the effects of practice was reported by Foxx and Jones (1978) in a study of spelling performance of regular elementary and junior high school students, whose baseline spelling scores averaged 85% or less. Baseline instructional procedures consisted of daily sessions focused on a spelling list taken from the basal series. A weekly spelling test was used to evaluate pupil performance. In addition, points exchangeable for prizes were earned or lost by pupils on this test. Three of the four grades (4, 7, and 8) took home notes to parents, as a means of communicating that week's spelling performance. During the first experimental condition, the weekly spelling lists were pretested on Wednesday, returned to pupils on Thursday, then tested finally on Friday. The goal of this condition was to provide pupils with feedback on their performance prior to the weekly test. The second condtion, "Test/Positive Practice," required that students perform remediation exercises on Monday on those spelling words missed on the previous Friday's test. Five exercises were specified for each word. A response cost (i.e., working on exercises during recess) was applied to students whose remediation was not completed by Tuesday. A combination intervention was evaluated during Condition 4. This consisted of the Wednesday pretest, remediation activities to be completed by Friday morning, and the usual Friday test.

During the final experimental phase of this study, all of the above interventions were to be completed by the Tuesday following the Friday test. The results indicated that this final condition was most effective in producing gains in weekly spelling scores for pupils in grades 4 and 8 (N = 16). The Test/Positive Practice procedures were most effective in the fifth grade (N = 4), and Test/Positive Practice produced greatest gains in the seventh grade (N = 9). Thus, conditions in which positive practice was employed were those of greater achievement. The use of a midweek pretest for providing feedback to pupils was ineffective in increasing weekly test scores. In a follow-up evaluation conducted during the subsequent school year, 15 or 22 students checked indicated maintenance of the instructional effects (mean spelling average = 91%). In addition, three of the four teachers were continuing to use the procedures, particularly with students encountering difficulty in spelling. In summary, the following conclusions may be drawn from this investigation:

1. The use of positive practice exercises increased significantly the spelling test scores of the majority of pupils.

2. The use of varied positive practice activities (i.e., requiring the pupil to find a word and its phonetic spelling, part of speech, and definition in a dictionary, and to copy the dictionary entry, and to use it in five different sentences) was more effective than a traditional remediation strategy (i.e., recopying each misspelled word ten times, as required during baseline).
3. The use of positive practice procedures was time- and cost-efficient, resulting in their continued use by teachers the following year.

The authors add to these findings the caution that "no positive practice program should be used unless a variety of positive consequences are programmed to follow spelling achievement [Foxx & Jones, 1978, p. 229]." (In the study described, this was accomplished through the use of traditional reinforcers such as prizes, positive written comments, and posting high-scoring tests.)

The importance of reinforcement in spelling instruction was demonstrated in a much earlier study by Lovitt, Guppy, and Blattner (1969). Thirty-two fourth graders, none of whom was handicapped, experienced traditional activities during the initial phase of the study. These practices included reading, saying, and writing the new words; taking a midweek test, completing additional practice exercises, and taking a final test each week. Report cards and approval by peers and teacher were the only contingencies in effect. During the second phase, however, scheduled lessons were dropped in lieu of simply assigning work to be completed within a certain time limit. "Final" tests were given on Tuesday through Friday of each week; pupils who scored 100% on any one of these tests were allowed, during subsequent testing periods, to select from several free time activities. A group contingency augmented these general procedures during the intervention: If all pupils scored 100% on a given day, the total group was allowed 15 min of radio listening. Out of 32 pupils, a mean of 12 perfect papers was recorded during Baseline 1. Interventions 1 and 2 produced averages of 25.5 and 30.0 papers, respectively. Thus, the group contingency of Intervention 2, while never realized, resulted in the greatest gains. This finding confirms that of Axelrod & Paluska (1975), who reported the Good Behavior Game as a successful group contingency procedure for spelling instruction of third and fourth graders.

In a departure from traditional practices, Kauffman *et al.* (1978) conducted two experiments to determine the effects of imitation of spelling errors on the performance of three mildly handicapped pupils. In the first study, two boys enrolled in a self-contained classroom for the educably mentally retarded were trained on 10 new words each week. Words were taken from the pupils' reading texts. Instruction consisted of different daily activities, including saying the words and writing them in different media. These activities remained constant throughout the study. Two teacher-mediated consequation tactics were alternated across the six phases of the investigation. The first consisted of praise for correctly spelled words, supplying a correctly written model for misspelled words, and requiring the pupil to recopy the word from the model ("Model

Only"). The second intervention, "Imitation Plus Model," required the teacher to write an exact imitation of the child's misspelled word with the accompanying verbal statement, "This is how you spelled the word [p. 218]." The teacher followed this imitation with the modeling procedure described above. As in the "Model Only" conditions, the child received praise for his correctly spelled words. Results indicated that the imitation–model combined strategy was the more effective: Acquisition was more rapid and led to higher levels of performance.

In the second study by Kauffman et al. (1978), one 12-year-old boy served as the subject. General teaching procedures included phonics drills, flash cards, and written exercises. Daily instruction and probes were continued throughout the study. In this study, the "Model Only" and "Imitation Plus Model" strategies were provided frequently each day, rather than solely after the instructional activity. Secondly, the teacher in the second investigation marked each incorrect letter in both the child's and in her imitation copy. Once more, the "Imitation Plus Model" tactic proved superior to the "Model Only" procedure: The difference in the performance levels was approximately 10%.

SUMMARY

The applied behavior analysis literature on instruction in spelling is a diverse yet small one (Lovitt, 1975). It is difficult therefore to draw firm conclusions from this literature. The following suggestions are supported by the investigations that have been reviewed:

1. While no clear guidelines can be suggested regarding the selection of spelling words to be taught, some data exist for selecting words according to common phoneme–grapheme patterns. Studies do not support the use of demon lists or word lists from other curricular areas such as social studies.
2. Students may assist one another in learning spelling words through a structured format, such as the Good Behavior Game, or through informal or formal peer tutoring (Axelrod & Paluska, 1975; Harris et al., 1972).
3. Distributed practice (Rieth et al., 1974) and positive practice (Foxx & Jones, 1978) are effective spelling review procedures for students.

Handwriting

In this section studies of cursive and manuscript penmanship will be reviewed. Subsumed under these two major categories will be research pertaining to the assessment of handwriting, remediation of digit and letter reversals, and general instructional procedures.

MANUSCRIPT WRITING

Manuscript writing, or printing, is typically offered in penmanship curricula before cursive writing instruction. Several procedures have been proposed for the instruction of printed letters: (*a*) copying (Birch & Lefford, 1967); (*b*) modeling and verbalizations (Furner, 1969); (*c*) kinesthetic approaches such as tracing, sandpaper letters, motor coordination exercises (Enstrom, 1966; Fernald, 1943; Green, 1967; Shea, 1956); (*d*) token reinforcement (Nichols, 1970); and (*e*) access to play activities (Hopkins, Schutte, & Garton, 1971; Rapport & Bostow, 1976; Salzberg, Wheeler, Devar, & Hopkins, 1971). A few of these procedures have been the subject of controlled experimental studies.

One of the first of such investigations was conducted by Hopkins *et al.* (1971). First graders printed a chalkboard assignment, while second graders wrote theirs in cursive. The 24 students, all in a regular classroom, were timed on the copying tasks, which averaged 194 letters for the younger group and 259 letters for the older children. In addition to the duration measure, each letter was scored as being correctly or incorrectly written. Eight criteria were used in recording letters: (*a*) omissions; (*b*) substitutions; (*c*) reversals; (*d*) partial omissions; (*e*) angle of strokes; (*f*) height of lower-case letters; (*g*) height of upper-case letters; and (*h*) lower-case letter extensions below the base line. Scoring was done by two observers whose agreements averaged 91%. Seven experimental conditions were employed to determine the effects on printing and writing of various consequation strategies. Following an initial baseline phase, pupils were allowed a 50-min free time upon completion and scoring of the assignment. The contingency during Phase 2, therefore, was simply one of completing work quickly to gain access to play activities. (In addition, pupils who were noisy in the playroom had to return to their seats. This occurred twice.) A reinstitution of baseline conditions followed this phase. Access to the playroom again was made available in the replication of Phase 2 that followed. After this reversal, three conditions were applied for the purpose of reducing the amount of play time made available to the pupils. The time was reduced to 45 min, to 40 min, and finally to 35 min in Phases 5, 6, and 7, respectively. Results of this study suggested that a traditional approach of requiring pupils to await the completion of work by their peers had a depressing effect on the rate of words written and printed. The contingent provision of free play activities, on the other hand, increased the written output of these primary school pupils. In addition to this improvement in writing rate, most of the pupils exhibited fewer errors in the reinforcement phases than in the two baseline conditions, despite the fact that access to the playroom was provided without regard to the quality of the work completed. (The authors did point out, however, that the teacher may have praised pupils differentially based on their scores. No control of teacher praise or criticism was attempted.) Finally, results were similar with respect to the two target responses, printing and cursive writing.

Salzberg and his colleagues (Salzberg *et al.*, 1971) pursued the question of how consequation affects handwriting in a study of six kindergarten pupils. Specially treated writing paper allowed the regular class teacher to produce a latent image of the letters over that printed by the pupils. Responses were scored correctly if they were within 1.5 mm of the guidelines. Additional scoring criteria were similar to those described by Hopkins *et al.* (1971). The general daily procedures also were similar to the earlier study: Following completion of a letter-copying assignment, pupils were allowed to play in an indoor or outdoor area. These procedures were in effect during the initial baseline phase. In the subsequent phase, pupils copied a letter on which they had previously received instructions as well as a noninstructed letter (Z). One-half of the pupils were selected randomly during each day of this condition to receive neutral feedback from the teacher, who scored their reproductions of the target letters. Nonselected students had immediate access to the play area. This condition was followed by a "feedback plus contingency–target" phase, in which the students randomly selected each day were required to meet a criterion score before being allowed to play. Again, the nontrained Z's were not scored. During the fourth experimental condition, feedback statements were provided to Z's only. Access to play was noncontingent. Phase 5 of the study, "feedback plus contingency–Z," required that selected pupils meet criteria on the nontrained Z letters before going to play. Instruction without subsequent feedback or grading continued on the target letters. The results of the intermittently applied contingency indicated that (*a*) instructions alone did not produce high quality of printing; (*b*) instruction and feedback together were ineffective in increasing the number of correctly formed letters; and (*c*) improvement occurred only on letters whose accurate production was reinforced. The latter two conclusions were based on printing of trained letters, as well as on the nontrained Z's. Of further interest was the finding that generalization from trained to nontrained letters did not take place as a result of any of the consequation procedures. Only two children showed improvement on the letter Z. This finding is in contradiction to that of Hansen and Lovitt (Note 1), who reported that pupils learning cursive letters at the Experimental Education Unit, University of Washington, required training on only 25% of the letters to write accurately all of the alphabet. This disparity in results might be explained by pupil differences: Those learning cursive, it would seem, have a longer history of instruction in handwriting than kindergarteners observed by Salzberg *et al.* (1971).

A more recent study reported by Rapport and Bostow (1976) again evaluated the effects of contingent reinforcement on writing. The performance of third graders improved slightly as a result of their being given access to recreational activities; admission to free play required scores of at least 80% correct on the handwriting and word copying tasks.

A noteworthy feature of all three of these studies is the ease with which a regular classroom teacher could implement the procedures. Free play or games centers occupy a portion of many existing classrooms; if necessary, these can be partitioned from the instructional area with a portable screen. And while the number of pupils targeted was different in each study (ranging from 6 to 24) it would appear that an entire classroom or instructional group could be instructed at once, as long as the teacher and/or teacher's assistant could score the assignments. (Alternatives to teacher scoring will be discussed in a later section.) Finally, individualized criteria, as used in the study by Salzberg *et al.* (1971) would allow for the successful integration of handicapped and non-handicapped pupils. Some differences in the effectiveness of the reinforcement procedures should be anticipated, as noted by Salzberg *et al.* (1971).

Generalization to the regular classroom setting was one goal of a multifaceted intervention attempted by Fauke, Burnett, Bowers, and Sulzer-Azaroff (1973). A 6-year-old pupil was nominated by his teacher on the basis of his behavior problems and poor performance in oral recall and printing of letters. Targeted for intervention were two uppercase and nine lowercase letters that comprised the child's name. Training was carried out in 40-min sessions held daily in the experimenter's home. The intervention procedures were as follows:

Phase 1: During this baseline condition, correct oral responses to the letters, correct and incorrect copying of model letters, and correctly written letters without a model were recorded.

Phase 2: Three types of tasks comprised the instruction during this period. In the first, the pupil was shown flash cards of letters, asked to name them, and was reinforced with candy for each correct answer. If the child made an error, he was asked to trace the letter on a yarn model. During subsequent testing activity, the boy was provided visual feedback on his performance. Contingent reinforcement for correct responses was offered again in the form of candy, which was given for increasingly higher percentages of correct answers. The second group of activities consisted of tracing worksheets of printed letters. Prompts for the correct formation of letters were provided by the experimenter (e.g., "*h* [is] a stick and a hump"). Prompts were gradually faded out. In the third daily activity of this phase, the child wrote his name without a model. Self-evaluation by the pupil using transparent overlays was the final task in this set.

Phase 3: A reinstitution of baseline conditions took place.

Phase 4: Procedures as described for Phase 2 were employed.

The data from this ABAB study were clear: The use of a three-part intervention package increased substantially the percentages of (a) correct letter recognition; (b) correctly written letters with a model; and, (c) correctly written letters without a model. Anecdotal reports from the regular classroom appeared favorable with respect to generalization of handwriting and copying skills, although formal measures were not taken. Although it is impossible to attribute effects differentially to the various components of the instructional package, it would appear that these results confirm those of previous writers who advocate the use of specific reinforcement for correctly printed responses (Hopkins et al., 1971; Rapport & Bostow, 1976; Salzberg et al., 1971).

LETTER AND DIGIT REVERSALS

A common handwriting problem is that of letter and digit reversals. The remediation of reversals has been described by several researchers as being accomplished effectively through behavior modification methods (Smith & Lovitt, 1973; Stromer, 1975, 1977). This approach to instruction contradicts the assumption expressed by Gallagher (1960) that "remediation is as likely to be accomplished through maturation as through specific interventions [p. 8]." A direct instruction approach also challenges the position that reversals are the permanent result of neurological impairment (Strauss & Lehtinen, 1947, p. 170).

The direct intervention strategy gained support in a study reported by Smith and Lovitt (1973). A 10-year-old pupil at the Experimental Education Unit, University of Washington, served as the single subject. This pupil was observed to have a specific problem with written reversals of b and d. As a result of initial assessments, the student was noted to have greatest difficulty with d placed as the initial consonant in a word. Other problems were b and d in the final position. By instructing the pupil to focus on the problem letters when presented in the words dam and bam the experimenter was able to reduce the pupil's errors to a zero level. Modeling, instructions, and praise were again successful when applied to the pupil's reversals of the numeral 9. Data also indicated that the ability to discriminate b and d generalized to other presentations of these letters and to other academic tasks.

Reversals of numerals and letters were also studied by Stromer (1975, 1977) in a series of experiments with learning disabled pupils. In the earlier study (Stromer, 1975) one- and two-digit reversals as well as single-letter reversals were remedied through the use of praise for correct responses and feedback for errors. Modeling of correct and incorrect letters, when combined with praise and feedback, improved the reversals of another pupil in this study (Stromer, 1975). Individual tutoring of a 7-year-old pupil focused on letter training in the more recent study (Stromer, 1977). Letters were dictated to the pupil, who was then requested to write them. Contingent visual prompts were provided through flashcard presentations when the pupil hesitated. Correct responses earned verbal praise, and incorrect responses were ignored during the subsequent exercises. These procedures proved effective in reducing substantially the number of errors made. The flashcard and feedback procedures were similarly successful in reducing the digit reversals of one pupil (Experiment 2) and in reducing *b–d* and *p–g* reversals in a small-group setting (Experiment 3). Post-checks conducted 1–4 months after each experiment showed that the pupils continued to make satisfactory letter and digit discriminations.

The manipulation of social approval was the procedure described by Hasazi and Hasazi (1972) in an ABAB study of digit reversals by an 8-year-old math pupil. When teacher attention was withdrawn for reversal errors in math computation problems, these errors were reduced to a low level ($\bar{x} = 2.5$). Upon reinstatement of teacher attention for these reversals (i.e., marking these answers as incorrect and providing the child with "extra help" until all sums were written correctly), they increased ($\bar{x} = 20$). When the teacher's attention subsequently was provided for correct digit formation in Phase 4 (i.e., digit reversals with no computation error marked as "correct"; correctly computed and written sums likewise marked and praised), the pupil's frequency of reversals fell to an average of 2.0.

In summary, these studies of written digit and letter reversals lend support to several conclusions. First, the notion of a generic disability resulting in pervasive written reversals across curricular areas was not supported. In each of the studies reported, the reversal problem was a discrete and measurable one, amenable to precise initial assessment procedures. Second, it appears that the reversal of written symbols was remedied effectively through behavior modification procedures, specifically, antecedent modeling, contingent prompting, feedback, and contingent reinforcement. Third, the use of such interventions resulted, in some cases, in improved performance in nontargeted academic areas and settings (e.g., regular classroom). Finally, the gains by pupils extended beyond the termination of treatment procedures, as evidenced in follow-up observations.

While the measurement of a written reversal is relatively simple, assessment of other printing problems are not. In fact, the reliable measurement of manuscript strokes and letters has been difficult to achieve through most handwriting scales (Anderson, 1965; Feldt, 1962). Recently several studies have addressed themselves to the assessment of illegibility in manuscript writing (Helwig, Johns, Norman, & Cooper, 1976; Johns, Trap, & Cooper, 1977; Stowitschek & Stowitschek, 1979). In the first of these (Helwig *et al.*, 1976) the authors reported the use of evaluative overlays designed to measure three degrees of errors: deviation of 0–1mm, 0–2mm, and 0–3mm from the guidelines of the transparent overlay. Six criteria were identified for use in scoring manuscript letters. Writing samples from six children were scored by 10 observers, whose interrater agreements averaged 89% (for trained observers) and 88% (for naive observers). Between four and six letters per minute were scored, thus suggesting that the procedure was not only reliable but efficient. (The reader is referred to the article for a description of the construction and cost of the overlays.)

To increase further the efficiency of such manuscript evaluation procedures was the goal of a study by Johns *et al.* (1977). First graders in a regular school were trained to use the evaluative overlays described by Helwig and his colleagues (1976). Training to a predetermined proficiency level was accomplished through the use of small instructional groups (N = 8) practicing on a set of three training sheets. The first group required 12 sessions to meet criterion (75% agreement with outside observers); the other groups required 4 and 6 sessions, respectively. Thus, within 80–120 min, all first graders were capable of scoring accurately their own manuscript strokes and letters.

The ongoing evaluation of handwriting (printing) was an integral component of an instructional program reported by Stowitschek and Stowitschek (1979). Evaluative templates were used to assist pupils to check their own performance. These templates were placed below the student's printing (which was done on a semitransparent, reusable worksheet). As a result of evaluating their own work in this manner, students in a field test demonstrated improvement averaging 1.68 letters per session. (The sessions lasted from 20 to 35 min.) The use of systematic evaluative materials as part of an ongoing handwriting program offers considerable assistance to regular classroom teachers who must rely on efficient teaching practices. Although more controlled research is clearly needed, the self-evaluation of pupils' printing yields great savings in a teacher's instructional time.

The value of self-correction in the instruction of printing was demonstrated again in a study by Clark, Boyd, and Macrae (1975). The specific task addressed by this study was the legible completion of biographical information on employment application forms. Subjects were six delinquent or mildly retarded students enrolled in a pre-occupational class. Applications were drawn at random from a pool; each required the completion of nine items (e.g., telephone number, address, date of birth, reference). Training on each item required five phases; tokens were issued for work completion throughout these conditions. The youths were trained to correct their own errors, which were circled by the teacher. To correct an item, the student was required to explain the error and its correction, then to rewrite the item. A model of the item was provided to students having difficulty on self-correction. Generalization of form completion skills was measured on nontrained applications. Pretraining data indicated that the youths completed items with an average of 12% accuracy. In posttests on untrained applications, the students averaged 84% accurate responses. Thus, a time-efficient, individualized program was demonstrated to be effective in training mildly retarded adolescents to print commonly requested biographical information.

CURSIVE WRITING

The accurate and reliable assessment of cursive writing has been a concern of researchers at the University of Washington's Experimental Education Unit. Hansen and Lovitt (Note 1) described a scoring method adapted from Pelander and Willis (Note 2), through which they were able to achieve 95.7% interrater reliability. For a description of this assessment procedure, the reader is referred to Haring *et al.* (1978).

Younger pupils studying cursive writing were employed as subjects in a pioneer study reported by Trap and her colleagues (Trap, Milner-Davis, Joseph, & Cooper, 1978). First graders in a regular classroom were trained to use laminated training sheets and evaluative overlays. Criteria for the correct formation of letters were adapted from Helwig *et al.* (1976). During the four phases of the multiple-baseline across-subjects design, pupils were provided with no feedback (Baseline), verbal feedback and praise from the teacher as well as visual feedback from the overlays (Intervention 1), verbal and visual feedback and praise as well as rewriting of incorrect letters (Intervention 2), and, finally, with visual and verbal feedback and a certificate of achievement (Intervention 3). Results indicated that the intervention package was highly effective in producing gains in cursive writing performance. Specific data were as follows: Baseline, X = 23.95% letter strokes written correctly; Intervention 1, 37.56%; Intervention 2, 59.80%; and Intervention 3, 71.68%. Thus, the addition of an achievement certificate during the fourth phase resulted in the highest performance recorded. A major contribution of this study was the demonstration of a reliable assessment of cursive writing. Mean interrater reliability on the measurement of correct strokes was 82%; for incorrect strokes, reliability averaged 98%.

While the number of published, applied behavior analytic studies of *cursive* handwriting instruction are few, there does appear to be considerable recent interest in systematic investigation of this important curricular area. Haring (1978) described in brief detail several pilot studies on the training of cursive writing. One such effort required students to evaluate their own cursive stokes, using the aforementioned scoring method. The five elementary-school-age subjects improved: The average rates of correctly formed strokes rose to 14.5 per min from an average level of 9.5 per min assessed before training.

SUMMARY

In this section, studies on the assessment and remediation of handwriting problems have been reviewed. The literature on handwriting supports the following conclusions:

1. Specific contingent reinforcement is an effective strategy for increasing the number of correctly written letters by elementary school children (Hopkins *et al.*, 1971; Salzberg *et al.*, 1971).
2. Conflicting data exists regarding the question of generalization from trained to nontrained letters (Salzberg *et al.*, 1971; Hansen & Lovitt, Note 1).
3. Modeling, instructions, and praise are useful strategies for remedying the problem of digit and letter reversals (Smith & Lovitt, 1973; Stromer, 1975).
4. The assessment of handwriting is facilitated through the use of evaluative overlays and/or a systematic scoring procedure (Helwig *et al.*, 1976).
5. Students can be trained to self-evaluate their writing through the use of evaluative overlays (Helwig *et al.*, 1976). Self-evaluation may serve to improve writing performances (Stowitschek & Stowitschek, 1979).

Creative Writing

The study of creative writing demands a great deal from researchers. First, it is necessary to wrestle with definitions of what is and is not "creative." Secondly, the researcher must challenge the traditional stance of many educators, expressed by Itten (1964): "Every correction in an essay has an offensive effect which destroys a child's natural storytelling [p. 117]." Finally, the investigator whose interest is handicapped pupils may discover that creative writing is overlooked in their curricula, with priority given instead to the more basic written language skills. Nevertheless, a small group of studies of creative writing have appeared in the applied behavior analysis literature. While written by different persons, the studies form a distinct line of research inquiry: What effects will reinforcement and feedback have on the quantity and quality of children's story writing?

One of the earliest applied studies of creative writing was conducted by Taylor and Hoedt (1966) with 105 fourth-grade pupils in a regular public school. Two groups were designated to receive different feedback on their creative writing papers. Group A received praise statements as well as a notation (i.e., red-penciled circle) of the best parts of their papers. Group B did not receive praise, but was given specific feedback on ways to improve problems, which were circled in red. An attempt was made to insure equal distribution of comments to both groups. All remarks were selected from a pool designated before the onset of the study. Outcomes of the two interventions were determined by (*a*) a self-report completed by each pupil as to his or her subjective evaluation of the writing experience; and (*b*) a 30-point creative writing scale, completed by three other teachers, which purported to reflect such dimensions as originality, humor, sensory content, divergent thinking, depth of feeling, and fluency. The results of the study showed that *both* groups of pupils improved on this qualitative measure. However, members of the praised group reported more favorable attitudes and appeared more independent and self-motivated. This latter group also produced more writing than the nonreinforced group. This study cannot be considered an applied behavior analytic design; yet it deserves inclusion for its pilot role in initiating subsequent inquiries—the demonstration that the manipulation of teacher responses to children's story writing will not result in a deterioration in the quality of those stories.

The creative writing of 13 fifth graders in an "adjustment" classroom attracted the research interest of Brigham and his colleagues (Brigham, Graubard, & Stans, 1972). During three intervention phases of this multiple baseline design, three pupils earned points for the number of total words written, for total words plus different words, and new words, respectively. In addition to these frequency counts, measures of the quality of themes were recorded by college student judges using a five-dimensional rating scale. The shift from the baseline condition (nonspecific praise for work-related responses) to the first intervention (points given for number of words) affected all pupils' performance in a positive direction. These increases were not noted during the new-words and different-words contingencies. The authors explained that pupils were observed, in fact, to be spending considerable portions of these writing periods searching for new words rather than committing their discoveries to paper. Quality ratings followed the same pattern: Improved scores were noted during the point-reinforcement condition. A final observation was that the pupils, who had previously been labeled poor writers, expressed increased enthusiasm for writing throughout the study.

This investigation by Brigham and his colleagues (1972) confirmed the findings of Taylor and Hoedt (1966) along three dimensions:

1. The experimental manipulation of reinforcement applied to story writing did not jeopardize the creative quality of that writing.
2. The application of reinforcement to specific aspects of composition did in one case increase those responses (number of words) targeted by the contingencies.
3. The stories written by children appeared to yield to an expert evaluation of quality, although more precise analyses of this process were lacking.

(Brigham *et al.* (1972) did not report interjudge reliabilities. Taylor and Hoedt

(1966) employed arbitration and a forced interrater consensus procedure for quality ratings.)

Further delineation of compositional variables was accomplished by Maloney and Hopkins (1973) in the first of two studies on creative writing of elementary school children. These variables were identified as the number of (a) different adverbs; (b) prepositional phrases; (c) different adjectives; (d) different action verbs; and (e) different sentence beginnings. The latter three variables were directly targeted during three intervention phases. Intervention was modeled after the Good Behavior Game (Barrish et al., 1969). Two teams of pupils were awarded points according to their use of targeted compositional items (e.g., for each different adjective, the pupil received 5 points during Phrase I.) Each member of the winning team then exchanged points for recess time and candy. To assist pupils in using the targeted compositional items, the teacher presented models of these items at the beginning of each class session. Behavioral measures included frequency counts of the five compositional items and subjective ratings by two graduate students.

In general the data indicated that a compositional item, when targeted for reinforcement, appeared at a rate dramatically higher than that observed during nontargeted phases. Of particular interest was a collateral increase observed in the frequency of use of adverbs during the phase in which only action verbs were reinforced. With respect to quality, improvement was noted in all intervention phases as compared with the baseline phase. Moreover, stories written during the action-verbs contingency were deemed most creative. Interjudge agreements occurred on 15 out of 54 of the evaluations.

In a later investigation Maloney, Jacobsen, and Hopkins (1975) observed the differential effects of lectures, requests, teacher praise, and free time on creative writing of 19 third graders. During each session of this study the classroom teacher projected a color slide about which the pupils were to write five-sentence stories. The time required for each pupil to complete the story was recorded by a time clock imprint on the pupil's paper. Access to at least 2 min of free time was made available to all students upon completion of their papers during the initial baseline condition. Following this, a condition was arranged wherein a teacher read a standard lecture on the definitions of nouns, action verbs, adjectives, and adverbs. Accompanying the lecture was a discussion of these parts of speech by the class members. Following a return to baseline conditions, the lecture procedure was reinstated. The next antecedent manipulation consisted of a request (e.g., "Please use five action verbs") written on the chalkboard immediately following the lecture and discussion. During the subsequent phase, this general procedure was followed with the request modified to read, "Please use five different action verbs and five different adjectives." In the final four stages of the investigation, the lecture and written request were continued. Moreover, access to free time was made contingent upon the pupil's use of that compositional item identified in the requests during the phase (i.e., action verb, adjective, adverb, and action verb and adjective, respectively.) An attempt also was made to reduce general teacher praise and to increase specific praise statements to pupils about the targeted part(s) of speech. In addition to frequency counts of compositional items, qualitative measures were provided by a team of four independent raters. As in the previous study (Maloney & Hopkins, 1973), a pupil's story was compared only with others that he had written. No interstudent evaluations were made. Data from the first four phases (Baseline I, Lecture I, Baseline 2, Lecture 2) were essentially uniform. However, the number of nouns decreased slightly during the first lecture condition. An even greater decline was observed during the Lecture 2 phase. The lecture-and-request conditions appeared to have no significant effect on the use of the targeted action verbs and adjectives. However, clearly differentiated effects were noted as modifications in teacher praise and free time were imposed during the final four conditions. When specific praise statements and free time were made contingent upon use of the targeted part(s) of speech, pupils responded accordingly. Nontargeted items did not increase, with the exception of adverbs and action verbs, which increased collaterally as the result of reinforcement to either one. Reliability of quality ratings averaged 55%, with highest scores awarded to stories written during the action-verb condition. These findings corroborated those of Maloney and Hopkins (1973).

To reduce the amount of teacher time spent on creative writing instruction, Ballard and Glynn (1975) examined the utility of pupil-managed instruction. Thirty-seven students in a public school third-grade class were trained (*a*) to check their work against a "good writing chart" of performance criteria; (*b*) to record the number of sentences, different describing words, and different action words; and (*c*) to reward themselves with points according to a teacher-designated system. A random sample of 14 students was monitored throughout the five phases of the multiple-baseline across-behaviors design. The teacher provided models of sentences, action words, and "describing words" at the beginning of each session. Students were then encouraged to use three writing charts to remind them of good writing rules as they worked. These general procedures were modified after an initial baseline period to include the self-assessment described earlier. The use of action words and describing words and the number of sentences was essentially equivalent for the baseline and self-assessment phases. The application of self-distributed points, however, more than doubled the number of words written. Each compositional item showed highest frequency of use when it was specifically targeted for reinforcement. It was during these conditions that independent quality ratings also increased. A finding of particular interest was that during the action-words condition, subjective ratings of creativity were highest. This is a similar result to that of Maloney and Hopkins (1973), who found that increased use of verbs improved quality ratings.

Of greatest utility in mainstreamed settings, perhaps, are the data on pupils' ability to manage their own instruction and reinforcement during the daily 25-min sessions. Throughout the study, all pupils were successful in reinforcing their own composition efforts, despite some reported inaccuracies in counting specific parts of speech. (Identifying adjectives presented the greatest difficulty.)

SUMMARY

Despite the paucity of research in this curricular area, it appears that several guidelines can be stated with confidence for those interested in improving the compositions of handicapped and nonhandicapped children:

1. The delineation of specific aspects of composition through lectures, requests, visual prompts, and models does not jeopardize the creative expression of elementary school pupils.
2. Certain compositional items (i.e., adjectives, adverbs, sentence beginnings, nouns, and action verbs) can be increased through the application of teacher-mediated and/or self-mediated reinforcement.
3. The increased use of these reinforced compositional items does not result in generalized use of nonreinforced items, with the exception of adverbs and action verbs, which increased collaterally in some instances.
4. A positive correlation exists between use of action verbs and subsequent creativity ratings of a story by independent judges.
5. High rates of interrater agreements on "creativity" are still impossible to achieve, although levels better than chance have been reported.
6. Traditional approaches to the teaching of creative writing (e.g., lectures, requests, self-assessment models, prompts) are ineffective without reinforcement for targeted responses if the goal of instruction is to produce stories deemed "creative" by independent judges.

Concluding Remarks

Providing adequate individualized instruction to exceptional students enrolled in regular classrooms is a serious problem for mainstream teachers. The problem is heightened by the fact that many regular classroom teachers have no access to or experience with the applied behavior analysis literature on academic interventions. This literature, as reviewed in the preceding sections, has a great deal to offer mainstream teachers. Specifically, empirical support exists for many easily implemented instructional modifications. These modifications in some instances are specific to a single curricular area (e.g., creative writing), although many are applicable to several academic areas.

Mainstream teachers who consult the applied behavior analysis literature on academic interventions may be faced with a number of confusing issues. First, target subjects are not described uniformly. This problem was discussed in detail by Lovitt and Jenkins, two prominent researchers in the area, in a 1979 article on defining populations for learning disabilities research. In their paper, Lovitt and Jenkins suggested that researchers consider four uniform characteristics for subject descriptions: situational variables, demographic features, instructional variables, and motivational level. Only when these types of information are available will practitioners be able to make a sensible decision about the utility of an empirically documented instructional procedure. A second source of confusion to consumers of the applied behavior analysis literature in academics is the selection of target behaviors. With few exceptions (e.g., the literature on creative writing) research subsumed under a curricular area does not follow a logical or comprehensive line of inquiry. Rather, studies represent extemely diverse pinpoints, frequently chosen at the discretion of an individual researcher with little or no regard for prior work in that academic area. The exception to this practice is the work of researchers who have collaborated on projects for a significant length of time (e.g., researchers conducting studies at the Experimental Education Unit at the University of Washington). The failure to establish a systematic approach to the selection of academic pinpoints is further reflected in the selection of measurement procedures for determining outcomes of treatment programs. There are no explicit guidelines available to researchers or practitioners on what constitutes accuracy, completeness, or fluency in academic performance. This lack of a clear standard for measuring treatment outcomes has resulted in the publication of studies with questionable results.

In conclusion, the applied behavior analysis literature on academic interventions has a great deal to offer teachers of mainstreamed students. In order to maximize this offering, however, researchers must focus more attention on the critical methodological issues of target behavior selection, population description, and systematic evaluation of childrens' performance.

Reference Notes

1. Hansen, C. L., & Lovitt, T. C. *Effects of feedback on content and mechanics of writing.* Paper read at the NIE symposium, Seattle, July 1973.
2. Pelander, J., & Willia, B. *Branching cursive penmanship programs.* Lakewood, Wash., Clover Park School District #400, 1970.

References

Anderson, D. W. Handwriting research: movement and quality. *Elementary English*, 1965, 42, 45–53.
Axelrod, S., & Paluska, J. A component analysis of the effects of a classroom game on spelling

performance. In E. Ramp & G. Semb (Eds.), *Behavior analysis: Areas of research and application.* Englewood Cliffs, N.J.: Prentice-Hall, 1975.

Ballard, K. O., & Glynn, T. Behavioral self management in story writing with elementary school children. *Journal of Applied Behavior Analysis,* 1975, 8, 387–398.

Barrish, H. H., Saunders, M., & Wolf, M. M. Good Behavior Game: Effects of individual contingencies on disruptive behavior in a classroom. *Journal of Applied Behavior Analysis,* 1969, 2, 119–124.

Birch, H. G., & Lefford, A. Visual differentiation, intersensory integration, and voluntary motor control. *Monographs of Society for Research in Child Development,* 1967, 32, 2.

Blankenship, C. C., & Lovitt, T. C. Story problems: Merely confusing or downright befuddling. *Journal of Research in Mathematics Education,* 1976, 7, 290–298.

Brigham, T. H., Graubard, P. S., & Stans, A. Analysis of the effects of sequential reinforcement contingencies on aspects of composition. *Journal of Applied Behavior Analysis,* 1972, 5, 421–429.

Broden, M., Beasley, A., & Hall, R. V. In-class spelling performance. *Behavior Modification,* 1978, 2, 511–529.

Burney, J. D., & Shores, R. E. A study of relationships between instructional planning and pupil behavior. *Journal of Special Education Technology,* 1979, 2, 16–25.

Cahen, L. S., Craun, M. J., & Johnson, S. K. Spelling difficulty: A survey of the research. *Review of Educational Research,* 1971, 41(4), 281–301.

Clark, H. B., Boyd, S. B., & Macrae, J. W. A classroom program teaching disadvantaged youths to write biographic information. *Journal of Applied Behavior Analysis,* 1975, 8, 67–75.

Conlon, M. F., Hall, C., & Hanley, E. M. The effects of a peer correction procedure on the accuracy of two elementary school children. In G. Semb (Ed.), *Behavior analysis and education,* 1972. Lawrence, Kans.: University of Kansas Support and Development Center for Follow Through, Department of Human Development, 1972.

Cox, L. S. Diagnosing and remediating systematic errors in addition and subtraction computations. *The Arithmetic Teacher,* 1975, 22, 151–157.

Davis, M. Effects of having one remedial student tutor another remedial student. In G. Semb (Ed.), *Behavior analysis and education,* 1972. Lawrence, Kans.: University of Kansas Support Development Center for Follow Through, Department of Human Development, 1972.

Dineen, J. P., Clark, H. B., & Risley, T. R. Peer tutoring among elementary students: Educational benefits to the tutor. *Journal of Applied Behavior Analysis,* 1977, 10, 231–238.

Enstrom, A. Out of the classroom. Handwriting for the retarded. *Exceptional Children,* 1966, 32, 385–388.

Fauke, J., Burnett, J., Bowers, M. A., & Sulzer-Azaroff, B. Improvement of handwriting and letter recognition skills: A behavior modification procedure. *Journal of Learning Disabilities,* 1973, 6, 296–300.

Feldt, L. S. The reliability of measures of handwriting quality. *The Journal of Educational Psychology,* 1962, 53, 288–292.

Felixbrod, J. J., & O'Leary, K. O. Effect of reinforcement on children's academic behavior as a function of self-determined and externally imposed contingencies. *Journal of Applied Behavior Analysis,* 1973, 6, 241–250.

Fernald, G. M. *Remedial techniques in basic school subjects.* New York: McGraw-Hill, 1943.

Fink, W. T., & Carnine, D. W. Control of arithmetic errors using informational feedback. *Journal of Applied Behavior Analysis,* 1975, 8, 461.

Fitzgerald, J. A. Words mispelled most frequently by children at the fourth, fifth, and sixth grade levels in life outside the school. *Journal of Educational Research,* 1932, 26, 213–218.

Foxx, R. M., & Jones, J. R. A remediation program for increasing the spelling achievement of elementary and junior high school students. *Behavior Modification,* 1978, 2 (2), 211–230.

Furner, B. A. Recommended instructional procedures in the method of emphasizing the perceptual motor nature of learning in handwriting. *Elementary English,* 1969, 46, 1021–1030.

Gallagher, H. H. *The tutoring of brain-injured mentally retarded children.* Springfield, Ill.: Charles C. Thomas, 1960.

Glicking, E. E., & Armstrong, D. L. Levels of instructional difficulty as related to on-task behavior, task completion and comprehension. *Journal of Learning Disabilities,* 1978, *11,* 559–566.

Glim, T. C. *The Palo Alto reading program: Sequential steps in reading.* New York: Harcourt, 1968.

Graham, R. T., & Rudorf, E. H. Dialect and spelling. *Elementary English,* 1970, *47,* 363–376.

Green, M. I. An introductory study of teaching handwriting to the brain injured child. *Exceptional Child,* 1967, *34,* 44–45.

Greenwood, C. R., Sloane, H. N., & Baskin, A. Training elementary aged peer behavior managers to control small group programmed mathematics. *Journal of Applied Behavior Analysis,* 1974, *7,* 103–114.

Hamblin, R. L., Hathaway, C., & Wodarski, J. Group contingencies, peer tutoring, and accelerating academic achievement. In E. A. Ramp & B. L. Hopkins (Eds.), *A new direction for education: Behavior analysis, 1971.* Lawrence: University of Kansas Support and Development Center for Follow Through, 1971.

Hanley, E. M. Review of research involving applied behavior analysis in the classroom. *Review of Educational Research,* 1970, *40,* 597–625.

Hanna, P. R., Hanna, J. S., Hodges, R. E., & Rudorf, E. H. *Phoneme-grapheme correspondence as cues to spelling improvement.* Washington, D.C.: U.S. Department of Health, Education and Welfare, Office of Education, 1966. OE32008.

Hanna, P. R., & Moore, J. T. Spelling—from spoken word to written symbol. *Elementary School Journal,* 1953, *53,* 329–337.

Haring, N. G., Lovitt, T. C., Eaton, M. D., & Hansen, C. L. *The fourth r: Research in the classroom.* Columbus, Ohio: Merrill, 1978.

Harris, V. W., & Sherman, J. A. Effects of peer tutoring and consequences on the math performance of elementary classroom students. *Journal of Applied Behavior Analysis,* 1973, *6,* 587–597.

Harris, V. W., Sherman, J. A., Henderson, D. G., & Harris, M. S. The effect of a tutoring procedure on the spelling performance of elementary classroom students. In G. Semb (Ed.), *Behavior analysis and education, 1972.* Lawrence: The University of Kansas Support and Development Center for Follow Through, Department of Human Development, 1972.

Hasazi, J. E., & Hasazi, S. E. Effects of teacher attention on digit-reversal behavior in an elementary school child. *Journal of Applied Behavior Analysis,* 1972, *5,* 157–162.

Haskett, G. T., & Lenfestey, W. Reading-related behavior in an open classroom: Effects of novelty and modeling on preschoolers. *Journal of Applied Behavior Analysis,* 1974, *7,* 233–241.

Haubrich, T. A., & Shores, R. E. The interrelationship of controlling attending behavior and academic performance of emotionally disturbed children. *Exceptional Children,* 1976, *42,* 337–338.

Helwig, J. J., Johns, J. C., Norman, J. E., & Cooper, J. O. The measurement of manuscript letter strokes. *Journal of Applied Behavior Analysis,* 1976, *9,* 231–236.

Hendrickson, J. M., Roberts, M., & Shores, R. E. Antecedent and contingent modeling to teach basic sight vocabulary to learning disabled children. *Journal of Learning Disabilities,* 1978, *11,* 524–528.

Hopkins, B. L., Schutte, R. C., & Garton, K. L. The effects of access to a playroom on the rate and quality of printing and writing of first and second grade students. *Journal of Applied Behavior Analysis,* 1971, *4,* 77–88.

Horn, E. Phonetics and spelling. *Elementary School Journal,* 1957, *57,* 424–432.

Horn, T. D. Spelling. *Encyclopedia of educational research* (4th ed.). London: Macmillan, 1969.

Hundert, J., & Bucher, B. Pupils' self-scored arithmetic performance for maintaining accuracy. *Journal of Applied Behavior Analysis,* 1978, *11,* 304.

Itten, J. Design and form. New York: A. Reinhold Publishing, 1964.

Johns, J., Trap, J., & Cooper, J. Students' self-recording of manuscript letter strokes. Journal of Applied Behavior Analysis, 1977, 10, 509–514.

Jenkins, J. R., Barksdale, A., & Clinton, L. Improving reading comprehension and oral reading: Generalization across behaviors, settings, and time. Journal for Learning Disabilities, 1978, 11, 607–617.

Johnson, M., & Bailey, J. S. Cross-age tutoring: Fifth graders as arithmetic tutors for kindergarten children. Journal of Applied Behavior Analysis, 1974, 7, 223–232.

Jones, W. F. Concrete investigation of the material of English spelling. Vermillion, S. D.: University of South Dakota, 1914.

Kauffman, J. M., Hallahan, D. P., Haas, K., Brame, T., & Boren, R. Imitating children's errors to improve their spelling performance. Journal of Learning Disabilities, 1978, 11(4), 217–222.

Kerr, M. M., & Strain, P. S. Use of precision planning techniques by teacher trainees with behaviorally disordered pupils. Monograph in Behavioral Disorders, 1978, 93–106.

Kirby, F. O., & Shields, F. Modification of arithmetic response rate and attending behavior in a seventh-grade student. Journal of Applied Behavior Analysis, 1972, 5, 79–84.

Knapczyk, D. R., & Livingston, G. The effects of prompting question asking upon on-task behavior and reading comprehension. Journal of Applied Behavior Analysis, 1974, 7, 115–12.

Lahey, B. B., & Drabman, R. S. Facilitation of the acquisition and retention of sight–word vocabulary through token reinforcement. Journal of Applied Behavior Analysis, 1974, 7, 307–312.

Lahey, B. B., McNees, M. P., & Brown, C. C. Modification of deficits in reading for comprehension. Journal of Applied Behavior Analysis, 1973, 6, 475–480.

Lovitt, T. C. Self-management projects with children with behavioral disabilities. Journal of Learning Disabilities, 1973, 6, 138–150.

Lovitt, T. C. Applied behavior analysis and learning disabilities. Journal of Learning Disabilities, 1975, 8, 504–518.

Lovitt, T. C., & Curtiss, K. A. Effects of manipulating an antecedent event on mathematics response rate. Journal of Applied Behavior Analysis, 1968, 1, 329–333.

Lovitt, T. C., & Curtiss, K. A. Academic response rate as a function of teacher- and self-imposed contingencies. Journal of Applied Behavior Analysis, 1969, 2, 49–53.

Lovitt, T. C., Eaton, M., Kirkwood, M., & Pelander, J. Effects of various reinforcement contingencies on oral reading rate. In E. A. Ramp & B. L. Hopkins (Eds.), A new direction for education: Behavior analysis. Lawrence: Kansas Press, 1971.

Lovitt, T. C., Guppy, T. E., & Blattner, J. E. The use of a free-time contingency with fourth graders to increase spelling accuracy. Behavior Research and Therapy, 1969, 7, 151–156.

Lovitt, T. C., & Hansen, C. L. Round one: placing the child in the right reader. Journal of Learning Disabilities, 1976, 9, 347–353.

Lovitt, T. C., & Hurlburt, M. Using behavior analysis techniques to assess the relationship between phonics instruction and oral reading. Journal of Special Education, 1974, 8, 57–72.

Lovitt, T. C., & Jenkins, J. R. Learning disabilities research: Defining populations. Learning Disability Quarterly, 1979, 2, 46–50.

Maloney, K. B., & Hopkins, B. L. The modification of sentence structure and its relationship to subjective judgment of creativity in writing. Journal of Applied Behavior Analysis, 1973, 6, 425–434.

Maloney, K. B., Jacobsen, C. R., & Hopkins, B. L. An analysis of the effects of lectures, requests, teacher praise, and free time on the creative writing behaviors of third-grade children. In E. A. Ramp & G. Semb (Eds.), Behavior analysis areas of research and application. Englewood Cliffs, N.J.: Prentice-Hall, 1975.

McCarty, T., Griffin, S., Apolloni, T., & Shores, R. E. Increased peer-teaching with group-oriented contingencies for arithmetic performance in behavior disordered adolescents. *Journal of Applied Behavior Analysis*, 1977, *10*, 313.

McCracken, G., & Walcutt, C. *Lippincott's basic reading*. Philadelphia: Lippincott, 1966.

Neef, N. A., Iwata, B. A., & Page, T. J. The effects of known-item interspersal on acquisition and retention of spelling and sight reading words. *Journal of Applied Behavior Analysis*, 1977, *10*, 738.

Nichols, S. Pupil motivation: A rewarding experience. *Modern English Journal*, 1970, *8*, 3641.

O'Leary, K. D., & Drabman, R. Token reinforcement programs in the classroom: A review. *Psychological Bulletin*, 1971, *75*, 379–398.

Ousley, O., & Russell, D. *Around the corner*. Boston: Ginn, 1961.

Parker, O., & Scannel, G. *SRA Reading Laboratories*. Chicago: Science Research Associates, 1961.

Ragland, E. U., Kerr, M. M., & Strain, P. S. Effects of teacher-mediated peer feedback on the social play of withdrawn children. *Behavior Modification*, in press.

Rainwater, N., & Ayllon, T. Increasing academic performance by using a timer as antecedent stimulus: A study of four cases. *Behavior Therapy*, 1976, *14*, 672–677.

Rapport, M. S., & Bostow, D. E. The effects of access to special activities on the performance in four categories of academic tasks with third grade students. *Journal of Applied Behavior Analysis*, 1976, *9*, 372.

Reavis, H. K., & Rice, J. A. Formative evaluation of academic tool teaching packages with student peers. *Journal of Special Education Technology*, 1978, *2*, 47–53.

Rieth, H. J., Axelrod, S., Anderson, R., Hathaway, F., Wood, K., & Fitzgerald, C. Influence of distributed practice and daily testing on weekly spelling tests. *Journal of Educational Research*, 1974, *68*, 73–77.

Rieth, H. J., Polsgrove, L., McLeskey, J., Payne, K., & Anderson, R. The use of self-recording to increase arithmetic performance of severely behaviorally disordered students. *Behavior Disorders*, Monograph Series No. 1, 1978, 50–58.

Rieth, H. J., Polsgrove, L., Raia, S., Patterson, N., & Buchman, K. The use of free time to increase the reading achievement of three students placed in programs for behavior disordered children. *Behavioral Disorders*, 1977, *3*, 45–54.

Roberts, A. H. A review by a specialist in the uses of computers in linguistic research. *Research in the Teaching of English*, 1967, *1*, 201–207.

Robertson, S. J., DeReus, D. M., & Drabman, R. S. Peer and college-student tutoring as reinforcement in a token economy. *Journal of Applied Behavior Analysis*, 1976, *9*, 169–177.

Salzberg, B. H., Wheeler, A. A., Devar, L. T., & Hopkins, B. L. The effects of intermittent feedback and intermittent contingent access to play on printing of kindergarten children. *Journal of Applied Behavior Analysis*, 1971, *4*, 163–171.

Shea, D. P. The case for the kinesthetic method. *Grade Teacher*, 1956, *74*, 60.

Slingerland, B. A. A multi-sensory approach to reading, writing and spelling. Cambridge, Mass.: Educators Publishing Service, 1969.

Smith, D. D., & Lovitt, T. C. The educational diagnosis and remediation of written b and d reversal problems: A case study. *Journal of Learning Disabilities*, 1973, *6*, 356–363.

Smith, D. D., & Lovitt, T. C. The differential effects of reinforcement contingencies on arithmetic performance. *Journal of Learning Disabilities*, 1975, *8*, 21–29. (a)

Smith, D. D., & Lovitt, T. C. The use of modeling techniques to influence the acquisition of computational arithmetic skills in learning-disabled children. In E. Ramp & G. Semb (Eds.), *Behavior analysis: Areas of research and application*. Englewood Cliffs, N.J.: Prentice-Hall, 1975, 183–308. (b)

Smith, D. A., Lovitt, T. C., & Kidder, J. D. Using reinforcement contingencies and teaching aids to alter subtraction performance of children with learning disabilities. In G. Semb (Ed.),

Behavior analysis and education, 1973. Lawrence, University of Kansas Support Development Center for Follow Through, Department of Human Development, 1973.

Smith, N. B. *Reading instruction for today's children.* Englewood Cliffs, N.J.: Prentice-Hall, 1963.

Solomon, H., & MacNeill, I. Spelling ability: A comparison between computer output based on the phonemic–graphemic algorithm and actual student performance in elementary grades. *Research in the Teaching of English,* 1967, *1,* 157–175.

Stowitschek, C. E., & Stowitschek, J. J. Evaluating handwriting performance: The student helps the teacher. *Journal of Learning Disabilities,* 1979, *12*(3), 203–206.

Strauss, A., & Lehtinen, L. *Psychopathology and education of the brain injured child.* New York: Grune & Stratton, 1947.

Stromer, R. Modifying letter and number reversals in elementary school children. *Journal of Applied Behavior Analysis,* 1975, *8,* 211.

Stromer, R. Remediating academic deficiencies in learning disabled children. *Exceptional Children,* 1977, *43,* 432–440.

Taylor, W. F., & Hoedt, K. C. The effect of praise upon the quality and quantity of creative writing. *Journal of Educational Research,* 1966, *60,* 80–83.

Trap, J. J., Milner-Davis, P., Joseph, S., & Cooper, J. O. The effects of feedback and consequences of transitional cursive letter formation. *Journal of Applied Behavior Analysis,* 1978, *11,* 381–393.

Van Houten, R., Hill, S., & Parsons, M. An analysis of a performance feedback system: The effects of timing and feedback, public posting, and praise upon academic performance and peer interaction. *Journal of Applied Behavior Analysis,* 1975, *8,* 449–457.

Van Houten, R., Morrison, E., Jarvis, R., & McDonald, M. The effects of explicit timing and feedback on compositional response rate in elementary school children. *Journal of Applied Behavior Analysis,* 1974, *7,* 547–555.

Van Houten, R., & Thompson, C. The effects of explicit timing on math performance. *Journal of Applied Behavior Analysis,* 1976, *9,* 227–230.

Willis, J., Crowder, J., & Morris, B. A. A behavioral approach to remedial reading using students as behavioral engineers. In G. Semb (Ed.), *Behavior analysis and education, 1972.* Lawrence: University of Kansas Support Development Center for Follow Through, Department of Human Development, 1972.

Zimmerman, E. H., & Zimmerman, J. The alteration of behavior in a special classroom situation. *Journal of the Experimental Analysis of Behavior,* 1962, *5,* 59–60.

Subject Index

A

Academic instruction, mainstreaming, *see* Mainstreaming, academic instruction
Administrator attitudes, mainstreaming, 51
Academic competence and peer attitudes, EMR, 58
Academic effects, placement, 1–10, *see also* Special versus regular class placement
Adult versus peer reinforcement, 114–116
Age and peer attitudes, 59
Aggression, peer modification, 113
Antecedent teaching strategies, *see* Teaching strategies, antecedent
Antisocial behavior, 13
Arithmetic and mainstreaming, 165–176
  antecedent teaching strategies, 167–171
  assessment and planning, 166–167
  behavior analysis research, 166–176
  demonstration plus permanent model, 169–171
  feedback, teacher, 171–172
  generalization of performance, 170–171
  instructional aids, 168
  peer-mediated strategies, 172–174
  permanent model, 169–171
  self-mediated strategies, 172–174
  teacher variables, 169–171
  timing effects, 167–168

Assessment
  educational placement, 25–31
  manuscript writing, 197–198
  peer social behavior, 103–104, 106–109
  social adjustment, 30
  social initiations, 110
  social interactions, 103–104, 111–112
  social isolation, 103–104
  spelling, 186–187
At risk children, 102, 122
Attitude modification, 39–40
Attitude scaling, 39
Attitudes of retarded, 19–20
Attitudes toward mentally retarded, 37–66
  attitude modification, 39–40
  attitude scaling, 39
  attribution theory, 43–44
  community, 41–44, 65
  expectancy paradigm, 40–41
  Head Start, 83
  and labeling, teachers, 52–57
  peers, 14–15, 20, 24, 57–66
  physical characteristics, 41–42
  professionals, 44–57, 65–66
  public opinion surveys, 38
  regular classroom teachers, 48–50
  research paradigms, 38
  versus slow learners, 42
  sociometric rating, 40, 60–65

stereotypes, investigations, 38–39
student teaching, effects, 48
teachers, 13–15, 41, 44–57, 65–66
teachers, special versus regular, 46–47, 51
Attribution theory, 43–44
Autism, mainstreaming, 79

B

Basal texts, reading, 176
Behavior generalization, 107–111, 114, 119,
    144
Behavior problems, classroom management,
    129–159
  contingency contracting, 145–146
  Good Behavior Game Procedure, 134–136
  group contingencies, 133
  home-based reporting, 146–148
  mainstream settings, 159
  peer-mediated feedback, 136–137
  praise, effects, 132
  rules, 131–134
  self-management, 140–145
  self-recording, 140–145
  standards for performance, 131–134
  target behaviors, 159
  teacher talk, 129–131
  teacher training, 152–159
  time out, 137–139
  token reinforcement, 148–152
Behavioral contingencies, *see* Contingencies,
    behavioral
Behavioral development and peer relations,
    102–105
  developmental delay, 102, 122
  social isolation, 102–103
Behavioral engineers, 183
Behavioral processes
  peer influence, 104
  reciprocity, 105–112
Behavioral ratings, EMR, 19–21, 30–31
Bilingual programs, mainstreaming, 79

C

California Achievement Test, 6–7
Classroom performance, 131
Classroom rules, 131–134
Center-based mainstreaming, 78

Community attitudes, 41–44
  attribution theory, 43–44
  mild versus severe retardation, 42–43
  physical causation, retardation, 41–42
  trends, 65
Consequation strategies
  handwriting, 194
  reading, 180–183
Consultation programs, teachers, 152–159,
    see also Teacher training
  and contingent attention, 153
  Prevention–Intervention Project, 157
  procedures, description, 158
  Program for Academic Survival Skills,
    155–156
  social skills, 154
  Vermont Consulting Teacher Model,
    157–158
Contingencies, behavioral, 120, 145–146
  behavior problems, 145–146
  group, 133–134
  handwriting, 193–195
  home-based, 147
  reading, 185
  and teacher attention, 153
Correlational studies, peer reinforcement, 112
Costs, mainstreaming, 82–83
Creative writing, 200–204
  pupil-managed instruction, 203–204
  reinforcement, 200–203
Curriculum, 6–9, 26
Cursive writing, 199–200

D

Deaf, see Hearing-impaired
Decertification, 51
Dehumanization, 24–25
Demand characteristics, experiments, 54
Demon. list method, 186–187
Demonstration-plus-permanent-model,
    169–171
  generalization, 170–171
Developmental delay, 102, 122
  peer social behavior, effects, 101–121
Differential reinforcement, 132–133, 138
Digital reversals, 196–199
Direct intervention, handwriting, 196
Discriminative stimuli, 119–120
Distributed practice, spelling, 190–191

E

Economics, mainstreaming, 82–83
Educable mentally retarded
  academic instruction, 165–205
  attitudes, 37–66
  mainstreaming, 1–32, 71–95
  outcomes, 85–89
  peer instruction, 101–122
  preschool mainstreaming, 71–95
  special class placement, 1–32
Educational factors, preschool mainstreaming,
  75–76
Educational level and peer attitudes, 59
Educational placement problems, 2–5, 9,
  28–29, 32
Error analysis, 166–167
Exceptional children, *see* Educable mentally
  retarded
Expectancy and attitudes, 53–57
Expectancy paradigm, 40–41

F

Family, effect of preschool mainstreaming,
  91–93
Feedback
  classroom behavior, 132–133
  creative writing, 200–203
  peer-mediated strategies, 136–137
Film-mediated models, 117–118
First Chance Projects, 87
Free time, 182–183
Functional analysis research, 107–109

G

Generalization of behavior change, 107–111,
  114, 144
  arithmetic, 170–171
  handwriting, 195–196
  reading, 181–182
  self-management, 144
  spelling, 190
Good Behavior Game, 134–136, 187
Group contingency, 133–135, *see also* Contingencies, behavioral
  arithmetic performance, 173

H

Handwriting
  assessment, 197–198
  cursive writing, 199–200
  digital reversals, 196–199
  instruction approaches, 193
  letter reversals, 196–199
  manuscript writing, 193–199
Head Start, 81–83
  case studies, 86
  costs, 82–83
  family, effects, 91–93
  handicapped preschoolers, 81–83
  legal factors, 75
  parent attitudes, 83, 91–93
  parents, effects, 91–93
  teacher attitudes, 82–83, 90
Hearing-impaired preschoolers, 83–85
  criteria for appropriateness, 84
  family, 91–93
  longitudinal studies, 86–87
  parents, 83, 85, 91–93
  programs, 83–85
High risk, *see* At risk children
Home-based education
  mainstreaming, 78
  reporting, 146–148
  tutoring, 189–190
Human development, *see* Behavioral development and peer relations

I

Illinois Index of Self-Derogation, 16–18, 21
Imitative behavior
  establishment, 119
  peer attitudes, 63
  spelling, 191–192
  variables affecting performance, 119–121
Individualized instruction
  Public Law 94–142, 9
  social adaptation, 21
Instructional process, 7–9, 26–27
  arithmetic aids, 168
  behavior, 130
  reading plan, 178–179
Integrated settings, *see* Mainstreaming

Intelligence Quotient
  school placement, 4
  social acceptance, 14

L

Labeling, 24
  college students, 55–56
  demand characteristics, experiments, 54
  and peer attitudes, 58, 62
  teacher evaluations, 52–57
Language models, 118–119
Least restrictive environment, 71, 75
Legal factors, preschool mainstreaming, 75
Letter reversals, 196–199
Location, school, 21
Longitudinal studies
  deaf, 86
  preschool mainstreaming, 86–87

M

Mainstreaming, *see also* Special versus regular
    class placement
  academic instruction, 165–205
  administrator attitudes, 51
  arithmetic, 165–176
  attitudes, 37–66
  costs, 82–83
  definition, 73–74
  Head Start, 81–83
  hearing-impaired, 83–85
  legal factors, 75
  parent attitudes, 83
  predictors of attitudes, 51–52
  preschool, 71–95
  problem behaviors, 159
  Public Law 94–142, 75
  reading, 176–186
  scaling studies, attitudes, 39
  spelling, 186–192
  teacher attitudes, 50, 82
  teacher selection, 51–52
Mainstreaming, academic instruction,
    165–205
  arithmetic, 165–176
  behavior analysis research, 165–205
  creative writing, 200–204
  handwriting, 192–200
  reading, 176–186
  spelling, 186–192

Mainstreaming, preschool
  autism programs, 79
  bilingual programs, 79
  case studies, 85–86
  center-based programs, 78
  child outcomes, 85–89
  definition, 73–75, 94
  educational factors, 75–76
  versus elementary, 72–73
  family effects, 91–93
  and Head Start, 81–83, 86
  hearing-impaired, 83–85
  home-based programs, 78
  as intervention strategy, 71–72
  legal factors, 75
  literature on, characterization, 72
  longitudinal studies, 86–87
  outcomes, 85–89
  parents, effects, 91–93, 77, 81
  peer attitudes, 81
  peers, imitation, 88
  program models, 78–79
  program outcomes, 78–81
  Public Law 94–142, 71
  rationale, 73–77
  research, implications, 95
  social factors, 76–77
  social interactions, 87–89
  success of predictors, 80, 94
  theory, 94–95
  visually handicapped, 79
Mainstreaming, preschool versus elementary,
    72–73
Maintenance of treatment effects
  definition, 111
  handwriting, 197
  peer strategies, 111, 136
  self-regulation, 141–142, 144
  spelling remediation, 188
  teacher training, 157
Manuscript writing, 193–199
  assessment, 197–198
  consequation, 194
  instruction, 193
  letter and digital reversals, 196–199
  and play, 193–194
Measurement, *see* Assessment
Mental retardation, *see* Educable mentally
    retarded
Methodology, placement studies, 25–31
  dependent measures, 29–31

independent variable, 25–28
subject selection, 28–29
Metropolitan Achievement Test, 7
Mild retardation, attitudes, 42–43
Minnesota Teacher Attitude Inventory, 48–49
Modeling, *see also* Peer modeling
  handwriting, 193, 197
  peer attitudes, 63
  preschool mainstreaming, 77
  spelling, 191–192
  of teachers, 131
Monetary reinforcement and reading,
  181–182

N

Number reversals, 196–199

O

Observational ratings, 30–31
Observational research, 105–107, 110–111
Ohio Social Acceptance Scale, 18, 21
On-task behavior, 26, 130
Outcome studies, EMR, 85–89
  case studies, 85–86
  longitudinal studies, 86–87
  peers, 88
  play, 87–88
  social interactions, analysis, 87–89
  teachers, 89–91

P

Parent attitudes, mainstreaming, 83, 91–93
Parents
  hearing-impaired, 83
  home-based instruction, 78, 146–148,
    189–190
  preschool mainstreaming, 91–93
Peer attitudes, 57–65
  description, 57
  and labeling, 58
  and modeling, 63
  and preschool mainstreaming, 81, 89
  regular versus integrative classes, effects,
    58–63
  remediation, 63–65
  toward retarded, 14–15, 20, 24, 57–65
  sex differences, 61

and social standing, 60–63
urban versus suburban, 62
Peer-mediated strategies
  arithmetic, 172–174
  problem behavior, 136–137
  reading, 183–184
  training packages, 173–174
Peer modeling
  film-mediation, 117
  imitative behavior, 119–121
  reinforcement, 119–120
  social behavior change, 116–121
  variables affecting, 119–121
Peer reinforcement
  versus adult reinforcement, 114–116
  and aggression, 113
  correlational studies, 112
  experimental analysis, 113–116
  and generalization, 107–111, 119
  imitative behavior, 119–121
  maintenance of effects, 111, 116
  modeling, 116–121
  preschools, 107–109, 112–116
  reciprocity of interaction, 106
  of socially withdrawn, 107–112
Peer social behavior, preschools, 101–121
  and aggression, 113
  assessment, 103–104, 106–109
  and behavior change, 105–113, 116–121
  and behavioral development, 102–103
  behavioral processes, 104–105
  clinical application issues, 109–112
  correlational studies, 112–113
  developmental potentials, 101–121
  experimental analysis, 113–116
  functional analysis research, 107–109
  generalization, 107–111, 114
  and imitation, 119–121
  instructional potentials, 101–121
  maintenance of effects, 111, 116
  modeling, 116–121
  observational research, 105–107, 110
  reciprocity, 105–112
  reinforcement, 107–109, 112–116
  social initiations, 107–112
  therapy, 107–109
Peer tutoring
  arithmetic, 170–171
  benefits to tutor, 188
  reading, 181–182
  spelling, 187–189

Performance, classroom, 131
Permanent model, 169–171
Phoneme–grapheme pattern, 187
Phonics instruction and reading, 179–180
Physical causation, retardation, 41–42
PL 94–142, see Public Law 94–142
Planning strategies, reading, 178–179
Play
  and handwriting, 193–194
  preschool mainstreaming, 87–88
Praise, 132, 141–142
Predictors of success, mainstreaming, 80, 94
Prereading, 180
Preschool mainstreaming, see Mainstreaming,
    preschool
Problem behavior, see Behavior problems,
    classroom management
Professionals' attitudes, 44–57, 65–66, see
    also Teacher attitudes
  experience, influence, 45
  training, effects, 45
Program outcomes, preschool mainstreaming,
    78–81
Prompting and reading, 179–180
Public Law 94–142
  least restrictive environment, 71, 75
  mainstreaming, 75
  zero reject, 71
Public opinion surveys, 38
Pupil-managed instruction, 203–204

R

Reading and mainstreaming, 176–186
  antecedent teaching strategies, 179–180
  basal texts, 176–177
  consequation strategies, 180–183
  free time, 182–183
  generalization, 181–182
  monetary reinforcement, 181–182
  peer strategies, 183–184
  phonics instruction, 179
  planning strategies, 178–179
  prereading, 180
  prompting, 179–180
  self-mediated strategies, 185
  teaching, 179–180
  token reinforcement, 180–181
Reciprocity of interaction, 105–112
  and aggression, 113
  functional analysis research, 107–109

observational research, 105–107, 110
  peer behavior change, 105–112
  peer therapists, 107–108
  predictors of success, 109
Regular classrooms, tokens, 148–152
Regular versus special classrooms, see also
    Mainstreaming
  peer attitudes, effects, 58–63
  and social standing, retarded, 60–63
Reinforcement
  creative writing, 200
  problem behavior, 132
  spelling, 191
Reinforcement, differential, 132–133, 138
Reinforcement, peer, see Peer reinforcement
Report cards, home-based, 146–148
Resource program schools
  peer attitudes, 61–62
  teacher attitudes, 47
Retardation, see Educable mentally retarded
Reverse mainstreaming, 74
Rosenthal effect, 52
Rucker-Gable Educational Programming
    Scale, 53
Rules, classroom, 131–134
  differential feedback, 132–133
  problem behavior, 131–134
  student performance, 131

S

School location, social factors, 21
Science Research Associates, 183
Self-concept
  long-term study, 17
  mainstreaming, 16–19, 21–25, 77
  special class placement, 16–19, 21–25
Self-fulfilling prophesy, teachers, 55
Self-instruction
  arithmetic, 175–176
  creative writing, 203–204
  handwriting, 198–199
  reading, 185
Self-management, 140–145
  academic instruction, 176
  accuracy, 143
  arithmetic, 175
  handwriting, 198–199
  maintenance of effects, 141–142, 144
  reading, 185
  teacher praise, 141–142

Self-ratings, 30
Self-recording, *see* Self-management
Self-scoring, arithmetic, 175–176
Sex differences
  class placement, 7
  peer attitudes, 61
  peer reinforcement, 116
Slow learners and attitudes, 42
Social acceptance
  effects of exposure, 64
  mainstreaming, 14–15, 18, 20–21, 23
  remediation, 63–65
  and school location, 21
  special versus regular classrooms, 14–15,
    18, 20–21, 23, 60–63
Social adjustment
  individualized instruction, 21
  measures, 30
  special versus regular classes, 15–16, 21–22
Social approval and handwriting, 197
Social behavior change
  film-mediated models, 117–118
  peer modeling, 116–121
Social behavior, preschool peers, *see* Peer so-
    cial behavior, preschools
Social consequences, placement, 10–25
  major findings, 22–25
  studies, era when conducted, 22–23
Social factors, preschools, 76–77
Social initiations, peers
  aggression, 113
  clinical application, 109–112
  functional analysis research, 107–109
  generalization of change, 107–111, 114
  maintenance of change, 111
  modeling, 116–121
  measurement, 110
  observational research, 105–107, 110–111
  predictors of success, 109
Social interaction
  assessment, 103–104, 111–112
  correlational studies, 112–113
  experimental analyses, 113–116
  peer modeling, 116–121
  peer therapists, 107–112, 174
Social interaction, preschoolers, 87–89, *see
    also* Peer social behavior, preschools
  behavioral processes, 104–105
  peers, 88–89
  play, 87–88
  teacher involvements, 87–88

Social isolation
  assessment, 103–104
  behavior development, 102–103
  film-mediated models, 117
  generalization of change, 107–108
  mainstreaming, 11
  maintenance of change, 111
  peer modeling, 116–121, 137
  peer therapists, 107–109, 137
  reciprocity of interaction, 105–107
Social standing, 11–12, 60–65
  educational placement, 11–12
  peer attitudes, 60–65
  remediation, 63–65
  sociometry, 60–63
  urban versus suburban, 62
Socioeconomic status, 12, 18–19
Sociometry, 40
  attitude remediation, 63–65
  class placement, effects, 11–12, 14, 17, 30
  peer ratings, 60–65
  preschool mainstreaming, 88
  and social isolation, 103
Special versus regular class placement
  academic consequences, 1–10
  achievement, 10
  antisocial behavior, 13
  attitudes of retarded, 19–20
  behavioral ratings, 19–21, 30–31
  civil liberties, 25
  controlled study, 5–6
  curriculum, 6–9, 26
  dehumanization, 24–25
  dependent measures, 29–31
  extraschool outcomes, 17
  independent variable, definition, 25–28
  individualized instruction, 7–8, 21
  instructional process, 7–9, 26–27
  I.Q., effects, 4
  major findings, 8–10
  methodological issues, 25–31
  peer attitudes, 13–15, 20
  retarded, attitudes, 19–20
  self-concept, 16–19, 21–25
  self-ratings, 30
  sex differences, 7
  social acceptance, 14–15, 18, 20–21
  social adjustment, 15–16, 21–22, 30
  social consequences, 10–25
  socioeconomic standing, 12, 18–19
  sociometric evaluation, 11–12, 14, 17, 30

studies, era when conducted, 22–23
subject placement problems, 2–5, 9,
        28–29, 32
subject selection, 28–29
teacher attitudes, 13–15
trends, 5, 8–10
Special teachers, *see* Teachers, special
Speech and modeling, 118–119
Spelling and mainstreaming, 186–192
    assessment, 186–187
    distributed practice, 190–191
    Good Behavior Game, 187–188, 192
    home-based tutoring, 189–190
    instructional strategies, 187
    modeling, 191–192
    peer tutoring, 187–189
    reinforcement, 191
Stereotypes, 38–39
Student teaching and attitudes, 48
Subject placement problems, 2–5, 9, 28–29,
        32
Suburban location, mainstreaming, 21

T

Teacher approval and disapproval
    arithmetic performance, 171–172
    consultation training, 156
    creative writing, 201–202
    loud versus soft reprimands, 130–131
    modeling, 131
    and peer-mediated strategies, 137
    rates of occurrence, 130–131
    and self-recording, 140–141
    token reinforcement, 152
Teacher attitudes, 13–15, 41, 44–57
    and decertification, 51
    demand characteristics, experiments, 54
    expectancy paradigm, 41, 53–54, 56
    experience, effects, 51–52
    Head Start, 82–83, 90
    instructional goals, 46
    and labeling, 52–57
    mainstreaming, 50–51
    predictors, 51–52
    preschool mainstreaming, 89–91
    and pupil performance, 52
    regular classroom, 48–51
    resource program schools, 47
    special classroom, 51
    special versus regular, 46–47, 50–51,
        53–54

student teaching, effects, 48
    trends, 65–66
Teacher expectancy effects, 41, 52–54
Teacher reinforcement, *see* Teacher approval
        and disapproval
Teacher training
    consultation programs, 152–159
    preschool mainstreaming, 89–91
    token reinforcement, 152
Teachers, special
    attitudes, 46–47, 51
    labeling, 53–54
    status, 50
Teaching plan, reading, 178–179
Teaching strategies, antecedent
    arithmetic, 167–171
    reading, 179–180
Time out procedures, 137–139
Timing and arithmetic, 167–168
Token reinforcement, 148–152
    basic components, 149
    behavior problems, 148–152, 182
    contingency contracting, 146
    critical issues, 151–152
    handwriting, 193
    reading, 180
    self-management, 143
    student management, 149–150
    teacher training, 156
Traditional mainstreaming, 74
Training, effects on professionals, 45
Treatment effects, maintenance, *see* Mainte-
        nance of treatment effects

U

Urban location, mainstreaming, 21

V

Verbal behavior, teachers, 129–131
Vicarious punishment, 120–121

W

Wide Range Achievement Test, 6–7
Withdrawal, *see* Social isolation
Writing, *see* Handwriting

Z

Zero reject, 71

EDUCATIONAL PSYCHOLOGY

continued from page ii

Thomas R. Kratochwill (ed.). Single Subject Research: Strategies for Evaluating Change

Kay Pomerance Torshen. The Mastery Approach to Competency-Based Education

Harvey Lesser. Television and the Preschool Child: A Psychological Theory of Instruction and Curriculum Development

Donald J. Treffinger, J. Kent Davis, and Richard E. Ripple (eds.). Handbook on Teaching Educational Psychology

Harry L. Hom, Jr. and Paul A. Robinson (eds.). Psychological Processes in Early Education

J. Nina Lieberman. Playfulness: Its Relationship to Imagination and Creativity

Samuel Ball (ed.). Motivation in Education

Erness Bright Brody and Nathan Brody. Intelligence: Nature, Determinants, and Consequences

António Simões (ed.). The Bilingual Child: Research and Analysis of Existing Educational Themes

Gilbert R. Austin. Early Childhood Education: An International Perspective

Vernon L. Allen (ed.). Children as Teachers: Theory and Research on Tutoring

Joel R. Levin and Vernon L. Allen (eds.). Cognitive Learning in Children: Theories and Strategies

Donald E. P. Smith and others. A Technology of Reading and Writing (in four volumes).

Vol. 1. *Learning to Read and Write: A Task Analysis (by Donald E. P. Smith)*

Vol. 2. *Criterion-Referenced Tests for Reading and Writing (by Judith M. Smith, Donald E. P. Smith, and James R. Brink)*

Vol. 3. *The Adaptive Classroom (by Donald E. P. Smith)*

Vol. 4. *Designing Instructional Tasks (by Judith M. Smith)*

Phillip S. Strain, Thomas P. Cooke, and Tony Apolloni. Teaching Exceptional Children: Assessing and Modifying Social Behavior